COOKING
WHOLE30®

COOKING WHOLE30®

Over 150 delicious recipes
for the Whole30 and beyond

MELISSA URBAN

PHOTOGRAPHY BY BRENT HERRIG

HOUGHTON MIFFLIN HARCOURT
Boston   New York   2021

CONTENTS

For my Whole30ers: you inspire me daily,
and I am so proud of you all

THIS BOOK PRESENTS THE RESEARCH AND IDEAS OF ITS AUTHOR. IT IS NOT
INTENDED TO BE A SUBSTITUTE FOR CONSULTATION WITH A PROFESSIONAL
HEALTHCARE PRACTITIONER. CONSULT WITH YOUR HEALTHCARE PRACTITIONER
BEFORE STARTING ANY DIET OR SUPPLEMENT REGIMEN. THE PUBLISHER AND
THE AUTHOR DISCLAIM RESPONSIBILITY FOR ANY ADVERSE EFFECTS RESULTING
DIRECTLY OR INDIRECTLY FROM INFORMATION CONTAINED IN THIS BOOK.

Originally published as THE WHOLE30 COOKBOOK

For information about permission to reproduce selections from this book,
write to trade.permissions@hmhco.com or to Permissions,
Houghton Mifflin Harcourt Publishing Company, 3 Park Avenue, 19th Floor,
New York, New York 10016.

hmhbooks.com

Library of Congress Cataloging-in-Publication Data is available.
ISBN 978-0-358-53992-6
ISBN 978-0-544-85444-4 (ebk)

Book design by Vertigo Design NYC
Additional design by Eugenie S. Delaney

Printed in the United States of America
DOC 10 9 8 7 6 5 4 3 2 1

FOREWORD

A Note from Whole30 CEO Melissa Urban and
Director of People & Culture Dr. Carrie Kholi-Murchison

Melissa: I co-founded the Whole30 in 2009, and by "co-founded" I mean "did a 30-day dietary self-experiment based on my own roughly sketched guidelines, was amazed at the results, and shared it on my BlogSpot." The program has obviously evolved throughout the years, and people often ask me, "How has the Whole30 changed since the early days?"

There are two answers to that question: not that much, and a heck of a lot. Not that much, in that the structure of the program has remained remarkably consistent since its first iteration. Even the foods we ask you to eliminate and reintroduce haven't changed much throughout the years, because the science and clinical evidence behind those recommendations still hold up. The small things we have changed (like adding white potatoes and green peas back into the program, or eliminating store-bought chips) were due to a better understanding of the science, or most often, our changing food landscape. No one could have predicted we'd turn cauliflower into gnocchi, pretzels, or pizza crust in 2009. What a time to be alive!

Kholi: On the other hand, so very much has changed.

Melissa: First, as the co-founder and CEO, I've grown tremendously. I've had a baby, gone through a difficult divorce and business split, sustained a life-changing concussion, and through it all rediscovered my true self and worth. I learned to develop empathy, compassion, and grace for myself, which led to greater empathy, compassion, and grace for those struggling in their own health journeys. The phrase "let good enough be enough" would never have left my lips in 2009, but with a toddler clinging to my leg as I tried to run a business as a single mom, it became my mantra.

Kholi: As an extension of Melissa's growth, our company has changed, too, beginning with the fact that I can say "*our* company." Whole30 has learned so much from our community since 2009, and has in many cases been called on to do more with our power and privilege to **serve** those who have historically been underrepresented and underserved. Our work together, and my service to you as Director of People & Culture, is to make Whole30 feel as much *ours* as *yours*. As such, we are deeply invested in our work in diversity, equity, inclusion, and accessibility. We're continuously growing in our ability to understand how to better serve all of you by recognizing our individual privileges in the health, wellness, and food space; building equity where possible and imagined; and wielding that privilege for good.

Melissa: We're also looking for areas of inaccessibility in our program, services, or recommendations, and actively working to ensure that everyone who wants to do a Whole30 feels welcomed, seen, heard, and represented in our efforts.

Cooking Whole30 was originally published in 2016 under the title *The Whole30 Cookbook*. It was my first stand-alone cookbook, and helped inspire hundreds of thousands of people to discover how simple, delicious, and satisfying Whole30 meals can be. The recipes are just as nourishing and flavorful today, and our community loves the meals we shared here just as much.

Kholi: Still, in the spring of 2020 Melissa and I decided that the book needed a page-by-page overhaul. Why?

Melissa: In 2015, when I was writing the book, I had little understanding of concepts like cultural appropriation or representation. As a result, our recipe titles and descriptions did not always do justice to the cultures from which these foods or ingredients came. Generalizing dish titles to ethnic regions (to which they may not even belong), failing to honor the cultural significance of certain ingredients or meals, and in some cases appropriating those recipes as our own likely left some community members feeling marginalized or overlooked.

We now know better, so we can do better. And we have.

This revision is a by-product of our followers' fierce advocacy and deep devotion to the program, Dr. Kholi's thoughtful leadership, guidance from cultural editor Redwood Hill, and my team's continued commitment to serve our community.

Kholi: We decided to revise *The Whole30 Cookbook* to make it reflective of our deep cultural appreciation of food, as well as its historical pathways and ingredients. We invited five new contributors from our community to showcase their culture and recipes in these pages, and reformatted it as a paperback to make it more cost-accessible.

Melissa: Working with Dr. Kholi and Redwood Hill—a reconstructor of culinary perspectives, and advocate for food sovereignty and the decolonization of food systems—we methodically went through every page; every word; every recipe title, description, and image. I researched dozens of meals and ingredients, learning so much about their origins and how they came to be incorporated into American cooking.

Kholi: Red sent us pages of notes on the cultural significance (and history of appropriation) of specific recipes, and made recommendations for changes that better reflect that history.

Melissa: We replaced words like "Whole30-compliant" with "Whole30-compatible" to better embody the spirit of autonomy and empowerment our program aims to provide its followers. We changed the recipe titles to respect the origins of the dishes, or clearly state where our inspirations came from. We inquired with our contributors as to their cultural connections to their recipes, to learn more about how best to represent their history with the food. And as Kholi mentioned, we added ten recipes from five new contributors, shining a spotlight on the rich diversity found within our Whole30 community.

I am immensely grateful to my team at HMH for taking what could have been a simple project and working with me to revise it in such a thoughtful and significant fashion. I have incredible respect for the knowledge and experience of Red, who taught me so much about food justice, culture, and appreciation, and worked nights and weekends to help me get these edits in on time. And I must again share my never-ending gratitude to Dr. Kholi, our leader in this space, for believing in our cause so much, and helping us make sure our impact lines up with all of our good intentions. We could not do, be, or inhabit this work without you.

And to you, dear reader . . . you might not know much about cultural appropriation and food, or even notice the changes we made to this book. But many of you will, and you are the people these changes impact the most. I hope you feel heard, and seen, and welcomed, and represented though this new text. Thank you for your support, your loyalty, and your faith in us and the Whole30.

Best in health,
Melissa & Kholi

WHAT IS THE WHOLE30?

Think of the Whole30 like pushing the reset button with your health, habits, and relationship with food.

The premise is simple: certain food groups could be having a negative impact on your body composition, health, and quality of life without you even realizing it. Are your energy levels inconsistent or nonexistent? Do you have aches and pains that can't be explained by overuse or injury? Are you struggling to fall asleep, stay asleep, or wake feeling rested? Do you have some sort of condition (like skin issues, digestive ailments, migraines, allergies, or fatigue) that are holding you back from feeling your best? These symptoms may be directly related to the foods you eat—even the "healthy" stuff.

So how do you know if (and how) these foods are affecting you? Eliminate them from your diet completely. Cut out food groups that are commonly psychologically unhealthy, hormone-unbalancing, gut-disrupting, or inflammatory for a full 30 days. Let your body heal and recover from whatever effects those foods may be causing. Push the "reset" button on your metabolism, systemic inflammation, and the downstream effects of the food choices you've been making. Learn once and for all how the foods you've been eating are actually affecting your day-to-day life and your long-term health.

How It Works

For a full 30 days, you completely eliminate the foods that scientific literature and 11 years of clinical experience have deemed the most commonly problematic in one of four areas—your cravings, metabolism, digestion, and immune system. During the elimination period, you'll be completely eliminating these foods for 30 straight days, experiencing what life is like without these commonly problematic triggers while paying careful attention to changes in energy, sleep, digestion, mood, attention span, self-confidence, cravings, chronic pain or fatigue, athletic performance and recovery, and any number of other symptoms or conditions. This elimination period will give you a new "normal"—a healthy baseline where, in all likelihood, you will look, feel, and live better than you ever imagined you could.

At the end of the 30 days, you then carefully and systematically reintroduce those foods you've been missing, again paying attention to any changes in your experience. Do your two p.m. energy slumps return? Does your stomach bloat? Does your face break out, your joints swell, your pain return? Does your Sugar Dragon rear his ugly head? The reintroduction period is just as important as elimination, as it shows you which specific foods are having a negative impact on how you look, feel, and perform.

Put it all together, and for the first time in your life, you'll be able to make educated decisions about when, how often, and in what amount you can include the foods you love back in your daily diet in a way that feels balanced and sustainable, but still keeps you feeling as awesome as you now *know* you can feel. Through the Whole30, you'll discover the perfect diet for YOU, and achieve true food freedom.

The Results

I cannot possibly put enough emphasis on this simple fact—the next 30 days can change your life. They can change the way you think about food, they most certainly will change your tastes, they will even change your habits and your cravings. They could, quite possibly, change the emotional relationship you have with food, and with your body. They have the potential to change the way you eat for the rest of your life. I know this because I did it, and millions of people have done it since, and it changed my life (and their lives) in a very permanent fashion.

The physical benefits of the Whole30 are profound. A full 96 percent of participants lose weight and improve their body composition without counting or restricting calories. Also commonly reported? Consistently high energy levels, better sleep, improved focus and mental clarity, a return to healthy digestive function, improved athletic performance, and a sunnier disposition. (Yes, many Whole30 alumni say they felt "strangely happy" during and after their program.)

The psychological benefits of the Whole30 may be even more dramatic. Through the program, participants report effectively changing long-standing, unhealthy habits related to food, developing a healthier body image, and dramatically reducing or eliminating cravings, particularly for sugar and carbohydrates. The words so many Whole30 participants use to describe this place?

"Food freedom."

Finally, thousands of Whole30 participants have shared stories of improving any number of lifestyle-related diseases and conditions through the program.

- high blood pressure • high cholesterol
- type 1 diabetes • type 2 diabetes
- asthma • allergies • sinus infections • hives
- skin conditions • endometriosis • PCOS
- infertility • migraines • depression
- bipolar disorder • heartburn • GERD
- arthritis • joint pain • ADHD
- thyroid dysfunction • Lyme disease
- fibromyalgia • chronic fatigue • lupus
- leaky gut syndrome • Crohn's • IBS
- celiac disease • diverticulitis • ulcerative colitis

THE WHOLE30 PROGRAM

The Whole30 Program is laid out in two phases: 30 days of elimination, and 10 days of reintroduction. For the first 30 days, you'll be eating meat, seafood, and eggs; lots of vegetables and fruit; and natural, healthy fats. The list of foods you'll eliminate may seem intimidating, but you've got 150 recipes here to see you through—and it's only 30 days. Below is a summary of Whole30 elimination. (Please refer to *The Whole30: The 30-Day Guide to Total Health and Food Freedom* for a comprehensive overview of the Whole30 Program, FAQs, recommendations, and troubleshooting.)

- **No added sugar, real or artificial.** This includes (but is not limited to) maple syrup, honey, agave nectar, coconut sugar, date syrup, monkfruit extract, stevia, Splenda, Equal, Nutrasweet, and xylitol. If there is added sugar in the ingredient list, it's out.

- **No alcohol in any form.** No wine, beer, champagne, vodka, rum, whiskey, tequila, etc., whether consumed on its own or used as an ingredient—not even for cooking.

- **No grains.** This includes wheat, rye, barley, oats, corn, rice, millet, bulgur, sorghum, sprouted grains, and all gluten-free pseudo-cereals like amaranth, buckwheat, or quinoa. This also includes all the ways we add wheat, corn, and rice into our foods in the form of bran, germ, starch, and so on. Again, read your labels.

- **No legumes.** This includes beans (black, red, pinto, navy, garbanzo/chickpeas, white, kidney, lima, fava, cannellini, lentils, adzuki, mung, cranberry, and black-eyed peas); peanuts (including peanut butter and peanut oil); and all forms of soy (soy sauce, miso, tofu, tempeh, edamame, soy protein, soy milk, or soy lecithin). The only exceptions are green beans and most peas (see The Fine Print, page 4).

- **No dairy.** This includes cow's-, goat's-, or sheep's-milk products such as cream, cheese, kefir, yogurt, ice cream, frozen yogurt, and sour cream. The only exceptions are clarified butter or ghee (see The Fine Print, page 4).

- **No carrageenan, MSG, or added sulfites.** If these ingredients appear in any form in the ingredient list of your processed food or beverage, it's out for the Whole30.

- **No recreating baked goods, "treats," or junk foods with approved ingredients.** No banana-egg pancakes, coconut-cassava tortillas, Paleo bread, or coconut milk ice cream. (See Let's Get Specific on page 4 for more details.) Your cravings and habits won't change if you keep eating these foods, even if they are made with Whole30 ingredients.

- **No stepping on the scale or taking measurements.** Your reset is about so much more than weight loss. Focusing on body composition means you'll miss out on the most dramatic and lifelong benefits this plan offers. As such, please don't weigh yourself, analyze body fat, or break out the tape measure during the 30-day elimination period. (You'll thank us.)

Let's Get Specific

Specific foods eliminated on the Whole30 include: pancakes, crepes, waffles, bread, tortillas, biscuits, muffins, cupcakes, cookies, brownies, alternative-flour pizza crust or pastas, granola, cereal, or ice cream. No commercially-prepared chips (potato, tortilla, plantain, etc.) or French fries, either. You may also decide to exclude additional foods that, despite being compatible with the program, promote cravings or make you feel out of control, like RXBARs or almond butter. (See page 95 in *The Whole30* for guidance.)

The Fine Print

These foods are exceptions and are allowed during your Whole30 elimination.

- **Clarified butter and ghee.** Clarified butter (see page 289) and ghee are allowed during Whole30 elimination, as they've had their milk solids rendered out.

- **Fruit juice.** Products or recipes that include orange, apple, or other 100% fruit juices are compatible with the program, even if they're used as a natural sweetener.

- **Certain legumes.** Green beans and most peas (including sugar snap peas, snow peas, green peas, yellow peas, and split peas) are allowed.

- **Vinegar and botanical extracts.** Most vinegar (including white, red wine, balsamic, apple cider, and rice) and alcohol-based botanical extracts (like vanilla, lemon, or lavender) are allowed during Whole30 elimination. (Just not malt-based vinegar or extracts, which will be clearly labeled as such, as they contain gluten.)

- **Coconut aminos.** All brands of coconut aminos (a brewed and naturally fermented soy sauce substitute) are acceptable, even if you see the words "coconut nectar" or "coconut syrup" in their ingredient lists.

- **Iodized salt.** All iodized salt contains a tiny amount of dextrose (sugar) as a stabilizer, but ruling out table salt would be unreasonable.

Reintroduction

Your Whole30 isn't over yet! Following the 30-day elimination, you'll enter phase two, a 10-day period (at least) of reintroduction. This is the fun part—where you get to bring back the food groups you've been missing, one at a time, and compare your experience. This is where you learn the most about which foods may be having a negative impact on your energy, sleep, mood, cravings, digestion, and more, so be thorough here!

In this phase, you'll reintroduce one food group at a time, then go back to the elimination phase for two days to reset (in case you have a negative experience). You'll reintroduce food groups in order of least likely to be problematic to most likely:

- (OPTIONAL) Added sugar
- (OPTIONAL) Gluten-free alcohol
- Legumes
- Non-gluten grains
- Dairy
- Gluten-containing grains

Reintroduction is where you'll learn which foods do and don't work for you, and create your perfect Food Freedom plan. For examples and detailed Reintroduction guidelines, see page 42 in *The Whole30* or Chapter 5 in *Food Freedom Forever*.

You Can Do Hard Things

The Whole30 is famous for its tough love, but don't be nervous—it's heavy on the love. At this point, many of you want to take on this life-changing self-experiment, but aren't sure you can really do it. If you've spent your whole life dieting, those efforts have likely left you discouraged, and skeptical that the Whole30 really is different. It is—I promise. And also, you're going to have to do the work. Here are a few key mindset shifts I want you to make heading into your Whole30, so you can step into your power, reclaim your confidence, and keep this promise to yourself.

- **This will be hard.** There are so many roadblocks to changing the way you eat. For some, it's emotional ties to comfort foods. For others, it's time or budget concerns. For still others, it's missing culturally significant foods. I honor the tremendous efforts many of you will go through just to complete the Whole30. And still, you have done harder things in your life. Losing a parent is hard. Fighting cancer is hard. Birthing a baby is hard. The Whole30 may also be hard, but you are more powerful than you give yourself credit for, and I know you can do this too.

- **Don't self-sabotage.** If you leave the program open to negotiation when you have a bad day or a special occasion, you are setting yourself up to fail. If you don't clean out your pantry; if you tell yourself, "One glass won't matter"; if you say, "I'll try to do all 30 days"; you are setting yourself up to fail. Language matters, and "I'll try" gives you an out. Wake up each day and say, "I am Whole30, and I will keep this promise to myself."

- **Hold your boundaries.** You never, ever, ever have to eat anything you don't want to eat. We're all grown-ups here, and someone else's feelings aren't as important as your physical and mental health. Practice saying, "No, thank you" or "I'm not drinking right now." Remember your "why" and come back to that when you're feeling pressured. Just because it's your sister's birthday, your best friend's wedding, or your company picnic does not mean you *have* to eat anything. Realizing the event is just as special, and your participation just as meaningful, without the wine or cake is a huge benefit of the program.

- **Changing your life requires effort.** Grocery shopping, meal planning, dining out, socializing, and dealing with stress will all prove challenging at some point during your program. We'll give you all the tools, guidelines, and resources you'll need in our books, website, newsletters, and social media feeds, but you also have to take responsibility for your own program. The Whole30 will challenge you in ways you don't expect, which is exactly why the benefits will carry over into every area of your life. Remember that when things get hard.

This is the journey you have been preparing for. You want to do this. You need to do this. You're ready for it. And I know that you can do it. So stop thinking about it, and take the first step. Right now, this very minute, commit to the Whole30.

Now take a deep breath, because you've already begun. I'm so excited to welcome you into our community and witness your journey. Even if you're not 100% sure the Whole30 will be as transformational for you as it has been for so many, all I ask is that you give it 30 short days and trust the process. What we do here is that important. I believe in it that much. It changed my life, and I want it to change yours, too.

Welcome to the Whole30.

GETTING STARTED WITH THE WHOLE30

Planning and preparation are the key to success on the Whole30. Here are some basic steps for getting your home and your head Whole30-ready. For a more detailed step-by-step plan for getting started with the program, see pages 17 to 31 in *The Whole30*.

Step 1: Choose Your Start Date

Start *as soon as you possibly can*, but plan carefully. If you've got a once-in-a-lifetime vacation, a trip to an unfamiliar location, or a wedding (especially your own!) in the near future, consider starting the Whole30 after those events. It's also important not to have your Whole30 end the day before a vacation, holiday, or special event. Reintroduction (see page 42 in *The Whole30*) is just as critical as the 30-day elimination. Ideally, allow a full 10 days after your 30-day elimination and carefully reintroduce *before* your special event.

Finally, take a look at your calendar during the proposed 30-day period and see what business or personal commitments you have in place. If you've got a family dinner, a business lunch, a road trip, or a bridal shower in your imminent future, excellent! Consider it an opportunity to take your Whole30 skills out on the town, and create a plan for how to handle it (see Step 4). You'll have to deal with lots of new situations during your program, so *don't* let them push your Whole30 off.

There will never be a "perfect" time to do the Whole30, so think about what you have coming up, choose a date, and circle it on your calendar in permanent marker. (Really—write it down. Habit research shows that putting your commitment on paper makes you more likely to succeed.)

Step 2: Build Your Support Team

Finding the right support network will be critical to keeping you motivated, inspired, and accountable during your program. The first step is sharing a bit about the program, leading with the things you *will* be eating. Say something like, "For thirty days, I'll eat lots of whole, fresh, nutritious foods—no calorie counting at all! Breakfast could be a vegetable frittata, fresh fruit, and avocado; lunch is a spinach salad with grilled chicken, apples, pecans, and Whole30 Elderberry Vinaigrette; and dinner is pulled pork carnitas with roasted sweet potato and a cabbage slaw."

You should also share with those close to you *why* you are choosing to embark upon this journey. Make it personal. Share your current struggles, your goals, and all the ways you believe the program will make you healthier and happier. Try something like, "Every day at three p.m., I feel like I need a nap. I'm hoping the Whole30 will help me keep my energy up without my usual afternoon soda and candy bar."

Finally, don't forget to *ask* for their support. Saying very directly, "Can I count on you to support me for the next thirty days?" lets them know how important these efforts are to you and how much you'd value their encouragement and help.

Still, despite all your best efforts, family and friends may be less than supportive of your Whole30 plan. If you're having a hard time talking to friends and family about the Whole30 or are dealing with pushback during your conversations, read the Friends, Family, and Food section in *Food Freedom Forever* for guidance.

Step 3: Get Your House Ready

First, get all the stuff you won't be eating out of the house. It's time to clean out the pantry—be thorough; throw out the foods you won't be eating, give them to a neighbor for safekeeping, or donate them to a local food bank.

If you're the only one at home doing the Whole30, dedicate an out-of-the-way cabinet or plastic storage tote for your family's sweets and treats, so you don't have to reach around the Oreos every time you need a can of coconut milk.

Even if you're not the planning type, make a plan for breakfast, lunch, and dinner for the first three to seven days of your Whole30. Then, go grocery shopping and buy everything you need for your first set of meals, plus Whole30 pantry staples. (See whole30.com/pdf-downloads for a detailed Shopping List.) Meal planning helps you save time and money, reduces stress, and keeps the pizza delivery guy off speed-dial.

Step 4: Plan for Success

Think about the next 30 days, and write down every potentially stressful, difficult, or complicated situation you may encounter during your Whole30. These may include business lunches, family dinners, travel plans, a long day at work, birthday parties, holiday celebrations, office gatherings, family stress, job stress, financial stress . . . anything you think might derail your Whole30 train. Then, make a plan for how you'll handle it. Use if/then statements when crafting plans. Some examples might include:

Business lunch: If my coworkers pressure me to have a drink, then I'll say, "Thanks, but I'm not drinking right now, I'll just have a mineral water, please."

Family dinner: If Mom invites me out for dinner, then I'll remind her I'm doing the Whole30 and ask if I can cook for her instead.

Travel day: If I get to the airport and my flight is delayed, then I'll snack on the EPIC bars, apples, carrot sticks, and individual-size packet of almond butter I brought in my carry-on.

Finally, plan three quick and easy "go-to" meals you can make in 10 minutes or less with foods you always have on hand. Write your list down and pin it to your fridge so you'll always have a plan for nights when things just get crazy. (My go-to: scrambled eggs, chicken sausage, roasted sweet potato, and avocado.)

Step 5: Toss That Scale

This is your last and final step in preparing for the Whole30—for the next 30 days, get rid of your scale. Put it in the garage, give it to a friend to "hold," or better yet, take it out back and introduce it to your sledgehammer in a fun little pre-Whole30 ritual.

We don't want you to ignore your body for the next 30 days—keep an eye on how your clothes are fitting, whether your stomach is flatter, your rings are looser, or your skin is clearer. You can also take before and after measurements, weigh yourself, or snap a photo on Day 0, and then again on Day 31. (But remember, none of this during your program.)

Ready, Set, Whole30!

And with that (and perhaps a quick refresher of the program details, FAQs, and Whole30 Timeline in *The Whole30*), you're ready to dive into your Whole30 program . . . and these delicious meals you'll find in the next seven chapters. *Bon appétit!*

WHOLE30 KITCHEN ESSENTIALS

If you're ready to invest in your Whole30 experience now, but aren't sure what you need, this is a detailed list of our essentials and "nice-to-haves."

POTS AND PANS

As for pots, buy a set of three or four—something that ranges from a small (1- to 2-quart) saucepan to a large (3- to 4-quart) Dutch oven. You'll want two skillets: one should be a cast-iron or oven-safe skillet. These are great for taking dishes straight from the stovetop to the oven and will last you a lifetime. It's also nice to have one nonstick pan for eggs. If you can buy one more pan, choose a large, high-walled sauté pan.

STRAINER

A strainer serves double-duty, allowing you to drain water from boiled vegetables or broths, and functioning as a steamer when placed inside a large stockpot. (You could also buy one large pot with a steamer/strainer insert, if you want to be really fancy.) It's nice to have two strainers—one fine-mesh handheld strainer to filter out smaller particles of food, and a larger one with bigger holes for straining out larger pieces and steaming.

MEASURING CUPS AND SPOONS

You'll need at least one basic set of measuring cups and spoons, but we highly recommend doubling up—you'd be surprised how many times you'll need a teaspoon as you cook your way through this book. It's also a good idea to have at least one larger glass measuring cup with a pouring spout—something that can handle three or four cups at a time.

BAKING SHEETS

You won't be making chocolate chip cookies on the Whole30, but you *will* be roasting and baking lots of meat and vegetables in the oven. Make sure you have at least two baking sheets, so you don't crowd your sweet potatoes when they're roasting.

CUTTING BOARDS

There is a lot of chopping in your future, so have at least three cutting boards—different sizes are also really nice. The best cutting boards are made from recycled wood fiber—they're eco-friendly, a snap to clean, and dry fast.

KNIVES

You'll want three basic knives—a paring knife for small cuts (like dicing an apple), an 8-inch chef's knife designed for chopping, and a long, thin slicing knife for carving. Look for knives that are all one piece (not a blade and handle joined together), and spend some money here. Trust us, this is one investment that will pay you back every single time you cook. (Don't forget the knife sharpener.)

SLOW COOKER OR INSTANT POT

A slow cooker or pressure cooker like the Instant Pot makes your Whole30 meals faster and easier. Throw your ingredients in by 7 a.m. and come home to a delicious-smelling dinner (with just one pot to clean), or whip up bone broth, baked sweet potatoes, or hard-boiled eggs in a flash.

FOOD PROCESSOR

A food processor is designed to take solid ingredients and chop, shred, or mix them to a perfect consistency. If you're cooking for one, you may be able to get away with a mini food processor for around $25, but there are plenty of 7- to 10-cup food processors available for between $40 and $100. Some are even combination blenders/food processors, saving you money and counter space.

MEAT THERMOMETER

Cooking meat and poultry to just the right degree takes time, attention, and lots of practice, but using a meat thermometer is like cheating in a good way. Make sure you get a meat thermometer (designed to tell you the internal temperature of meat) and not an oven thermometer (designed to tell you how hot your oven really is on the inside). Look for something that says "instant read" (even though these actually take about 20 seconds to get up to the right temperature)—you should be able to find one for around $10.

PARCHMENT PAPER

Aluminum foil can stick to delicate meats and veggies. Parchment paper is moisture-resistant and specially treated for oven use, keeping your dishes clean and your food from sticking. At about $3 a roll, this is a great investment for easy Whole30 kitchen cleanup.

GARLIC PRESS

Peel the clove, put it in the press, squeeze the handle, and you've got perfectly minced garlic in 10 seconds. They key to this tool is making sure you rinse the leftover garlic pulp out of the press as soon as you're done (before it dries and hardens), and use a kitchen brush or toothbrush to keep the holes clean.

JULIENNE PEELER OR SPIRAL SLICER

This looks just like a normal peeler (and works the same way), but its special grooved blades turn vegetables into long, thin strings, just like noodles. You can find them for under $10 at any kitchen store, and it only takes about a minute to julienne an entire zucchini. If you want to splurge a bit here, you could also buy a fancy tool called a spiral slicer for about $40. This nifty gadget slices, grates, or juliennes nearly any vegetable or fruit.

CITRUS JUICER

Squeezing lemons and limes by hand is messy, and doesn't ever get all the juice out. Why go through the mess when you can buy a handheld combination lemon/lime squeezer for around $10?

ZESTER OR MICROPLANE

Many of our recipes call for citrus zest—very finely grated lemon, lime, or orange peel mixed right into the dish. Zest adds a ton of flavor, but getting to it can be a pain without the right tool. A zester has tiny holes designed to remove long, skinny pieces of skin as you scrape it down the outside of your citrus fruit, no extra chopping required. Or, for about $15, buy a Microplane—a multifunctional fine-toothed rasp grater perfect for zesting fruit or grating spices (like nutmeg) or roots (like ginger).

MEAT TENDERIZER

This handy and inexpensive kitchen tool is one easy way to make tougher cuts more tender, or to ensure that those who prefer well-done meat aren't chewing for hours. It's also a great way to speed up cooking times and get more consistent results.

For our complete kitchen recommendations, including brands and models we like, visit whole30.com/whole30kitchen.

EGGS

BISTRO BREAKFAST SALAD

This riff on the classic French bistro salad, *frisée aux lardons*, is a whole new way to eat eggs and bacon in the morning—with a healthy dose of greens dressed in a garlicky mustard vinaigrette.

SERVES 2

PREP: 10 minutes   **COOK:** 20 minutes   **TOTAL:** 30 minutes

4 cups packed curly endive (see Tip)

1½ tablespoons extra-virgin olive oil

1 tablespoon apple cider vinegar

1 teaspoon Whole30-compatible Dijon mustard

¼ teaspoon minced garlic

Salt and black pepper

4 slices Whole30-compatible bacon, cut into ¼-inch pieces

2 teaspoons white vinegar

4 large eggs

Wash and dry the endive. Place in a shallow salad bowl and chill until needed.

Combine the oil, apple cider vinegar, mustard, and garlic in a small jar with a lid. Season with salt and pepper. Cover and shake vigorously to combine. Set aside.

Cook the bacon in a small amount of water in a small skillet over medium-high heat for 5 minutes. Drain the bacon and dry the skillet. Return the bacon to the dry skillet and cook over medium heat until browned and crisp.

Meanwhile, fill a wide saucepan with 3 inches of water. Add the white vinegar and 1 teaspoon salt. Bring to a boil over high heat. Crack each egg into a separate small bowl or cup. Gently pour each egg into the boiling water. Remove the pan from the heat, cover, and let sit until the whites are firm but the yolks are still runny, about 4 minutes. Remove the poached eggs from the skillet with a slotted spoon and place on a paper towel–lined plate to drain.

Drizzle the endive with the vinaigrette, tossing to coat well. Divide the endive between two plates. Top each with two poached eggs and sprinkle with the bacon. Season with pepper and serve immediately.

TIP Curly endive is sometimes called frisée. Use only the pale and tender leaves from the interior of the bunch, so buy a little more than 4 cups (a little more than 4 ounces). Discard the dark green outer leaves.

BST (BACON, SPINACH, TOMATO) BREAKFAST SALAD

A warm bacon dressing slightly wilts the spinach in this yummy salad topped with poached eggs. If you like the yolk to run out over the greens, let the eggs sit in the hot water for just 3 minutes. If you like firmer yolks, go longer.

SERVES 2

PREP: 10 minutes   **COOK:** 15 minutes   **TOTAL:** 25 minutes

6 cups baby spinach (about 6 ounces)

1 ripe avocado, halved, pitted, peeled, and sliced

½ cup grape or cherry tomatoes, halved

4 slices Whole30-compatible bacon

1 small shallot, finely chopped

3 tablespoons extra-virgin olive oil

2 tablespoons red wine vinegar

¼ teaspoon dry mustard

⅛ teaspoon black pepper

2 teaspoons white vinegar

1 teaspoon salt

4 large eggs (see Tip)

Sliced green onions (optional)

Divide the spinach, avocado, and tomatoes between two serving bowls.

Cook the bacon until browned and crisp in a large skillet over medium heat. Drain the bacon on paper towels, reserving 3 tablespoons of the drippings in the skillet. Crumble the bacon and set aside.

Cook the shallot in the reserved bacon drippings over medium heat, stirring frequently, until tender, about 3 minutes. Remove from the heat; whisk in the oil, red wine vinegar, dry mustard, and pepper.

Meanwhile, fill a wide saucepan with 3 inches of water. Add the white vinegar and salt and bring to a boil over high heat. Crack each egg into a separate small bowl. Gently slide each egg into the boiling water. Remove the pan from the heat, cover, and let sit for 3 minutes for very soft yolks or 5 minutes for firm yolks. Remove the cooked eggs from the pan with a slotted spoon and place on a paper towel–lined plate to drain.

Top each bowl of the spinach mixture with two poached eggs and divide the crumbled bacon and the dressing evenly between them. If desired, sprinkle with green onions.

TIP Adding a little vinegar to the water when poaching eggs helps the whites coagulate and firm up so you get a nicely shaped—not raggedy—edge. If you'd like to take the guesswork out of making perfect poached eggs, you can use poaching cups instead.

GREEN EGG OMELET

The Charred Tomatillo Salsa that gets spooned on top of these veggie-packed omelets is a great all-purpose salsa verde that tastes terrific on grilled chicken, steak, pork, or fish.

SERVES 2

PREP: 10 minutes   **COOK:** 45 minutes   **TOTAL:** 55 minutes

FOR THE CHARRED TOMATILLO SALSA

3 cloves garlic, unpeeled

4 tomatillos, husked, rinsed, and dried

1 medium poblano chile, stemmed, seeded, and quartered

½ small onion, cut into thin wedges

2 tablespoons snipped fresh cilantro

1 tablespoon fresh lime juice

½ teaspoon coarse salt

¼ teaspoon ground cumin

FOR THE OMELET

4 teaspoons extra-virgin olive oil

2 green onions, thinly sliced

½ cup thin bite-size strips green bell pepper

6 large eggs

2 tablespoons water

¼ teaspoon coarse salt

¼ teaspoon black pepper

1 cup coarsely chopped baby spinach

MAKE THE SALSA: Wrap the garlic in aluminum foil. Place the packet on a rack in the lower third of the oven. Adjust top oven rack to 4 or 5 inches from the broiler. Preheat the broiler. Line a baking pan with foil and combine the tomatillos, poblano, and onion on the pan. Place the pan on the top oven rack and broil for 8 to 10 minutes, turning the tomatillos once or twice, until the tomatillos and poblano skins are charred. Place the pan on a wire rack. Bring the foil up and around vegetables to fully enclose them. Let stand until cool. Change the oven setting to 400°F. Roast the garlic for 10 minutes more, then set on a wire rack to cool. Using a sharp knife, peel the skin off the cooled poblano quarters. Peel the cooled garlic. In a food processor, combine the poblano, tomatillos, onion, and garlic. Pulse until finely chopped. Transfer to a medium bowl. Stir in the cilantro, lime, juice, salt, and cumin.

MAKE THE OMELET: Heat 2 teaspoons of the olive oil in an 8-inch ceramic nonstick skillet with flared sides over medium heat. Add the green onions, reserving some of the green tops for garnish, and the bell pepper and cook, stirring occasionally, until the pepper is crisp-tender, 3 to 5 minutes. Transfer the bell pepper mixture to a small bowl.

Meanwhile, in a 2-cup glass measure, beat the eggs, water, salt, and black pepper until well combined. In the same skillet, heat 1 teaspoon of the olive oil over medium heat. Add half the egg mixture to the skillet. Cook and stir the eggs, pushing the cooked portion toward the center with a spatula and allowing the uncooked egg to flow under, until the eggs are set and have formed an even layer in the skillet. Spoon half the bell pepper mixture and half the spinach over one side of the egg. Fold the opposite side over the filling. Transfer the omelet to a serving plate and keep warm. Repeat with the remaining olive oil, egg mixture, bell pepper mixture, and spinach to make a second omelet.

Spoon ¼ cup of the Charred Tomatillo Salsa over each omelet. Top with the reserved green onion.

MUSHROOM, LEEK, AND SPINACH FRITTATA

This vegetarian frittata goes together so quickly, you can enjoy it on even the busiest weekday mornings—but it also makes a terrific quick dinner at the other end of the day, served with a fresh green salad.

SERVES 2 OR 3

PREP: 10 minutes   **COOK:** 10 minutes   **TOTAL:** 20 minutes

2 medium leeks (white and light green parts only)

6 large eggs, lightly beaten

1 tablespoon full-fat coconut milk

2 teaspoons fresh thyme, finely chopped, or ½ teaspoon dried thyme, crushed

¼ teaspoon salt

¼ teaspoon red pepper flakes

2 tablespoons extra-virgin olive oil

1½ cups sliced fresh mushrooms

1 bag (about 6 ounces) baby spinach, roughly chopped

1 clove garlic, minced

2 tablespoons thinly sliced green onions

Trim the roots and wilted leaves from the leeks. Cut the leeks in half lengthwise, then cut them crosswise into ¼-inch-thick pieces. Rinse well with cold water. Drain and dry the leeks and set aside.

Preheat the broiler (or preheat the oven to 500°F). In a medium bowl, combine the eggs, coconut milk, thyme, salt, and red pepper flakes; set aside.

Heat the olive oil in a large oven-safe skillet over medium heat; add the leeks and mushrooms and cook, stirring frequently, until softened, 5 to 8 minutes. Add the spinach and garlic and let the spinach wilt for 30 seconds.

Pour the egg mixture into the skillet and cook over medium heat. As the egg mixture sets, run a spatula around edge of skillet, lifting the cooked egg so the uncooked egg flows underneath. Cook until the egg is beginning to set (the surface will still be moist).

Transfer the pan with the eggs to the oven and broil 4 to 5 inches from the heat (or bake in the preheated oven for 1 to 3 minutes), until the top is set and lightly browned. Top with the green onions. Cut into wedges and serve hot, directly out of the pan.

TIP This recipe will work well with just about any produce you have in the fridge, but you can also get creative with seasonal combinations. Try asparagus, fennel, and sweet onion in spring; grape tomatoes, zucchini, and green beans in summer; butternut squash, fresh cranberries, and Swiss chard in fall; or kale and sweet potato topped with pomegranate seeds in winter.

PESTO-PEPPER FRITTATA WITH SQUASH

While the nutritional yeast is optional, it will give this pesto a nutty, cheesy flavor without the use of Parmesan, which is traditional in a classic *pesto alla genovese*. Toasting the pine nuts or walnuts also boosts flavor.

SERVES 2

PREP: 10 minutes   **COOK:** 15 minutes   **TOTAL:** 25 minutes

1 cup firmly packed fresh basil leaves

¼ cup pine nuts or chopped walnuts, toasted (see Tip)

3 cloves garlic, chopped

1 tablespoon nutritional yeast (optional)

¼ teaspoon coarse salt

¼ teaspoon black pepper

4 tablespoons extra-virgin olive oil

1 small red or green bell pepper, cut into thin bite-size strips

¼ cup very thinly sliced onion

6 large eggs

⅓ cup thawed frozen pureed butternut squash

Preheat the oven to 375°F.

In a food processor, combine the basil, nuts, garlic, nutritional yeast (if using), ⅛ teaspoon of the salt, and ⅛ teaspoon of the black pepper. Cover and pulse until very finely chopped. With the food processor running, pour 3 tablespoons of the oil through the feed tube, processing until well combined and nearly smooth.

Heat the remaining 1 tablespoon oil in an oven-safe 6-inch nonstick skillet with flared sides over medium heat. Add the bell pepper and onion and cook, stirring occasionally, until the vegetables are tender, about 5 minutes. Meanwhile, in a medium bowl, whisk together the eggs, squash, remaining ⅛ teaspoon salt, and remaining ⅛ teaspoon black pepper.

Reduce the heat under the skillet to medium-low. Add the egg mixture and cook, without stirring, until the eggs begin to set. Cook, stirring, for 1 minute more. Remove the skillet from the heat. Spoon half the pesto in mounds onto the egg mixture; fold gently to partially mix the pesto into the egg. Spread the egg mixture into an even layer.

Transfer to the oven and bake for 6 to 9 minutes, until completely set. Let sit for 5 minutes before serving. Cut into four wedges. Divide the wedges between two serving plates. Top evenly with the remaining pesto.

TIPS Try doubling the pesto recipe and tossing it with steamed veggie noodles (such as zucchini or spaghetti squash) for a quick and flavorful side dish.

To toast nuts, spread them in a single layer on a rimmed baking sheet. Toast in a preheated 375°F oven, stirring once, until fragrant and lightly browned, 5 to 7 minutes. Let cool before chopping.

SAUSAGE-MUSHROOM FRITTATA

Smoked paprika (also called *pimentón* de la Vera in its native Spain) is an almost magical ingredient. Made from peppers that are slowly dried over a fire of burning oak, it comes in both sweet and hot varieties. (If the label doesn't specify that it's hot or "picante," it's made with sweet peppers.) Just a little bit infuses foods with smoky, woodsy, complex flavor. Here, it adds great taste to homemade Italian sausage.

SERVES 4

PREP: 10 minutes **COOK:** 15 minutes **TOTAL:** 25 minutes

8 large eggs

¾ teaspoon salt

⅛ teaspoon black pepper

8 ounces ground pork

1 teaspoon Italian seasoning, crushed

¼ teaspoon smoked paprika

⅛ teaspoon fennel seeds

⅛ teaspoon red pepper flakes

2 tablespoons extra-virgin olive oil

2 cups sliced white or cremini mushrooms

2 cloves garlic, minced

3 cups roughly chopped arugula

1 cup chopped tomato

¼ cup sliced green onions

Whole30-compatible hot sauce (optional)

Preheat the broiler. In a medium bowl, beat the eggs with ½ teaspoon of the salt and the black pepper; set aside.

In a medium bowl, combine the pork, Italian seasoning, paprika, fennel seeds, red pepper flakes, and remaining ¼ teaspoon salt; mix well.

Heat the olive oil in a large oven-safe skillet over medium heat. Add the pork mixture and cook, stirring frequently, until the meat is browned. Add the mushrooms and garlic. Cook, stirring, until the mushrooms are tender, 3 to 4 minutes. Stir in the arugula and cook until wilted, about 1 minute. Pour the egg mixture into the skillet. As the mixture sets, run a spatula around the edge of the skillet, lifting the egg mixture so the uncooked egg flows underneath. Cook until almost set, 2 to 3 minutes more.

Place the skillet under the broiler, 4 to 6 inches from the heat, and broil for 1 to 2 minutes, until the top is set.

To serve, top the frittata with the tomato and green onions. Cut into quarters and serve hot, directly from the skillet. Pass hot sauce alongside, if desired.

SAUTÉED GREEN BEANS AND MUSHROOMS WITH FRIED EGGS

With three eggs per serving and a whole mess of veggies and greens, this tasty breakfast will keep you going strong until lunchtime. A quick lemon-shallot vinaigrette is drizzled over everything to give the dish great flavor.

SERVES 2

PREP: 10 minutes   **COOK:** 15 minutes   **TOTAL:** 25 minutes

6 tablespoons extra-virgin olive oil

2 cups sliced fresh mushrooms

12 ounces fresh green beans, trimmed and cut into 2-inch pieces

1 sprig fresh thyme

1 clove garlic, minced

1 teaspoon salt

4 cups arugula (2 to 3 ounces)

6 large eggs

½ teaspoon grated lemon zest

1 tablespoon fresh lemon juice

2 tablespoons finely chopped shallot

Black pepper

Heat 2 tablespoons of the olive oil in a large non-stick skillet over high heat. Add the mushrooms and cook, stirring occasionally, until just beginning to brown, about 3 minutes. Reduce the heat to medium and stir in the green beans, thyme, garlic, and ½ teaspoon of the salt. Cook, stirring frequently, for 2 minutes. Cover and cook, stirring once or twice, until the beans are crisp-tender, about 5 minutes. Remove and discard the thyme.

Spread the arugula on a large platter or in a large shallow bowl. Top with the hot vegetables. Let stand until the arugula wilts, about 5 minutes.

Meanwhile, wipe out the skillet. Heat 2 tablespoons of the oil in the skillet over medium-high heat. Fry the eggs in the hot oil until the whites are set and the yolks are cooked to your desired doneness, flipping the eggs if desired.

In a small bowl, whisk together the lemon zest and juice, the remaining 2 tablespoons oil, and the shallot.

Toss together the wilted arugula and vegetables. Drizzle with the dressing and top with the fried eggs. Sprinkle with the remaining ½ teaspoon salt and black pepper to taste.

SCRAMBLED EGG BREAKFAST TACOS WITH QUICK CIDER-CHIPOTLE BREAKFAST SAUSAGE

Spicy, smoky sausage and creamy scrambled eggs are tucked into tender butterhead lettuce leaves and topped with pico de gallo or hot sauce—and avocado and cilantro, if you like. They may be "breakfast" tacos, but they taste just as good at dinner.

SERVES 4

PREP: 15 minutes   **COOK:** 15 minutes   **TOTAL:** 30 minutes

FOR THE SAUSAGE

¼ cup apple cider

1 teaspoon kosher salt

1 teaspoon ground chipotle chile pepper

1 teaspoon dried sage, crushed, or 1 tablespoon finely chopped fresh sage

½ teaspoon dried thyme, crushed

½ teaspoon black pepper

½ teaspoon garlic powder

½ teaspoon onion powder

1 pound ground pork

FOR THE EGGS

1 tablespoon Clarified Butter (page 289) or ghee

8 large eggs

Kosher salt and black pepper

12 butterhead lettuce leaves

Whole30-compatible pico de gallo or hot sauce

Chopped avocado (optional)

Fresh cilantro leaves (optional)

MAKE THE SAUSAGE: In a large bowl, combine the apple cider, salt, chipotle, sage, thyme, black pepper, garlic powder, and onion powder. Add the ground pork and use your hands to thoroughly mix in the seasonings.

In a large skillet, cook the sausage over medium-high heat until browned, using a wooden spoon to break up the meat into small pieces as it cooks. Use a slotted spoon to transfer the sausage to a bowl. Pour off any fat remaining in the skillet and wipe out the skillet.

MAKE THE EGGS: Set the skillet in which you cooked the sausage over medium heat and add the butter. In a medium bowl, whisk the eggs just until the yolks are broken. Pour the eggs into the skillet. Cook, stirring often, until they reach the desired doneness. Season with salt and black pepper.

Divide the sausage and eggs among the lettuce leaves. Top with pico de gallo and, if desired, avocado and cilantro.

SHAKSHUKA

This dish of spicy tomato sauce is eaten all over North Africa and the Middle East. Using fire-roasted tomatoes instead of regular crushed tomatoes gives it another layer of flavor.

SERVES 2

PREP: 10 minutes   **COOK:** 25 minutes   **TOTAL:** 35 minutes

2 tablespoons extra-virgin olive oil

½ cup chopped onion

1 cup chopped red bell pepper

4 cloves garlic, minced

1 can (28 ounces) Whole30-compatible fire-roasted crushed tomatoes

1 to 2 tablespoons Whole30-compatible harissa (see Tip)

1 teaspoon ground cumin

½ teaspoon salt

6 large eggs

Black pepper

3 tablespoons chopped fresh parsley

Heat the oil in a large skillet over medium heat. Add the onion and cook, stirring, until slightly wilted, about 2 minutes. Add the bell pepper and garlic and cook, stirring, until the onion and pepper are tender, 4 to 5 minutes more. Add the tomatoes, harissa, cumin, and salt; bring to a boil. Reduce the heat to low and simmer, stirring occasionally, until the sauce has thickened, 10 to 15 minutes.

Use the back of a spoon to make six depressions in the sauce. Crack one egg into a small bowl and carefully slide the egg into one depression in the sauce. Repeat with the remaining eggs. Cook, covered, until the egg whites are completely cooked and the yolks begin to thicken but are not hard, 6 to 8 minutes. Remove from the heat. Season with black pepper and sprinkle with the parsley before serving.

TIP Harissa is a red chile-based Tunisian condiment that features prominently in Moroccan cuisine. Usually made with chiles, garlic, cumin, coriander, caraway, and olive oil, harissa is most often fiery hot, but there are mild versions as well. Choose mild or spicy based on your taste. See page 263 for our version with fire-roasted jalapeños.

SWEET POTATO BREAKFAST STACKS

This morning meal runs a gamut of delicious, complementary flavors. There's sweetness from the sweet potatoes, smokiness and saltiness from the bacon, and, if you like, vinegary heat from a drizzle of hot sauce.

SERVES 2

PREP: 5 minutes   **COOK:** 20 minutes   **TOTAL:** 25 minutes

2 tablespoons extra-virgin olive oil

1 medium sweet potato, peeled and cut into eight ½-inch-thick rounds (see Tip)

¼ teaspoon salt

¼ teaspoon black pepper

2 teaspoons white vinegar

4 large eggs

1 clove garlic, minced

4 cups baby spinach

4 slices Whole30-compatible bacon, cooked until crisp

Whole30-compatible hot sauce

Heat 1 tablespoon of the olive oil in a large skillet over medium heat. Add the sweet potato rounds in a single layer and cook until fork-tender and browned on both sides, 3 to 5 minutes per side. Remove the sweet potatoes from the skillet and sprinkle with ⅛ teaspoon of the salt and ⅛ teaspoon of the pepper.

Meanwhile, fill a wide saucepan with 3 inches of water. Add the vinegar and bring to a boil over high heat. Crack each egg into a separate small bowl. Gently slide each egg into the boiling water. Remove the pan from the heat, cover, and let sit for 3 minutes for very soft yolks or 5 minutes for firm yolks. Remove the cooked eggs from the pan with a slotted spoon and place on a paper towel-lined plate to drain.

Heat the remaining 1 tablespoon oil in the large skillet over medium heat. Add the garlic and cook, stirring, until fragrant, about 30 seconds. Stir in the spinach and cook, stirring, until wilted, about 1 minute. Stir in the remaining ⅛ teaspoon salt and ⅛ teaspoon pepper.

On each plate, top four of the cooked sweet potato rounds with spinach, bacon, and two poached eggs. Serve with hot sauce for drizzling.

TIP Choose a thick, round sweet potato. Store any extra sweet potato rounds in an airtight container in the refrigerator for up to 3 days, or cook them while you're at the stove and use the leftovers as an easy side for lunch or dinner.

RED
MEAT

FAUX PHO BEEF ZOODLE SOUP

This Whole30 take on Vietnamese pho subs in zucchini noodles for the classic rice noodles but features the same flavorful ginger-garlic beef broth and toppings—Thai basil, cilantro, sliced green onion, jalapeño, and lime wedges—so you can customize it to your taste. It also uses coconut aminos, a soy-free seasoning made from coconut sap that imparts a savory, soy sauce-like flavor to food.

SERVES 4

PREP: 15 minutes   COOK: 10 minutes   TOTAL: 25 minutes

2 tablespoons coconut oil

1 small onion, halved and thinly sliced

6 ounces fresh shiitake mushrooms, stemmed and sliced

2 cloves garlic, minced

2 teaspoons minced fresh ginger

5 cups Beef Bone Broth (page 285) or Whole30-compatible beef broth

2 tablespoons coconut aminos

2 teaspoons Red Boat fish sauce

1 teaspoon salt

2 medium zucchini

12 ounces boneless beef sirloin steak, thinly sliced across the grain (see Tip)

TOPPINGS

Fresh Thai basil leaves

Fresh cilantro leaves

Sliced green onion

Sliced jalapeño

Lime wedges

In a large pot, heat the coconut oil over medium heat. Add the onion and cook, stirring, until softened, about 2 minutes. Add the mushrooms and cook, stirring, for about 3 minutes. Add the garlic and ginger and cook, stirring, until fragrant, about 30 seconds. Add the broth, coconut aminos, fish sauce, and salt. Bring to a boil; reduce the heat to medium-low and simmer, uncovered, for 5 minutes.

Meanwhile, use a spiral slicer or julienne peeler to cut the zucchini lengthwise into long, thin strands (or use a regular vegetable peeler to cut the zucchini lengthwise into thin ribbons). Add the zucchini noodles to the simmering soup and cook until just tender, about 2 minutes. Add the sliced steak and simmer until just cooked, 30 to 60 seconds. Ladle the soup into bowls and serve with the toppings of your choice.

TIP Freeze the steak for 15 minutes for easier slicing.

BEEF AND SWEET POTATO CHILI

Sweet meets heat in this savory chili. Smoky ground chipotle chile gives it just enough heat to be interesting without being blistering. Make it with your choice of meat—beef, bison, or lamb.

SERVES 4

PREP: 20 minutes   **COOK:** 25 minutes   **TOTAL:** 45 minutes

1 tablespoon olive oil

1 pound ground beef, bison, or lamb

2 cups chopped onion

1 medium serrano chile, seeded and finely chopped

3 cloves garlic, minced

1 can (28 ounces) Whole30-compatible fire-roasted diced tomatoes, undrained

1 cup Beef Bone Broth (page 285) or Whole30-compatible beef broth

1 large sweet potato, peeled and cut into ¾-inch chunks (about 2 cups)

1 cup chopped red bell pepper

2 tablespoons chili powder

½ teaspoon ground chipotle chile pepper

½ teaspoon salt, plus more as needed

Chopped fresh cilantro (optional)

Sliced green onions (optional)

Heat the olive oil in a large pot over medium-high heat. Add the ground beef, onion, serrano chile, and garlic and cook, stirring frequently and breaking up the meat with a wooden spoon, until the meat is browned, about 5 minutes.

Stir in the tomatoes with their juices, broth, sweet potato, bell pepper, chili powder, chipotle, and salt and bring to a boil. Reduce the heat to low, cover, and simmer, stirring occasionally, until the sweet potato is tender, 20 to 25 minutes. If desired, season with additional salt. Serve the chili topped with cilantro and green onions, if desired.

BEEF AND BEET BORSCHT

This jewel-toned Russian-Polish soup is a real tablecloth stainer—but so worth the bit of mess it takes to make. It's absolutely packed with veggies—beets, cabbage, carrots, celery, and mushrooms—and has a fresh, clean taste.

SERVES 4, WITH LEFTOVERS

PREP: 30 minutes   **COOK:** 45 minutes   **TOTAL:** 1 hour 15 minutes

2 tablespoons extra-virgin olive oil

12 ounces sirloin steak, cut into ½-inch cubes

½ teaspoon salt

Freshly ground black pepper

8 ounces fresh mushrooms, sliced

½ teaspoon caraway seeds

4 medium beets (about 1 pound total), peeled and shredded

2 cups shredded red or green cabbage

1 cup shredded carrots

1 cup finely chopped celery

1 small onion, finely chopped

3 tablespoons red wine vinegar

6 cups Beef Bone Broth (page 285) or Whole30-compatible beef broth

1 cup tomato sauce

¼ cup chopped fresh dill, plus more for serving

1 tablespoon Whole30-compatible prepared horseradish or grated fresh horseradish

Chopped fresh parsley

Heat 1 tablespoon of the olive oil in a Dutch oven or stockpot over medium-high heat. Add the steak. Season with the salt and pepper to taste and cook, stirring occasionally, until the meat is browned, 3 to 4 minutes. Transfer to a bowl.

Add 1½ teaspoons of the remaining oil to the pot and reduce the heat to medium. Add the mushrooms and caraway seeds and cook, stirring, until the mushrooms begin to brown, 3 to 5 minutes. Transfer to another bowl.

Add the remaining 1½ teaspoons oil to the pot. Add the beets, cabbage, carrots, celery, and onion and cook, stirring frequently, until the vegetables begin to soften, 8 to 10 minutes. Add the vinegar and scrape up any browned bits from bottom of the pot. Stir in the mushrooms, broth, and tomato sauce and bring to a boil. Reduce the heat to low, cover, and simmer, stirring occasionally, until the vegetables are tender, about 30 minutes.

Add the beef and simmer, covered, until heated through, 1 to 2 minutes. Stir in the dill and horseradish. Taste and adjust the seasoning. Serve topped with parsley and additional dill.

BISON BURGERS WITH ROASTED SHAVED BRUSSELS SPROUTS AND CRISPY SHALLOTS

FROM JENN BUMB OF *PRETEND IT'S A DONUT*

Bison. Check. Roasted Shaved Brussels. Check. Crispified Shallots. CHECK. This is the burger that has been missing in your life. Until now. Bison has a slightly sweeter taste than regular ground beef, and when it's paired with roasted Brussels sprouts and shallots, the flavor becomes out-of-this-world good. Another variation would be to place the shaved Brussels sprouts into a bowl, then top them with the bison burger and crispy shallots, and make yourself a burger bowl.

SERVES 4

PREP: 25 minutes   **COOK:** 20 minutes   **TOTAL:** 45 minutes

1½ pounds ground bison (also called ground buffalo)

4 tablespoons extra-virgin olive oil

1½ tablespoons balsamic vinegar, plus more for serving

1 teaspoon dried rosemary, crushed

1 teaspoon dried thyme, crushed

½ teaspoon red pepper flakes

Salt and black pepper

1 pound Brussels sprouts, trimmed and coarsely shaved (see Tip)

2 tablespoons Clarified Butter (page 289) or ghee, melted

2 large shallots, thinly sliced

Preheat the oven to 400°F.

In a large bowl, combine the bison, 2 tablespoons of the olive oil, vinegar, the rosemary, thyme, red pepper flakes, 1 teaspoon salt, and black pepper to taste. Form the meat mixture into four ¾-inch-thick patties.

Spread the Brussels sprouts in an even layer on a large rimmed baking sheet. Drizzle with the butter and season with salt and black pepper. Toss until well coated. Roast for 20 to 25 minutes, stirring once or twice, until the sprouts are lightly browned and crisp on the edges.

Meanwhile, heat the remaining 2 tablespoons oil in a large heavy skillet (cast iron works well) over medium-high heat. Add the shallots and season lightly with salt and black pepper. Reduce the heat to medium and cook, stirring occasionally, until the shallots are crispy, about 10 minutes. Remove the shallots from the skillet and drain on paper towels.

(Continued)

Add the bison patties to the hot skillet and cook, turning once, until they register 160°F in the center, 12 to 14 minutes. Remove the burgers from the skillet and let rest for 5 minutes before serving.

Serve the burgers topped with the Brussels sprouts and crispy shallots and drizzled with balsamic vinegar.

TIP You often can find packaged shredded fresh Brussels sprouts at the supermarket. Or use the slicing blade on a food processor to coarsely shred trimmed whole sprouts. To trim the sprouts, cut very thin slices off the stem ends, being careful not to cut so much off that the sprouts fall apart.

JENN BUMB

Jenn Bumb lives in the San Francisco Bay area with her husband and five little kids. In June 2014, after having her fifth child and reading *It Starts With Food*, she completed her first Whole30. The program completely changed her family's eating habits, and Jenn hasn't looked back since. She started her blog, *Pretend It's a Donut*, and Instagram account in November 2014, focusing on Paleo and Whole30 family-friendly recipes and sticking to a healthy-eating budget when you have a plethora of mouths to feed. In her spare time, she loves camping and traveling with her family, creating recipes, kickboxing, and artichokes.

BRAISED BEEF SHORT RIBS WITH PORCINI MUSHROOM SAUCE

This is the perfect dish to make for a winter dinner party. It's hearty, so delicious—and for the two hours the meat simmers into a meltingly tender texture, you can be doing other things. Start things off with Spinach-Stuffed Mushrooms (page 276), and serve with Dukkah-Crusted Brussels Sprouts (page 224) and Skin-On Garlic Mashed Potatoes (page 249).

SERVES 2

PREP: 30 minutes   **COOK:** 2 hours 15 minutes   **TOTAL:** 2 hours 45 minutes

3 tablespoons extra-virgin olive oil

1 cup chopped carrots

½ cup thinly sliced celery

½ cup chopped onion

4 to 6 bone-in beef short ribs
(1 to 1¼ pounds total)

1 cup Beef Bone Broth (page 285) or Whole30-compatible beef broth

¾ teaspoon salt

Black pepper

¼ cup dried porcini mushrooms

Boiling water

1 cup sliced cremini mushrooms

1 clove garlic, minced

2 teaspoons coconut aminos

1 teaspoon Whole30-compatible coarse-grain mustard

Preheat the oven to 325°F.

Heat 1 tablespoon of the olive oil in a 3- to 4-quart brazier or oven-safe skillet over medium heat. Add the carrots, celery, and onion to the hot oil and cook, stirring occasionally, for 5 minutes. Use a slotted spoon to transfer the vegetables to a bowl. Add the short ribs to the pan. Brown the ribs, turning to brown all sides evenly. Spoon the vegetables around the ribs in the pan. Add ½ cup of the broth. Sprinkle the meat and vegetables with ½ teaspoon of the salt and pepper to taste. Bring to a boil. Cover the pan with the lid, transfer to the oven, and cook for 2 to 2½ hours, until the meat is very tender.

Place the dried mushrooms in a small bowl and add just enough boiling water to cover them. Let stand for 10 minutes. Drain the mushrooms in a fine-mesh sieve set over a bowl to catch the soaking liquid; set the liquid aside. Rinse the mushrooms well and chop them.

In a medium saucepan, heat the remaining 2 tablespoons oil over medium heat. Add the porcini and cremini mushrooms and cook, stirring occasionally, until tender and lightly browned, 6 to 8 minutes. Add the garlic and cook, stirring, for 1 minute more.

In a small bowl, whisk together the coconut aminos and mustard. Add the mustard mixture to the pan with the mushrooms. Stir in the remaining ½ cup broth and the mushroom soaking liquid. Bring to a boil. Reduce the heat to medium-low and simmer, uncovered, until the liquid has

reduced slightly, 3 to 5 minutes. Add the remaining ¼ teaspoon salt and pepper to taste.

Transfer the ribs to a serving platter. Use a slotted spoon to transfer the vegetables to the pan with the mushrooms. Skim the fat off the top of the cooking juices in the brazier. Add the cooking juices to the mushroom mixture and bring just to a boil. Spoon the vegetables and sauce over the ribs to serve.

CHURRASCO SKIRT STEAK WITH GRILLED TOMATOES AND CILANTRO SAUCE

Churrasco is a popular dish in South America and features prominently in many styles in the diverse cuisines of Brazil, Uruguay, and Argentina. The term refers to beef cooked on a spit over an open fire or grilled over an open flame. Here the smoky meat is drizzled with a savory green herb sauce similar to chimichurri.

SERVES 2

PREP: 10 minutes   **MARINATING:** 1 hour   **COOK:** 10 minutes   **TOTAL:** 20 minutes plus marinating

2 tablespoons fresh lime juice

2 tablespoons finely chopped onion

1 tablespoon plus 2 teaspoons extra-virgin olive oil

2 teaspoons finely chopped fresh ginger

3 cloves garlic, minced

½ teaspoon coarse salt

¼ teaspoon black pepper

1 (12-ounce) beef skirt or scored flank steak (see Tip)

16 cherry tomatoes

1 cup fresh cilantro leaves

½ cup fresh parsley leaves

2 tablespoons fresh oregano leaves

¼ cup avocado oil or extra-virgin olive oil

2 teaspoons red wine vinegar

¼ teaspoon red pepper flakes

Lettuce leaves, for serving (optional)

In a shallow dish, combine the lime juice, onion, 1 tablespoon of the olive oil, the ginger, one-third of the garlic, ⅛ teaspoon of the salt, and ⅛ teaspoon of the black pepper. Add the steak and turn to coat. Cover and marinate in the refrigerator for 1 to 4 hours, turning the meat occasionally.

If using wooden skewers, soak them in water to cover for 30 minutes to 1 hour to prevent them from burning.

In a medium bowl, combine the tomatoes, remaining 2 teaspoons olive oil, ⅛ teaspoon of the salt, and remaining ⅛ teaspoon black pepper. Toss to coat. Thread the tomatoes evenly on two 10- to 12-inch skewers, leaving ¼ inch of space between the tomatoes.

Preheat a grill to medium (350 to 375°F). Remove the steak from the marinade and discard the marinade. Grill the steak over direct heat until the internal temperature reaches 145 to 150°F, 10 to 12 minutes for skirt steak or 15 to 17 minutes for flank steak. Grill the tomatoes for 4 to 6 minutes, or until softened and browned. Remove the steak and tomatoes from the grill. Cover the steak with aluminum foil and let rest for 5 minutes.

Meanwhile, in a food processor or blender, combine the cilantro, parsley, avocado oil, oregano, vinegar, remaining ⅛ teaspoon salt, the red pepper flakes, and remaining garlic. Process or blend until the mixture is well combined and finely chopped, but not completely smooth.

Thinly slice the steak across the grain. Serve on plates with the tomatoes. Spoon the cilantro sauce evenly over all. If desired, serve with lettuce leaves to make lettuce wraps. (Use any leftover cilantro sauce on your morning eggs.)

TIP If using flank steak, use a sharp knife to score the steak in a 1-inch diamond pattern on both sides, making long, shallow cuts.

GRILLED FLANK STEAK WITH AVOCADO CREMA AND CUCUMBER SLAW

This summery supper features a whole bunch of complementary flavors, textures, and temperatures. Warm, juicy, marinated grilled steak is topped with a creamy avocado-mayo mixture and served with a side of cool, crunchy, spicy slaw.

SERVES 2 OR 3

PREP: 20 minutes   MARINATING: 1 hour   COOK: 20 minutes   TOTAL: 40 minutes plus marinating

FOR THE STEAK

2 tablespoons extra-virgin olive oil

1 tablespoon fresh lime juice

2 cloves garlic, finely chopped

1 teaspoon chili powder

½ teaspoon ground cumin

¼ teaspoon salt

1 (1¼- to 1½-pound) beef flank steak

FOR THE AVOCADO CREMA

1 ripe avocado, halved, pitted, peeled, and chopped

¼ cup Basic Mayonnaise (page 287)

2 teaspoons fresh lime juice

Salt and black pepper

FOR THE CUCUMBER SLAW

1 English cucumber, seeded and chopped

1 cup shredded red cabbage

⅓ cup roughly chopped fresh cilantro

1 small jalapeño, seeded and finely chopped

2 tablespoons fresh lime juice

1 tablespoon extra-virgin olive oil

Salt and black pepper

MARINATE THE STEAK: In a shallow dish or 1-gallon resealable plastic bag, mix together the olive oil, lime juice, garlic, chili powder, cumin, and salt. Place the steak in the dish or bag and turn to coat the steak with the marinade. Cover the dish or seal the bag and marinate in the refrigerator for at least 1 hour but no longer than 24 hours.

MAKE THE AVOCADO CREMA: In a food processor, combine the avocado, mayonnaise, and lime juice and pulse until smooth. Transfer the crema to a bowl and season with salt and pepper. Cover and chill until ready to serve.

MAKE THE CUCUMBER SLAW: In a medium bowl, combine the cucumber, cabbage, cilantro, jalapeño, lime juice, and olive oil. Season with salt and pepper.

Remove the steak from the refrigerator 30 minutes before cooking. Preheat a grill to medium (350 to 375°F).

Remove the steak from the marinade and discard the marinade. Grill the steak over direct heat, turning once, for 17 to 21 minutes for medium (160°F). Remove the steak from the grill and let it rest for 5 minutes.

Thinly slice the steak diagonally across the grain. Serve the steak with the Avocado Crema and Cucumber Slaw.

SLOW-COOKER ITALIAN BEEF ROAST

Seasoned with fennel, garlic, and a blend of dried oregano, basil, thyme, and rosemary, this hearty roast captures the classic flavors of Italian cooking. The first night, serve it with a blend of potatoes, carrots, and fennel bulb cooked under the roast. Use the leftovers to make three more delicious meals.

SERVES 2, WITH LEFTOVERS

PREP: 25 minutes   **COOK:** 10 hours (low) or 5 hours (high)   **TOTAL:** 10 hours 25 minutes

6 small Yukon Gold or other yellow-fleshed potatoes, peeled

3 carrots, halved and cut into chunks

1 fennel bulb, halved, trimmed, and cut into wedges

1 large onion, cut into wedges

1½ tablespoons dried parsley

1 tablespoon Italian seasoning, crushed

1 tablespoon fennel seeds, crushed

1 teaspoon garlic salt

1 teaspoon black pepper

1 bone-in beef chuck or other pot roast (5 pounds)

1 tablespoon avocado oil or extra-virgin olive oil

⅔ cup Beef Bone Broth (page 285), Whole30-compatible beef broth, or water

2 tablespoons quick-cooking tapioca, crushed

Place the potatoes, carrots, fennel bulb, and onion in a 4-quart slow cooker.

In a small bowl, combine the parsley, Italian seasoning, fennel seeds, garlic salt, and pepper and rub the mixture on all sides of the beef.

Heat the oil in a large skillet over medium-high heat. Add the beef and brown on all sides. Transfer the beef to the slow cooker. Add ⅓ cup of the broth to the hot skillet and bring to a boil, stirring to scrape up any browned bits from the bottom of the skillet. Pour the hot broth over the beef in the slow cooker. Combine the remaining ⅓ cup broth and the tapioca in a bowl and add to the slow cooker.

Cover and cook on low for 10 to 12 hours or on high for 5 to 6 hours.

Divide the beef roast into four equal pieces, removing and discarding the bone. Transfer one piece to a serving platter and the remaining three pieces to separate storage containers to use in Remix recipes. With a slotted spoon, transfer two of the potatoes and one-third of the other vegetables to the serving platter. Transfer the four remaining potatoes and ½ cup of the other vegetables to one storage container for Potato Patties with Shredded Beef and Poached Eggs with Salsa Verde (page 44) and the remaining vegetables to another storage container for Easy Beef, Mushroom, and Rosemary Ragout (page 47). The remaining meat portion is for Beef and Broccoli Slaw Lettuce Wraps (page 48). Skim the fat from the sauce in the slow cooker; spoon half the sauce over the vegetables in the ragout Remix container. Seal the containers, label with the designated Remix recipe, and refrigerate.

Drizzle the remaining sauce over the meat and vegetables on the serving platter and serve immediately.

POTATO PATTIES WITH SHREDDED BEEF AND POACHED EGGS WITH SALSA VERDE

This super-quick dish makes an excellent breakfast or brunch as well as dinner. It not only takes advantage of leftover meat from Slow-Cooker Italian Beef Roast, but also the leftover potatoes, carrots, and fennel, which are transformed into crispy potato cakes.

SERVES 4

PREP: 5 minutes   **COOK:** 25 minutes   **TOTAL:** 30 minutes

Reserved meat and vegetables from Slow-Cooker Italian Beef Roast (page 43)

5 large eggs

¼ teaspoon salt

2 to 3 teaspoons Clarified Butter (page 289) or ghee

4 tablespoons Charred Tomatillo Salsa (see page 15) or Whole30-compatible salsa verde

---

Preheat the oven to 200°F.

In a food processor, combine the potatoes and vegetables from the Slow-Cooker Italian Beef Roast, 1 of the eggs, and the salt. Pulse until the potatoes and vegetables are chopped into very small chunks.

Heat the butter in a large skillet over medium-high heat. Working in batches, drop rounded tablespoons of the potato mixture into the skillet, flattening them slightly. Cook the patties, turning them once, until browned on both sides, 3 to 4 minutes per side. (You should have 12 patties.) Keep the potato patties warm on a baking sheet in the oven.

Meanwhile, fill a wide saucepan with 3 inches of water. Add the white vinegar and 1 teaspoon salt. Bring to a boil over high heat. Crack each egg into a separate small bowl or cup. Gently pour each egg into the boiling water. Remove the pan from the heat, cover, and let sit until the whites are firm but the yolks are still runny, about 4 minutes. Remove the poached eggs from the skillet with a slotted spoon and place on a paper towel-lined plate to drain.

Use two forks to shred the meat from the Slow-Cooker Italian Beef Roast and place it in the skillet used to cook the potato patties. Warm the beef over medium heat.

Divide the potato patties among four serving plates; top them evenly with the warm beef and finish each serving with a poached egg and 1 tablespoon of the salsa.

TIP Salsa verde or "green sauce" is a salsa made from lemony-tart tomatillos, chiles, lime juice, garlic and/or onion, and cilantro. It can be made from fresh, uncooked tomatillos and chiles or vegetables that have been lightly charred.

EASY BEEF, MUSHROOM, AND ROSEMARY RAGOUT

In France, a *ragoût* is a thick, long-simmered, and well-seasoned stew of meat and vegetables. This hearty beef ragout with mushrooms and tomatoes tastes like it's been cooking all day, but thanks to leftovers from Slow-Cooker Italian Beef Roast, it takes just 20 minutes, start to finish.

SERVES 2 OR 3

PREP: 5 minutes   **COOK:** 15 minutes   **TOTAL:** 20 minutes

2 teaspoons extra-virgin olive oil

2 cups sliced fresh cremini or assorted mushrooms

2 cloves garlic, minced

1 can (14.5 ounces) diced tomatoes, undrained

1 to 2 tablespoons chopped fresh rosemary

Reserved meat and vegetables from Slow-Cooker Italian Beef Roast (page 43)

Salt and black pepper

1 tablespoon balsamic vinegar (optional)

1 spaghetti squash, cooked and shredded into noodles (optional; see Tip)

Heat the oil in a large skillet over medium heat. Add the mushrooms and garlic and cook, stirring occasionally, until the mushrooms are tender, about 3 minutes. Add the tomatoes with their juices and the rosemary. Bring to a boil, then reduce the heat to maintain a simmer.

Use two forks to shred the meat from the Slow-Cooker Italian Beef Roast. Cut the reserved vegetables into large bite-size pieces. Add the beef and vegetables to the tomato mixture in the skillet. Simmer, uncovered, until the mixture reaches the desired consistency, about 10 minutes. Season with salt and pepper. Stir in the vinegar (if using) and serve over spaghetti squash noodles, if desired.

TIP For spaghetti squash noodles, cut a spaghetti squash in half lengthwise and remove the seeds. Place the halves, cut-side down, in a baking dish. Bake, uncovered, in a preheated 350°F oven for about 45 minutes, or until tender. (Alternatively, add a little water to the baking dish, cover, and microwave on high for about 15 minutes.) Use a fork to pull the squash pulp into shreds, or "noodles."

BEEF AND BROCCOLI SLAW LETTUCE WRAPS

When you are really in a hurry, you can still eat a delicious, wholesome meal—and these tasty beef wraps topped with a warm Asian-inspired slaw are proof. Using planned leftovers from the Slow-Cooker Italian Beef Roast, they take just 10 minutes from start to finish.

SERVES 2

PREP: 5 minutes   **COOK:** 5 minutes   **TOTAL:** 10 minutes

1 tablespoon coconut oil

1 clove garlic, minced

2 cups shredded broccoli slaw mix

2 green onions, sliced

1 teaspoon finely grated fresh ginger

Reserved meat from Slow-Cooker Italian Beef Roast (page 43), shredded with 2 forks

2 tablespoons coconut aminos

1 tablespoon rice vinegar

4 to 6 large-leaf lettuce or butterhead lettuce leaves

Heat the coconut oil in a large skillet over medium-high heat. Add the garlic and cook, stirring, for 30 seconds. Add the broccoli slaw mix, green onions, and ginger and cook, stirring, until the broccoli slaw is crisp-tender, about 3 minutes. Stir in the shredded beef, coconut aminos, and vinegar and cook until the beef is heated through.

Spoon the beef and broccoli mixture onto the lettuce leaves. Wrap the leaves around the filling and secure with toothpicks. Serve immediately.

JICAMA TACOS WITH BARBACOA

FROM KENDRA CARDOZA OF *PALEO PAPARAZZI*

Tacos were birthed in taquerias in Mexican working-class neighborhoods in the late 19th century. They were brought to the U.S. by Mexican migrants working in mines and on railroads in the early 1900s, and were eventually popularized by San Antonio's street-vendor Chili Queens and early tamale pushcart entrepreneurs in Southern California. Today, Mexican food and Mexican-American tacos are typically adaptations of indigenous and traditional ingredients, as opposed to the ones available in the American food industry. I grew up in Southern California, immersed in the culture of Mexican-American food, and love to be inspired in the kitchen by this intermixture of cultural flavors. These grain-free tacos with spicy, smoky barbacoa use jicama in place of traditional tortillas.

SERVES 4 (5 TACOS PER SERVING), WITH LEFTOVER MEAT

PREP: 25 minutes   COOK: 8 hours (low) or 4 hours (high)   TOTAL: 8 hours 25 minutes

1 tablespoon extra-virgin olive oil

3 pounds boneless beef chuck roast

3 dried chile peppers (mild chile pods), stemmed and seeded

1 cup Beef Bone Broth (page 285) or Whole30-compatible beef broth

½ cup canned crushed tomatoes

¼ teaspoon cayenne pepper

1 cup finely chopped white onion

4 cloves garlic, minced

1 can (4 ounces) chopped green chiles

Juice of 2 limes (about ¼ cup)

4 bay leaves

2 tablespoons apple cider vinegar

2 tablespoons ground cumin

1 tablespoon salt

2 teaspoons dried oregano, crushed

1 teaspoon Red Boat fish sauce

1 teaspoon granulated garlic

½ teaspoon crushed or ground cloves

¼ teaspoon smoked paprika

¼ teaspoon red pepper flakes

¼ teaspoon black pepper

1 medium jicama (see Tip), peeled

Whole30-compatible salsa

Guacamole (page 271)

Chopped fresh cilantro

Heat the olive oil in a Dutch oven or heavy skillet over medium-high heat. Add the beef and sear on all sides, turning the meat to brown it evenly. Place the beef in a 3½- to 5-quart slow cooker.

In the Dutch oven or skillet, cook the dried chiles over medium-high heat, stirring frequently, until

(Continued)

slightly darkened and fragrant, 3 to 5 minutes (don't let them smoke). Add ½ cup of the broth, the tomatoes, and the cayenne and bring to a boil. Reduce the heat to medium-low and simmer, uncovered, for 5 to 6 minutes. Transfer to a blender and puree until smooth (be careful, as the mixture will be hot).

Add the pureed tomato mixture to the slow cooker along with the remaining ½ cup broth, the onion, garlic, canned chiles, lime juice, bay leaves, vinegar, cumin, salt, oregano, fish sauce, granulated garlic, crushed cloves, smoked paprika, red pepper flakes, and black pepper. Cover and cook on low for 8 hours or on high for 4 hours, until the beef is tender and falls apart when shredded with a fork.

Turn off the slow cooker. Remove and discard the bay leaves. Use two forks to shred the meat in the cooker. Season the meat mixture with salt. (You should have about 6 cups meat.)

Use a mandoline to thinly slice the jicama into ⅛-inch-thick disks to use as your taco shells. (You should have about 20 taco shells.) Using tongs or a slotted spoon, fill each taco shell with about 2 tablespoons of the meat. Top with salsa, guacamole, and cilantro.

Store the remaining meat (about 2½ cups) in an airtight container in the refrigerator for up to 3 days or freeze for up to 1 month. Serve over Simple Cauliflower Rice (page 291) or cooked zucchini noodles.

TIP It is important to choose a medium jicama that will just fit onto your mandoline so that you have evenly thick slices—about ⅛ inch. If you don't have a mandoline, substitute 20 lettuce leaves for the jicama.

KENDRA CARDOZA

Kendra Cardoza is the founder and chef of the whole food recipe and lifestyle blog *Paleo Paparazzi*. A self-taught real food chef, she started her journey of exploring how to heal her and her family's bodies with nutritious foods after her husband suffered a stroke and she was diagnosed with an autoimmune disease (endometriosis) in 2011. In 2013 she stumbled upon the Whole30 program and the Paleo lifestyle. This sparked her passion for nutrition, recipe creation, and food photography. Kendra lives in Northern California with her husband, and when they aren't cooking, they love to spend their time cycling and giving back to their community by volunteering for various local charities.

BISON BURGERS
WITH GRILLED GREEN ONIONS
AND RIPE TOMATOES

An aromatic combination of spices—coriander, cumin, and cinnamon—imparts a warm, slightly exotic flavor to these smoky grilled burgers. Served atop slices of juicy ripe tomatoes with a dollop of mayo on top and crispy charred onions on the side, they are the essence of summer.

SERVES 4

PREP: 15 minutes   **COOK:** 10 minutes   **TOTAL:** 25 minutes

¼ cup chopped fresh parsley

1 teaspoon ground coriander

½ teaspoon ground cumin

½ teaspoon coarse salt

¼ teaspoon ground cinnamon

¼ teaspoon black pepper

1 pound ground bison

1 large egg, lightly beaten

⅓ cup finely chopped onion

2 tablespoons extra-virgin olive oil

2 bunches green onions

1 large ripe tomato, cut into 4 thick slices

4 teaspoons Basic Mayonnaise (page 287)

Chopped fresh chives, basil, and/or thyme

Preheat a grill to medium (350 to 375°F).

In a small bowl, combine the parsley, coriander, cumin, salt, cinnamon, and pepper. Place the bison in a medium bowl and add the parsley-spice mixture, the egg, chopped onion, and 1 tablespoon of the olive oil. Mix with your hands just until combined. Shape the meat mixture into four ¾-inch-thick patties. Use your thumb to make a slight indentation in the center of each patty.

Grill the patties over direct heat for 10 to 12 minutes, turning once, until they register 160°F.

Toss the green onions with the remaining 1 tablespoon olive oil and lightly season with salt and pepper. Grill the green onions, turning them once, until tender and lightly charred, about 4 minutes.

Place a tomato slice on each of four serving plates and top each with a bison burger. Divide the charred green onions among the plates. Top the patties with mayonnaise and sprinkle chopped herbs over all.

GRILLED LAMB CHOPS AND FINGERLINGS WITH ARUGULA PESTO

Lamb chops are super juicy and loaded with meaty flavor. Here they get a simple seasoning of garlic and thyme and a topping of peppery arugula pesto. Boiling the potatoes and then grilling them yields a creamy interior and wonderfully crisp exterior.

SERVES 2

PREP: 10 minutes   **COOK:** 25 minutes   **TOTAL:** 35 minutes

FOR THE CHOPS

4 lamb loin or rib chops (about 1 pound)

1 clove garlic, halved

2 teaspoons snipped fresh thyme

Coarse salt and black pepper

FOR THE POTATOES

6 fingerling potatoes

Coarse salt

1 tablespoon extra-virgin olive oil

Black pepper

FOR THE PESTO

2 cups packed arugula

½ cup almonds, toasted (see Tip, page 19)

½ cup walnut oil or extra-virgin olive oil

1 teaspoon grated lemon zest

1 tablespoon fresh lemon juice

1 clove garlic, minced

¼ teaspoon coarse salt

⅛ teaspoon cayenne pepper

Preheat a grill to medium (350 to 375°F).

MAKE THE CHOPS: Trim the fat from the chops. Rub both sides of the chops with the garlic. Lightly season the chops with the thyme and salt and black pepper to taste, rubbing in the seasoning with your fingers. Let stand at room temperature while you prepare the potatoes and pesto.

MAKE THE POTATOES: Put the potatoes in a large saucepan with enough water to cover. Lightly salt the water. Bring to a boil and cook until the potatoes can be pierced with the tip of a knife but are not completely tender, 9 to 10 minutes. Drain. When cool enough to handle, cut the potatoes in half lengthwise and toss with the olive oil and salt and black pepper to taste.

MAKE THE PESTO: In a food processor, combine the arugula, almonds, walnut oil, lemon zest and juice, garlic, salt, and cayenne. Process until smooth.

Grease the grill rack. Place the chops and potatoes on the greased rack over direct heat. Cover and grill the chops, turning once, for 12 to 14 minutes for medium-rare (145°F) or 15 to 17 minutes for medium (160°F). Grill the potatoes, turning once, for 10 minutes, or until they are tender and have grill marks.

Serve the lamb chops with the pesto and grilled potatoes.

TACO-STYLE TWICE-BAKED POTATOES

FROM KENDRA CARDOZA OF *PALEO PAPARAZZI*

These are not your ordinary baked potatoes. Delicious potatoes baked twice with a wonderful Mexican flair, they are stuffed with a spicy cauliflower "rice" and taco-flavored beef and topped with guacamole and salsa.

SERVES 2

PREP: 40 minutes **BAKE:** 1 hour **TOTAL:** 1 hour, 40 minutes

3 large baking potatoes

FOR THE TACO MIX

2 tablespoons chili powder

1 tablespoon ground cumin

2 teaspoons salt (optional)

1 teaspoon black pepper

1 teaspoon smoked paprika

1 teaspoon ground coriander

½ teaspoon garlic powder

½ teaspoon red pepper flakes

FOR THE TACO MEAT

1 teaspoon extra-virgin olive oil

8 ounces lean ground beef

¼ cup chopped onion

2 cloves garlic, minced

¾ teaspoon Whole30-compatible hot sauce

⅛ teaspoon apple cider vinegar

FOR THE CAULIFLOWER RICE

1½ cups cauliflower florets

½ cup Chicken Bone Broth (page 284) or Whole30-compatible chicken broth

¼ cup canned crushed tomatoes

¼ cup chopped onion

1½ teaspoons Whole30-compatible hot sauce

2 cloves garlic, minced

¼ teaspoon ground cumin

Pinch of cayenne pepper

⅛ teaspoon red pepper flakes

TO SERVE

Whole30-compatible salsa

Guacamole (page 271)

Snipped fresh cilantro

Preheat the oven to 400°F.

Scrub the potatoes and pat them dry. Pierce the potatoes all over with a fork and wrap them individually in aluminum foil. Set them on a baking sheet and bake for 1 hour, until tender when pierced with a fork.

MAKE THE TACO MIX: While the potatoes are baking, in a small bowl, combine the chili powder, cumin, salt (if using), black pepper, paprika, coriander, garlic powder, and red pepper flakes.

MAKE THE TACO MEAT: Heat the olive oil in a large skillet over medium-high heat. Add the beef, onion, garlic, hot sauce, vinegar, and 1 tablespoon of the Taco Mix. Cook, stirring frequently, until the meat is browned, about 8 minutes. Transfer the taco meat to a bowl.

MAKE THE CAULIFLOWER RICE: Pulse the cauliflower in a food processor until it is broken down to the size of rice. Transfer the cauliflower rice to the skillet in which you cooked the meat and add the broth, tomatoes, onion, hot sauce, garlic, cumin, cayenne, and red pepper flakes. Cook over medium-high heat until the liquid cooks down and the cauliflower is tender, 10 to 15 minutes. Transfer the cauliflower rice to a bowl.

Remove the potatoes from the oven (keep the oven on) and let cool for 5 to 10 minutes. Slice each potato in half lengthwise. Using a large spoon, scoop out the center of each potato, leaving about ¼ inch of flesh around the skins. Place the potato flesh in a large bowl. Add the taco meat and cauliflower rice and stir to combine. Scoop the filling back into the potato shells and return them to the baking sheet. Bake for 10 minutes, until heated through.

Serve the potatoes topped with salsa, guacamole, and cilantro.

MUSHROOM-STUFFED BEEF ROULADE WITH GARLICKY GREEN BEANS

Roulade is the French term for a thin piece of meat rolled around a savory filling of some combination of vegetables, bread crumbs, and cheese. This Whole30 Approved roulade features a yummy stuffing of sautéed cremini mushrooms, onions, and red bell pepper flavored with garlic, oregano, basil, and lemon zest.

SERVES 4

PREP: 25 minutes   **COOK:** 25 minutes   **TOTAL:** 50 minutes

5 tablespoons extra-virgin olive oil

8 ounces cremini mushrooms, finely chopped

1 cup finely chopped red onion

½ cup finely chopped red bell pepper

4 cloves garlic, minced

1 tablespoon chopped fresh oregano

¾ cup chopped fresh basil

1 tablespoon almond flour

1 teaspoon grated lemon zest

1 teaspoon salt

1 pound green beans, trimmed

½ teaspoon red pepper flakes

1 beef sirloin or round steak (1¼ to 1½ pounds)

2 tablespoons Whole30-compatible tomato paste

1 cup Beef Bone Broth (page 285) or Whole30-compatible beef broth

Preheat the oven to 400°F.

Heat 1 tablespoon of the olive oil in a large skillet over medium-high heat. Add the mushrooms and cook, stirring occasionally, until lightly browned, about 3 minutes. Add ½ cup of the onion and the bell pepper. Cook, stirring occasionally, until the onion is tender, 3 minutes. Add half the garlic and the oregano. Cook, stirring, for 1 minute more. Remove from the heat and stir in ½ cup of the basil, the almond flour, lemon zest, and ½ teaspoon of the salt. Transfer the mushroom mixture to a bowl and set aside to cool slightly. Rinse and dry the skillet.

Trim away any excess fat from the edges of the steak. Place the steak on a work surface. With the notched edge of a meat mallet, pound the steak to about ¼ inch thick. Spread the mushroom mixture over the steak to within ½ inch of the edges. Starting on a long side, roll up the meat and tie it with 100% cotton kitchen string.

In a medium bowl, combine the green beans, 2 tablespoons of the oil, the remaining garlic, and the remaining ½ teaspoon salt and toss. Spread the beans evenly on a large baking sheet. Roast for 18 to 20 minutes, until the beans are lightly browned and crisp-tender.

In the same skillet, heat the remaining 2 tablespoons olive oil over medium-high heat. Sear the meat in the hot oil and cook, turning occasionally, to sear evenly on all sides. Remove the meat from the skillet. Add the remaining ½ cup onion to the skillet. Cook, stirring, until softened, about 5 minutes. Stir in the tomato paste, then whisk in the broth. Bring the broth to a boil. Return the meat to the skillet and spoon some of the sauce over the meat. Cover and reduce the heat to medium-low. Simmer gently, turning once, until the internal temperature of the roulade is 160°F, 8 to 10 minutes. Sprinkle with the remaining ¼ cup basil.

Transfer the roulade to a cutting board and let rest for 5 to 10 minutes. Remove the string and cut into ½-inch-thick slices. Serve the meat and sauce with the green beans.

SLOW-COOKED MOROCCAN-SPICED SHREDDED BEEF WITH MOROCCAN CAULIFLOWER RICE

What makes this dish Moroccan? A heavenly combination of aromatic spices like cumin, turmeric, cloves, and cayenne, and the use of dried fruits for a touch of sweetness. Look to your local Middle Eastern or North African market for these ingredients.

SERVES 4

PREP: 15 minutes   **COOK:** 11 hours (low) or 5½ hours (high)   **TOTAL:** 11 hours 15 minutes

1 teaspoon coarse salt

1 teaspoon ground coriander

1 teaspoon ground cumin

½ teaspoon black pepper

½ teaspoon ground ginger

¼ teaspoon ground cloves

¼ teaspoon cayenne pepper

1 boneless beef chuck pot roast (2 to 2½ pounds), trimmed of fat

1 tablespoon extra-virgin olive oil

1 small onion, cut into wedges

½ cup water

4 lemon slices

4 orange slices

Simple Cauliflower Rice (page 291)

½ cup unsulfured raisins

¼ cup slivered almonds

¼ teaspoon ground turmeric

¼ teaspoon ground cinnamon

1 green onion

4 unsulfured dried apricots, thinly sliced

Combine the salt, coriander, ½ teaspoon of the cumin, the black pepper, ginger, cloves, and cayenne in a small bowl. Sprinkle the spice mixture over the roast and rub it in with your fingers. In a large skillet, heat the olive oil over medium heat. Add the roast and cook until browned, turning it to brown all sides evenly.

Place the onion wedges in a 3½- or 4-quart slow cooker and add the water. Set the meat in the slow cooker and arrange the lemon and orange slices over the meat. Cover and cook on low for 11 to 12 hours or on high for 5½ to 6 hours.

Meanwhile, prepare the cauliflower rice and stir in the remaining ½ teaspoon cumin, the raisins, almonds, turmeric, and cinnamon.

Remove the meat from the slow cooker. Using two forks, shred the meat; discard the fat and the citrus slices. If desired, add the onions from the cooker to the meat. Add some of the cooking juices to the meat to moisten it.

Thinly slice the green top from the green onion. Spoon the meat onto serving plates and sprinkle with the green onion tops and dried apricots. Serve with the cauliflower rice.

SPICY PINEAPPLE STEAK KABOBS

Pork isn't the only meat that pairs perfectly with pineapple. These skewers feature chunks of juicy pineapple and bell peppers threaded alternately with steak that has soaked up the fabulous flavors of a sweet-spicy marinade made from pineapple juice, coconut aminos, lemon juice, serrano chile, ginger, and garlic.

SERVES 4

PREP: 25 minutes   **MARINATING:** 1 to 24 hours   **COOK:** 10 minutes   **TOTAL:** 35 minutes plus marinating

2 pounds lean beef steak (sirloin, flank, strip), cut into 1-inch pieces

¼ cup unsweetened pineapple juice

3 tablespoons coconut aminos

2 tablespoons fresh lemon juice

1 serrano chile pepper, seeded and thinly sliced

2 teaspoons grated fresh ginger

1 clove garlic, minced

¼ teaspoon salt

¼ teaspoon black pepper

1 small pineapple, peeled, cored, and cut into 1½-inch chunks

2 bell peppers, seeded and cut into 1½-inch pieces

1 onion, cut into 8 wedges

Place the steak in a resealable plastic bag or non-reactive bowl with a lid and add the pineapple juice, coconut aminos, lemon juice, serrano chile, ginger, garlic, salt, and black pepper. Toss the steak to coat thoroughly with the marinade. Seal the bag or cover the bowl and marinate the steak in the refrigerator for 1 to 24 hours.

If using wooden skewers, soak them in water for 30 minutes to 1 hour to prevent them from burning.

Remove the steak from the refrigerator 30 minutes before cooking. Preheat a grill to medium (350 to 375°F).

Drain the steak, reserving the marinade. Prepare the kabobs by threading the steak, pineapple, bell peppers, and onion onto the skewers, leaving a ¼-inch space between each piece. Brush the kabobs with the marinade.

Grill the kabobs over direct heat, brushing them with the marinade and turning them once or twice, for 8 to 12 minutes, until the vegetables are tender and steak is cooked to the desired doneness. Discard any remaining marinade.

TIP If fresh pineapple isn't in season, use 4 cups canned unsweetened pineapple chunks in pineapple juice. Bonus—you can use the juice from the can, too.

TOMATO BUN SLOPPY JOES WITH ANCHO-SPICED BUTTERNUT SQUASH

Although you won't need as many napkins to eat these bunless, knife-and-fork sandwiches as you would for a traditional sloppy joe, they're every bit as saucy and delicious as the original.

SERVES 2 OR 3

PREP: 5 minutes   **COOK:** 25 minutes   **TOTAL:** 30 minutes

1 portion Ground Beef Base (recipe follows)

3 tablespoons Whole30-compatible tomato paste

½ teaspoon dried thyme, crushed

1 cup apple cider

1 cup Beef Bone Broth (page 285) or Whole30-compatible beef broth

2 tablespoons Whole30-compatible yellow mustard

2 medium tomatoes or 1 large tomato, cut into ½-inch-thick slices

Chopped fresh parsley

1 portion Ancho-Spiced Roasted Butternut Squash (recipe follows)

Place the Ground Beef Base in a large skillet. Add the tomato paste and thyme. Cook, stirring, until heated through. Stir in the apple cider, broth, and mustard and bring to a boil. Reduce the heat, cover, and simmer for 20 minutes. If necessary, remove the lid and simmer, uncovered, until the mixture reaches the desired consistency.

Spoon the beef mixture onto the tomato slices. Top with parsley. Serve with the Ancho-Spiced Butternut Squash.

GROUND BEEF BASE

MAKES 3 PORTIONS (3 CUPS EACH)

PREP: 10 minutes   **COOK:** 20 minutes   **TOTAL:** 30 minutes

3 pounds ground beef

2 red, yellow, and/or green bell peppers, seeded and chopped

2 large onions, chopped

4 cloves garlic, minced

2 teaspoons dried oregano, crushed

2 teaspoons salt

1 teaspoon black pepper

In a very large skillet, cook the ground beef over medium heat, stirring and breaking it up with a wooden spoon, until browned. Add the bell peppers, onions, garlic, oregano, salt, and black pepper. Cook, stirring occasionally, until the onions have softened, about 5 minutes.

Divide the beef mixture into three equal portions (about 3 cups each). Place two portions in separate airtight containers for Beef and Squash Collard Green Enchiladas (page 68) and Triple-Chile Butternut Squash Chili with Lime Slaw (page 67). Cover and chill for up to 3 days or freeze for up to 6 months (if frozen, thaw in the refrigerator before using). Use the remaining portion for the sloppy joes.

ANCHO-SPICED ROASTED BUTTERNUT SQUASH

MAKES 3 PORTIONS (2 CUPS EACH)

PREP: 15 minutes   **COOK:** 30 minutes   **TOTAL:** 45 minutes

2 medium butternut squash, peeled, halved, seeded, and cut into 1-inch cubes

¼ cup extra-virgin olive oil

2 teaspoons ground ancho chile

1 teaspoon garlic powder

1 teaspoon salt

Preheat the oven to 400°F.

In a large roasting pan, combine the squash, olive oil, ancho chile, garlic powder, and salt. Toss to combine. Roast for 30 to 40 minutes, stirring once or twice, until the squash is browned and tender.

Divide the squash into three equal portions (about 2 cups each). Place two portions in separate airtight containers for Beef and Squash Collard Green Enchiladas (page 68) and Triple-Chile Butternut Squash Chili with Lime Slaw (page 67). Cover and chill for up to 3 days or freeze for up to 6 months. Serve the remaining portion with the sloppy joes.

TRIPLE-CHILE BUTTERNUT SQUASH CHILI WITH LIME SLAW

Three kinds of fresh chiles—poblano, banana, and jalapeño—give this chili interest and mild heat. A cool and crisp topping of lime-dressed cabbage-jicama slaw gives it crunch.

SERVES 4

PREP: 15 minutes   **COOK:** 35 minutes   **TOTAL:** 50 minutes

1 portion Ground Beef Base (page 64)

1 fresh poblano pepper, seeded and chopped

1 fresh banana pepper or Anaheim chile, seeded and chopped

1 fresh jalapeño, seeded and chopped

1 can (28 ounces) diced tomatoes, undrained

1 cup Beef Bone Broth (page 285) or Whole30-compatible beef broth

1 portion Ancho-Spiced Roasted Butternut Squash (page 65)

1 tablespoon chili powder

3 cups finely shredded green cabbage

1 cup shredded jicama or carrots

¼ cup finely chopped fresh cilantro

Grated zest and juice of 1 lime

In a large saucepan, heat the Ground Beef Base over medium heat until heated through. Add the poblano, banana pepper, and jalapeño and cook, stirring, until softened, about 5 minutes. Stir in the tomatoes with their juices, the broth, butternut squash, and chili powder. Bring to a boil. Reduce the heat, cover, and simmer for 30 minutes.

Meanwhile, in a medium bowl, combine the cabbage, jicama, cilantro, lime zest, and lime juice. Let stand at room temperature for 10 minutes.

Serve the chili topped with the slaw.

BEEF AND SQUASH COLLARD GREEN ENCHILADAS

These enchiladas come to the table bubbling in a delicious, fresh-tasting chili sauce. Sturdy collard green leaves—with their generous size—heartily hold the savory-sweet filling of spicy ground beef and roasted butternut squash. Not only do they stand in beautifully for tortillas, but they boost nutrition, too.

SERVES 4

PREP: 25 minutes   **COOK:** 30 minutes   **TOTAL:** 55 minutes

8 large collard green leaves, stemmed

1 portion Ground Beef Base (page 64)

1 portion Ancho-Spiced Roasted Butternut Squash (page 65)

½ teaspoon ground cumin

½ teaspoon ground coriander

1 can (16 ounces) Whole30-compatible tomato sauce

1½ teaspoons chili powder

1 to 2 teaspoons Whole30-compatible hot sauce

½ cup Cashew Cream (page 72)

½ cup chopped fresh cilantro

Preheat the oven to 400°F.

Fill a large pot with water and bring to a boil. Fill a large bowl with ice water. Working with 4 collard green leaves at a time, blanch the leaves in the boiling water until just softened, about 30 seconds. Immediately plunge the leaves into the ice water to cool and stop the cooking. Drain the leaves and pat dry.

In a medium bowl, combine the Ground Beef Base, butternut squash, cumin, and coriander. Divide the beef filling among the collard green leaves. Roll up the leaves and arrange the rolls in a 9 x 13-inch baking dish seam side down.

In a medium bowl, combine the tomato sauce, chili powder, and hot sauce. Pour the mixture over the rolls. Cover the dish with aluminum foil and bake for 30 minutes, until bubbling. Drizzle with the Cashew Cream and sprinkle with the cilantro before serving.

STEAK WITH CARAWAY-PEPPERCORN RUB AND CHARRED GREEN BEANS

Grinding your own spices from whole seeds makes a huge difference in the freshness and intensity of their flavors. Toasting the peppercorns and the caraway and coriander seeds for the spice rub before grinding them enhances their aromas and flavors even more!

SERVES 4

PREP: 25 minutes   **CHILLING:** 4 hours   **COOK:** 20 minutes   **TOTAL:** 45 minutes plus chilling

FOR THE SAUCE

1 cup Cashew Cream (recipe follows)

¼ cup Whole30-compatible prepared horseradish (see Tip) or grated fresh horseradish

1 tablespoon Whole30-compatible Dijon mustard

1 teaspoon white vinegar

1 small clove garlic, minced

¼ teaspoon salt

¼ teaspoon black pepper

FOR THE STEAK

2 tablespoons caraway seeds

2 to 3 teaspoons black peppercorns

¼ teaspoon coriander seeds

2 teaspoons sweet paprika

1 teaspoon salt

½ teaspoon grated lemon zest

1¼ to 1½ pounds beef flank steak

FOR THE GREEN BEANS

12 ounces fresh green beans, trimmed if desired

2 tablespoons olive oil

¼ teaspoon salt

MAKE THE SAUCE: In a small bowl, combine the Cashew Cream, horseradish, mustard, vinegar, garlic, salt, and pepper. Whisk until the sauce is smooth and creamy. Cover and refrigerate for at least 4 hours or overnight to allow the flavors to blend.

MAKE THE STEAK: Preheat a grill to medium (350 to 375°F). In a small skillet, toast the caraway seeds, peppercorns, and coriander seeds over medium heat until fragrant, 1 to 2 minutes. Let cool. Grind the toasted seeds and peppercorns in a spice grinder. Place the ground spices in a small bowl and stir in the paprika, salt, and lemon zest. Lightly score the steak on both sides. Sprinkle the spice mixture over both sides of the meat and rub it in with your fingers. Grill the steak over direct heat, with the lid closed, turning once, for 15 to 17 minutes for medium-rare (145°F) or 17 to 19 minutes for medium (160°F). Cover the steak with aluminum foil and let rest for 5 minutes.

MAKE THE GREEN BEANS: Meanwhile, fill a large saucepan two-thirds full with water and bring to a boil. Fill a large bowl with ice water. Blanch the green beans in the boiling water for 3 minutes. Use a slotted spoon to transfer the green beans to the ice water to cool and stop the cooking; let cool

(Continued)

for 5 minutes, then drain. Transfer the beans to a paper towel–lined tray to dry. Heat a grill wok over direct heat for 5 minutes. Toss the green beans with the olive oil and ¼ teaspoon salt. Add the beans to the wok. Cover the grill and cook the green beans for 8 minutes, stirring occasionally, until tender and lightly charred and blistered.

Cut the steak across the grain into ¼-inch-thick slices. Serve the steak with the charred green beans and horseradish sauce. (Use any leftover sauce on grilled or roasted meats and vegetables later in the week.)

Cashew Cream

Rinse 1 cup raw cashews; drain and place in a bowl. Add enough water to cover by 1 inch. Cover; let stand at room temperature for at least 4 hours and preferably overnight. Drain the cashews, then rinse under cold water. Place the cashews in a high-speed blender; add ¾ cup water and blend until smooth, stopping the blender and scraping down the sides a few times. Add additional water, 1 tablespoon at a time, to reach the desired consistency. Store in an airtight container in the refrigerator for up to 1 week. Makes about 2 cups.

TIP Look for Whole30-compatible prepared horseradish that contains only horseradish, vinegar, and salt—and sometimes a little mustard oil (no sugar, preservatives, or dairy products). It's available at both regular supermarkets and at natural- and whole-foods stores. If you can't find any, it's not difficult to grate your own.

STRIP STEAK WITH BLACKENED CABBAGE

Strip steak—also called New York strip—is a particularly tender cut of meat, with a strip of fat along one edge that gets delightfully crisp and charred on the grill. The fresh basil leaves that are placed between the layers of the grilled cabbage wedges wilt slightly from the heat, making the cabbage taste wonderful and smell amazing!

SERVES 2

PREP: 10 minutes   **COOK:** 20 minutes   **TOTAL:** 30 minutes

½ small head green cabbage

Extra-virgin olive oil

1 pound strip steak, about 1 inch thick

1 clove garlic, halved

Salt and black pepper

8 fresh basil leaves

Caesar-Style Dressing (page 257)

Preheat a grill to medium (350 to 375°F).

Remove the tough outer leaves from the cabbage and cut the cabbage into four wedges, keeping the stalk and inner core intact. Lightly brush the wedges with olive oil.

Rub the steak with the cut sides of the garlic clove and 1 tablespoon olive oil. Season with salt and pepper.

Place the steak and cabbage wedges on the grill rack over direct medium heat. Cover and grill the steak for 10 to 12 minutes for medium-rare (145°F) or 12 to 15 minutes for medium (160°F). Remove the steak from the grill; let rest while the cabbage finishes cooking. Grill the cabbage for 12 to 15 minutes, until the cut sides are blackened and the cabbage is beginning to soften. Carefully turn the wedges over. Cover and grill for 5 to 7 minutes more, until a metal or bamboo skewer easily slides through the layers.

Remove the cabbage from the grill. Place the basil leaves between layers of cabbage; let stand until the basil leaves soften, 2 minutes. Drizzle the cabbage with the Caesar dressing.

STRIP STEAK WITH CRISPY SALT-AND-VINEGAR SMASHED POTATOES

These tarragon butter–topped steaks are served with potatoes inspired by the "chips" (deep-fried potato wedges) served in English pubs that are salted and sprinkled with malt vinegar. To make these, baby Yukon Gold potatoes are boiled in salted water with vinegar until soft, tossed in melted ghee, smashed flat, and baked at high heat until crisp—then seasoned with additional salt and vinegar right before serving.

SERVES 2 OR 3

PREP: 15 minutes   **COOK:** 1 hour   **TOTAL:** 1 hour 15 minutes

FOR THE TARRAGON BUTTER

4 tablespoons Clarified Butter (page 289) or ghee

1 tablespoon minced green onion

1 teaspoon minced fresh tarragon

1 clove garlic, minced

½ teaspoon grated lemon zest

½ teaspoon Whole30-compatible whole-grain mustard

⅛ teaspoon salt

⅛ teaspoon black pepper

FOR THE POTATOES

6 baby Yukon Gold potatoes (about 12 ounces)

1 cup white vinegar

1 tablespoon salt

1 tablespoon Clarified Butter (page 289) or ghee, melted

1 tablespoon extra-virgin olive oil

FOR THE STEAKS

2 strip steaks (about 8 ounces each; see Tip)

Salt and black pepper

1 tablespoon Clarified Butter (page 289) or ghee

1 tablespoon white vinegar

Chopped fresh chives

MAKE THE TARRAGON BUTTER: In a small bowl, combine the butter, green onion, tarragon, garlic, lemon zest, mustard, salt, and pepper. Stir until well combined. Cover and refrigerate until needed.

MAKE THE POTATOES: Preheat the oven to 400°F. Line a large rimmed baking sheet with parchment paper. In a 2-quart saucepan, combine the potatoes, vinegar, and salt. Add enough water to cover the potatoes by an inch. Bring to a boil, then reduce the heat to medium-low and simmer until the potatoes are tender, about 25 minutes. Drain the potatoes and return them to the saucepan. Add the butter and toss gently to coat. Arrange the potatoes in a single layer on the prepared baking sheet. Using a heavy mug or glass, smash each potato to about ½-inch thickness. Bake for 20 minutes. Gently turn each potato over with a spatula. Brush with the olive oil and bake for 15 to 20 minutes more, until golden brown and crisp.

MAKE THE STEAKS: Pat the steaks dry with a paper towel. Season with salt and pepper. In a large oven-safe skillet, melt the butter over medium-high heat.

Sear the steaks until the exterior is nicely browned, 2 to 3 minutes per side. Transfer the skillet to the oven. Roast the steaks to the desired doneness, 5 to 6 minutes for medium-rare (145°F).

Transfer the steaks to serving plates. Top each steak with 1 tablespoon of the tarragon butter (cover and refrigerate any leftover butter). Let stand for 5 minutes.

Sprinkle the potatoes with the vinegar (about ½ teaspoon on each potato) and chives. Season with salt and pepper. Serve the potatoes with the steaks.

TIP Let the steaks stand at room temperature for 30 minutes before cooking, if possible.

RED BEEF CURRY WITH GREEN BEANS

FROM GUEST BLOGGER ARSY VARTANIAN OF *RUBIES & RADISHES*

Fifteen minutes of prep in the morning will reward you with a warm, flavor-packed, and satiating meal at the end of a long day. Serve this curry over cauliflower rice or enjoy it as is!

SERVES 4

PREP: 25 minutes   **COOK:** 7 hours (low) or 3½ hours (high) plus 30 minutes (high)   **TOTAL:** 7 hours 25 minutes

1 tablespoon coconut oil, plus more as needed

2 pounds charcoal steak (see Tip), cut into 1-inch cubes

1 teaspoon coarse salt

½ teaspoon black pepper

1 yellow onion, sliced

3 cloves garlic, minced

1 can (14 ounces) full-fat coconut milk

3 tablespoons Whole30-compatible Thai red curry paste

2 teaspoons Red Boat fish sauce

1 pound fresh green beans, trimmed

Heat the coconut oil in a heavy skillet over medium-high heat. Season the steak with the salt and pepper. Add the beef to the skillet and cook, stirring occasionally, until browned on all sides, about 5 minutes. Place the meat in a 5- to 6-quart slow cooker.

Cook the onion in the same skillet, adding additional coconut oil if needed. Cook, stirring, until the onion is soft, 4 to 5 minutes. Add the garlic and cook, stirring, until fragrant, about 30 seconds. Add the coconut milk and curry paste, stirring to scrape up any brown bits from the bottom of the skillet. Stir in the fish sauce. Transfer to the slow cooker.

Cover and cook on low for 7 to 8 hours or on high for 3½ to 4 hours. Add the green beans and cook on high for 30 minutes more, until the beans are crisp-tender.

TIP Charcoal steak is cut from the side of the sirloin tip. It's a very lean steak that can be on the tough side if it's just grilled (without marinating), but turns butter-knife tender after braising in the slow cooker all day.

ARSY VARTANIAN

Arsy Vartanian is the founder and chef of the Paleo recipe and lifestyle blog *Rubies & Radishes* and the author of the cookbooks *The Paleo Foodie* and *The Paleo Slow Cooker*. In an effort to achieve optimal health and wellness, she began a Paleo diet and a CrossFit program in 2008. Arsy started feeling better than ever and was eventually able to recover from health issues that she had struggled with for almost a decade. Arsy deeply enjoys spending time in her kitchen creating healthy, grain-free recipes for her family and her blog readers. She resides in a quaint beach town in California with her husband and daughter.

PORK

CIDER-BRINED ROASTED PORK TENDERLOIN WITH APPLE-SAUERKRAUT SLAW

A 6- to 8-hour soak in a brine made of apple cider, salt, bay leaves, garlic, caraway, and peppercorn infuses the pork with amazing flavor and makes it super juicy. Toss together the crunchy, sweet-tart slaw at least 2 hours before you plan to eat to allow time for the flavors to blend.

SERVES 3

PREP: 40 minutes   **BRINING:** 6 to 8 hours   **COOK:** 15 minutes   **TOTAL:** 55 minutes plus brining

FOR THE PORK

2 cups apple cider

3 tablespoons salt

2 bay leaves

2 cloves garlic, crushed

2 teaspoons caraway seeds

1 teaspoon black peppercorns

1 pork tenderloin (1¼ to 1½ pounds)

FOR THE SLAW

¼ cup apple cider

2 tablespoons extra-virgin olive oil

1 tablespoon apple cider vinegar

1 teaspoon caraway seeds

1 teaspoon Whole30-compatible coarse-grain mustard

¼ teaspoon salt

1 jar (16 ounces) Whole30-compatible sauerkraut, drained well

1 red or green bell pepper, seeded and finely chopped

1 large carrot, coarsely shredded

½ small sweet onion, finely chopped

1 stalk celery, finely chopped

1 tablespoon extra-virgin olive oil

Black pepper

MAKE THE PORK: In a small saucepan, combine the apple cider, salt, bay leaves, garlic, caraway, and peppercorns. Bring to a boil, stirring to dissolve the salt. Remove from the heat and let stand for 15 minutes. Stir in ½ cup ice cubes. Let stand until completely cool.

Trim the pork tenderloin, removing any tough silver skin. Place in a resealable plastic bag and pour in the cooled brine. Squeeze any air from the bag and seal. Place the bag in a dish and refrigerate for 6 to 8 hours.

MAKE THE SLAW: In a medium bowl, whisk together the apple cider, olive oil, vinegar, caraway, mustard, and salt. Add the sauerkraut, bell pepper, carrot, onion, and celery; toss to coat. Cover and chill for at least 2 hours before serving.

Preheat the oven to 425°F. Remove the pork from the brine and pat it dry with paper towels (discard the brine). Rub the pork with the olive oil and sprinkle with black pepper. Heat a large oven-safe skillet over medium-high heat. Sear the pork on all sides until lightly browned. Transfer the skillet to the oven and roast the tenderloin for 15 to 20 minutes or until the internal temperature is 145°F. Let rest for 10 minutes.

Thinly slice the pork and serve it over or alongside the slaw.

CUBAN-SPICED PORK TENDERLOIN WITH WATERCRESS SALAD

Both the marinade for the pork and the vinaigrette for the salad feature the flavors of a classic Cuban *mojo* (pronounced MO-ho), a sauce made with olive oil, garlic, orange or lime juice, and cumin.

SERVES 2 OR 3

PREP: 15 minutes   **MARINATING:** 2 hours   **COOK:** 25 minutes   **TOTAL:** 40 minutes plus marinating

---

FOR THE VINAIGRETTE

¼ cup extra-virgin olive oil

2 tablespoons apple cider vinegar

1 tablespoon fresh orange juice

1 teaspoon fresh lime juice

1 clove garlic, minced

Salt and black pepper

FOR THE PORK

1 cup fresh orange juice

¼ cup fresh lime juice

1¾ teaspoons ground cumin

1 teaspoon salt

1 teaspoon smoked paprika

½ teaspoon dried oregano, crushed

2 cloves garlic, minced

1 pork tenderloin (1 to 1¼ pounds)

2 teaspoons orange zest

½ teaspoon black pepper

1 tablespoon extra-virgin olive oil

FOR THE SALAD

1 tablespoon extra-virgin olive oil

3 rings fresh pineapple (1 inch thick)

2 bunches watercress, thick stems removed, or 3 cups baby arugula

½ ripe avocado, peeled and cubed

Red onion slivers

MAKE THE VINAIGRETTE: In a small bowl, whisk together the olive oil, vinegar, orange juice, lime juice, and garlic. Season with salt and pepper. Cover and refrigerate until ready to serve.

MAKE THE PORK: In a resealable plastic bag or nonreactive bowl with a lid, combine the orange juice, lime juice, ¾ teaspoon of the cumin, ½ teaspoon of the salt, the paprika, oregano, and garlic. Add the pork to the bag or bowl and turn the meat to coat it with the marinade. Seal the bag or cover the bowl and marinate in the refrigerator, turning occasionally, for 2 hours.

Preheat the oven to 425°F. Remove the pork from the marinade and pat it dry with paper towels (discard the marinade).

In a small bowl, combine the orange zest, the remaining ½ teaspoon salt, remaining 1 teaspoon cumin, and the pepper. Rub the mixture over the pork with your fingers.

Heat the olive oil in a large oven-safe skillet over medium-high heat. Add the pork and sear on both sides, about 10 minutes. Transfer the skillet to the oven and roast for 15 minutes, until the internal temperature is 145°F. Transfer the pork to a cutting board and let rest for 5 minutes before slicing.

MAKE THE SALAD: In a ceramic nonstick skillet, heat the olive oil over medium heat. Add the pineapple rings and cook, turning once, until caramelized, 5 to 8 minutes. Let the pineapple cool slightly and then cut it into bite-size pieces. Place the watercress in a medium bowl and toss with half the vinaigrette. Arrange the watercress on a platter and top with the pineapple and avocado. Drizzle with the remaining vinaigrette and sprinkle with red onion.

Serve the pork with the salad.

GREEN PORK AND CAULIFLOWER CURRY

Thankfully, there are premade curry pastes that are Whole30 compatible and very widely available. Thai Kitchen makes a green curry paste that is just green chile, garlic, lemongrass, galangal (Thai ginger), salt, shallot, spices, and kaffir lime. Just a couple of spoonfuls adds awesome flavor to this coconut-milk curry.

SERVES 4

PREP: 10 minutes　　**COOK:** 25 minutes　　**TOTAL:** 35 minutes

2 teaspoons coconut oil

2 tablespoons Whole30-compatible green curry paste

1 pound pork tenderloin, sliced into bite-size strips

1 small onion, chopped

1 Thai chile, seeded and finely chopped (optional)

3 cups bite-size cauliflower florets

¾ cup diced orange bell pepper

1 cup full-fat coconut milk

¾ cup Chicken Bone Broth (page 284) or Whole30-compatible chicken broth

1½ teaspoons Red Boat fish sauce or coconut aminos

4 fresh basil leaves (preferably Thai basil), rolled and sliced crosswise into thin ribbons

Lime wedges

Heat the coconut oil in a large nonstick skillet over medium-high heat. Add the curry paste and cook, stirring, for 1 minute. Add the pork and cook, stirring occasionally, until no longer pink, 3 to 5 minutes. Transfer the pork to a bowl and cover to keep warm.

Add the onion and the chile (if using) to the same skillet and cook over medium-high heat, stirring occasionally, until tender, 3 to 4 minutes. Add the cauliflower and bell pepper and cook, stirring occasionally, for 2 minutes more. Stir in the coconut milk and broth. Bring to a simmer. Cover and simmer for 8 minutes. Stir in the pork and fish sauce and cook, uncovered, until the pork is heated through, about 2 minutes. Garnish with the sliced basil and serve with lime wedges.

PORK POSOLE WITH TOSTONES

Posole is a hearty soup popular in Mexico made with pork or chicken and hominy—dried corn that has had the hull and germ removed. This Whole30 version forgoes the hominy and is served with tostones—crisp, pan-fried slices of green plantains served as a side dish in the Afro-Caribbean.

SERVES 2, WITH LEFTOVER PORK

PREP: 1 hour   **COOK:** 9 hours (low) or 4 hours 30 minutes (high) plus 15 minutes (high)   **TOTAL:** 10 hours 45 minutes

FOR THE POSOLE

1 boneless pork shoulder roast (2 pounds)

2 teaspoons dried oregano, crushed

2 teaspoons sweet paprika

1 teaspoon coarse salt

1 teaspoon ground coriander

½ teaspoon ground cumin

¼ teaspoon cayenne pepper

1 tablespoon extra-virgin olive oil

1 cup diced celery root or turnip

1 medium onion, cut into thin wedges

½ cup water

2 cloves garlic, thinly sliced

1 fresh medium poblano chile, quartered and seeded

1 small green bell pepper, quartered and seeded

1¼ cups Chicken Bone Broth (page 284) or Whole30-compatible chicken broth

¼ cup chopped fresh cilantro

½ cup full-fat coconut milk (see Tip)

1 teaspoon salt

FOR THE TOSTONES

2 tablespoons coconut oil

1 small green plantain, peeled and cut into ¾-inch-thick slices

⅛ teaspoon salt

Lime wedges

Thinly sliced radishes

MAKE THE POSOLE: Trim some of the fat off the pork. In a small bowl, combine the oregano, paprika, salt, coriander, cumin, and cayenne. Sprinkle the spice mixture all over the pork and rub it in with your fingers. Heat the olive oil in a large skillet over medium heat. Add the pork and cook, turning to brown all sides evenly.

Combine the celery root, onion, water, and garlic in a 3½- or 4-quart slow cooker. Place the pork on top of the vegetables. Cover and cook on low for 9 to 10 hours or on high for 4½ to 5 hours.

Meanwhile, preheat the oven to 450°F. Line a baking sheet with aluminum foil. Place the poblano and bell pepper quarters, cut sides down, on the baking sheet. Roast for 12 to 15 minutes, or until the skins are well charred. Carefully wrap the foil around the peppers to fully enclose them and

(Continued)

let stand until cool enough to handle, about 20 minutes. Using a small sharp knife, peel off and discard the charred skin and cut the peppers into thin bite-size strips.

Using a slotted spoon, remove the meat from the slow cooker. Using two forks, coarsely shred the meat (discard any fat). Divide the meat into three equal portions (about 1 cup each). Return one portion to the slow cooker. Transfer the remaining two portions to two separate airtight containers to use for Apple-Cabbage and Pork Hash (page 90) and Shredded Pork Lettuce Wraps with Cashew-Coconut Cream Sauce (page 89); seal and refrigerate for up to 3 days or freeze for up to 3 months.

Combine half the poblano and bell peppers, the broth, and 2 tablespoons of the cilantro in a blender and puree until smooth. Add the pepper mixture to the pork in the slow cooker. Add the remaining roasted pepper strips. Stir in the coconut milk and salt.

Cover the slow cooker and cook on high to heat through, about 15 minutes.

MAKE THE TOSTONES: In a heavy medium skillet, heat the coconut oil over medium heat. Add the plantain slices. Cook until lightly browned, turning once, 3 to 4 minutes. Drain on paper towels. Working with one plantain slice at a time, place the slice on a cutting board and use the bottom of a small heavy skillet to flatten the slice to ¼-inch thickness. Use a thin metal spatula to lift and scrape the tostón off the cutting board.

In the same skillet, cook the flattened plantain slices, in batches, until golden brown, turning once, 3 to 4 minutes. Drain on paper towels. Sprinkle with the salt.

To serve, ladle the soup into two bowls. Garnish with the remaining cilantro, lime wedges, and radishes. Serve with the tostones alongside.

TIP Canned coconut milk separates in the can, with the cream rising to the top. Make sure to whisk the coconut milk well before measuring the amount called for here.

SHREDDED PORK LETTUCE WRAPS WITH CASHEW–COCONUT CREAM SAUCE

The Cashew-Cilantro Topper is optional, but it takes no time to make and really adds crunch and flavor to these bahn mi–inspired wraps.

SERVES 2

PREP: 30 minutes   TOTAL: 30 minutes

¼ cup raw cashews

Boiling water

1 tablespoon toasted sesame oil

2 teaspoons rice vinegar

1 teaspoon coconut aminos

1 teaspoon Red Boat fish sauce

⅛ to ¼ teaspoon red pepper flakes

½ cup shredded broccoli slaw mix

¼ cup shredded carrot

6 fresh snow peas, trimmed and thinly sliced lengthwise

2 tablespoons slivered red onion

¼ cup fresh orange juice

¼ teaspoon ground ginger

⅛ teaspoon coarse salt

2 tablespoons coconut cream (see page 286)

1 portion meat from Pork Posole with Tostones (page 87), warmed

6 medium butterhead lettuce leaves

Cashew-Cilantro Topper (recipe follows; optional)

In a medium bowl, combine the cashews and boiling water to cover by 1 inch. Cover and let sit for 20 minutes.

Meanwhile, in a medium bowl, whisk together the sesame oil, vinegar, coconut aminos, fish sauce, and red pepper flakes. Add the broccoli slaw mix, carrot, snow peas, and onion. Toss well to coat.

Drain the cashews and transfer to a blender or food processor. Add the orange juice, ginger, and salt. Cover and blend or process for several minutes, until the mixture is very smooth. Add the coconut cream and blend or process until combined.

To assemble the wraps, divide the warmed meat evenly among the lettuce leaves. Top with the broccoli slaw mixture. Sprinkle with the Cashew-Cilantro Topper, if desired. Drizzle with the sauce and wrap the lettuce leaves up around the filling.

Cashew-Cilantro Topper

In a small bowl, combine ¼ cup toasted chopped raw cashews, ¼ cup chopped fresh cilantro, 2 tablespoons thinly sliced green onion tops, and 1 teaspoon grated lime zest.

APPLE, CABBAGE, AND PORK HASH

With a total prep time of 20 minutes, this hearty hash makes a great meal for a busy weeknight—or a stick-to-your-ribs breakfast before you run out the door.

SERVES 2

PREP: 10 minutes   **COOK:** 10 minutes   **TOTAL:** 20 minutes

6 small red or yellow potatoes (about 1½ inches in diameter)

2 tablespoons Clarified Butter (page 289) or ghee

¼ cup thinly sliced onion

2 cups shredded green cabbage

1 medium cooking apple (see Tip), peeled, if desired, quartered, cored, and thinly sliced

1 teaspoon snipped fresh thyme

¼ teaspoon caraway seeds, crushed

¼ teaspoon coarse salt

⅛ teaspoon black pepper

1 portion meat from Pork Posole with Tostones (page 87)

Fresh thyme (optional)

Scrub the potatoes and thinly slice them crosswise. In a large skillet, heat the butter over medium heat. Add the potatoes and onion and cook, stirring occasionally, for 6 minutes. Stir in the cabbage and apple. Cover and cook, stirring once, for 2 minutes. Uncover and cook, stirring occasionally, until the potatoes and apple are just tender, 2 to 3 minutes more.

Sprinkle the potato mixture with the snipped thyme, caraway seeds, salt, and pepper. Add the shredded meat and toss to combine. Cook until heated through, 1 to 2 minutes. Divide the potato mixture between two serving plates. Garnish with additional thyme, if desired.

TIP   Shredding cabbage can be done in a food processor fitted with a shredding blade, or simply with a sharp chef's knife. Just quarter and core the cabbage, then slice a quarter very thinly until you get the amount of cabbage you need.

Some apple varieties are better for cooking than others because they hold their shape and don't get mushy when exposed to heat. Good varieties for cooking include Granny Smith, Jonathan, Jonagold, Winesap, and Royal Gala.

GRILLED CHOPS WITH MASHERS AND PEPITA PESTO

The unusual pesto that tops these simple grilled chops packs a punch of flavor. It's perfect with the mild, slightly sweet flavor of the mashers: a creamy blend of Yukon Gold potatoes and parsnips.

SERVES 4

PREP: 25 minutes   **COOK:** 20 minutes   **TOTAL:** 45 minutes

FOR THE PESTO

½ cup extra-virgin olive oil

1 bunch curly kale, stemmed

½ cup unsalted roasted pepitas (pumpkin seeds)

1 tablespoon lemon juice

1 tablespoon Whole30-compatible prepared horseradish

1 teaspoon grated lemon zest

½ teaspoon coarse salt

FOR THE MASHERS

2 pounds Yukon Gold potatoes, peeled, if desired, and quartered

1 pound parsnips, peeled and cut into 2-inch pieces

¼ cup Clarified Butter (page 289) or ghee

½ cup Chicken Bone Broth (page 284) or Whole30-compatible chicken broth

½ teaspoon coarse salt

½ teaspoon black pepper

FOR THE CHOPS

4 bone-in pork loin chops (6 to 8 ounces each), cut ½ to 1 inch thick

Coarse salt and black pepper

Finely chopped fresh chives

MAKE THE PESTO: In a food processor, combine the olive oil, kale, pepitas, lemon juice, horseradish, lemon zest, and salt. Process until smooth. Refrigerate until ready to serve (see Tip).

MAKE THE MASHERS: Place the potatoes and parsnips in a large saucepan or Dutch oven. Add cold water to cover and bring to a boil. Reduce the heat to low and simmer until tender, 20 to 25 minutes. Drain and return the vegetables to the hot saucepan. In a small saucepan, heat the butter and broth over medium-low heat until hot. Add the hot broth mixture to the vegetables. Add the salt and pepper. Mash with a potato masher until smooth.

MAKE THE CHOPS: While the potatoes are cooking, preheat a grill to high (400 to 450°F). Lightly season the chops with salt and pepper. Sear the chops on the grill over direct heat until a crust forms, 1 to 2 minutes per side. Reduce the grill temperature to medium (350 to 375°F) or move the chops to indirect heat. Close the grill lid and cook until the internal temperature of the chops is 145°F, about 5 minutes. Let the chops rest for 3 to 5 minutes.

Sprinkle the potato-parsnip mashers with chives and serve alongside the pork chops, topped with the pesto.

TIP Place any leftover pesto in a tightly sealed container and store in the refrigerator for up to 3 days.

PORK CHOPS WITH APPLES AND GREENS

There are so many wonderful flavors that come together in this dish—tart apples, the sweetness of apple cider, and the piquancy of shallot and whole-grain mustard. It makes a perfect fall supper. (Be sure to drizzle everything with generous amounts of the pan sauce!)

SERVES 2

PREP: 20 minutes   **COOK:** 15 minutes   **TOTAL:** 35 minutes

2 tart red apples, cored and sliced

3 tablespoons extra-virgin olive oil

2 bone-in pork chops (about 8 ounces each)

¼ teaspoon salt

¼ teaspoon black pepper

2 tablespoons finely chopped shallot

½ cup Chicken Bone Broth (page 284) or Whole30-compatible chicken broth

¼ cup apple cider

1 teaspoon Whole30-compatible whole-grain mustard

4 cups packed fresh spinach

Preheat the oven to 425°F.

Toss the apple slices with 1 tablespoon of the olive oil in a bowl. Spread the apple slices in a single layer on a rimmed baking sheet. Bake for 10 minutes.

Meanwhile, heat 1 tablespoon of the oil in a medium skillet over medium heat. Pat the pork chops dry with paper towels and sprinkle both sides with the salt and pepper. Add the pork chops to the hot skillet. Cook until browned, about 2 minutes per side. Transfer the chops to the baking sheet with the apples and roast for 10 to 15 minutes, until the internal temperature of the chops is at least 145°F and the apples are tender.

Combine the remaining 1 tablespoon oil and the shallot in the same skillet used to brown the pork chops. Cook over medium heat until the shallot is translucent, 2 to 3 minutes. Add the broth, apple cider, and mustard. Bring to a boil, stirring to scrape up any brown bits from the bottom of the skillet. Reduce the heat and simmer, uncovered, until reduced by half, 3 to 4 minutes. Stir in the spinach and cook, stirring, until wilted, about 30 seconds.

Using a slotted spoon, divide the wilted spinach between two plates. Top with the pork chops and apples. Serve with the remaining pan sauce, if desired.

TIP Apple varieties run the sweet-tart spectrum. For this dish, you want a tart red apple such as Cortland, Jonathan, or Braeburn. Even Honeycrisp—despite its name—works well, as it has tart undertones.

GRILLED PORK RIB CHOPS WITH TARRAGON-MUSTARD RUB AND VEGGIE KABOBS

A blend of olive oil, tarragon, coarse-grain mustard, and black pepper does double duty here. One half is used as a marinade for the pork chops. With a little lemon juice added, the other half becomes a brush-on for the veggie kabobs.

SERVES 2

PREP: 20 minutes   **MARINATING:** 30 minutes to 1 hour   **COOK:** 10 minutes   **TOTAL:** 30 minutes plus marinating

2 tablespoons extra-virgin olive oil

2 tablespoons Whole30-compatible coarse-grain mustard

¼ teaspoon black pepper

1 tablespoon chopped fresh tarragon

2 bone-in pork rib chops, cut ¾ inch thick

1 large zucchini

12 to 14 cherry tomatoes

1 tablespoon fresh lemon juice

Pinch of salt

In a small bowl, stir together the olive oil, mustard, tarragon, and pepper. Spoon half the marinade into a second small bowl.

Brush half the marinade over both sides of the chops. Place the chops on a plate and cover with plastic wrap. Marinate in the refrigerator for 30 minutes to 1 hour.

If using wooden skewers, soak them in water for 30 minutes to 1 hour to prevent them from burning.

Preheat a grill to high (500°F).

Use a vegetable peeler or mandoline to slice the zucchini lengthwise into long, thin strips (you should have 12 strips). Thread the zucchini strips accordion-style on the skewers, placing the tomatoes between the zucchini. Stir the lemon juice and salt into the reserved marinade. Drizzle or brush the marinade over the kabobs.

Grill the chops over direct heat until they are seared on both sides and easily come off the grill, 4 to 6 minutes. Reduce the grill temperature to medium (or move the chops to indirect heat). Grill until the internal temperature is 145°F, 3 to 5 minutes. Let the chops rest for 3 to 5 minutes.

Grill the kabobs over direct heat, turning occasionally, until the zucchini is just tender and starting to brown, 3 to 4 minutes.

Serve the chops with the kabobs.

GRILLED PORK CHOPS WITH WATERMELON SALAD

Here's the perfect dish for a beautiful summer evening, when watermelon is ripe and plentiful and grilling out is a pleasure.

SERVES 4

PREP: 15 minutes   **COOK:** 10 minutes   **TOTAL:** 25 minutes

FOR THE PORK CHOPS

2 teaspoons chili powder

½ teaspoon salt

¼ teaspoon black pepper

2 tablespoons extra-virgin olive oil

2 teaspoons fresh lime juice

4 boneless pork loin chops (6 ounces each), cut 1 inch thick

FOR THE SALAD

4 cups chopped seedless watermelon, chilled

¼ cup thinly sliced red onion

2 tablespoons chopped fresh cilantro

1 tablespoon extra-virgin olive oil

1 tablespoon fresh lime juice

¼ teaspoon salt

⅛ teaspoon black pepper

Lime wedges and chopped fresh cilantro, for serving (optional)

MAKE THE PORK CHOPS: Preheat a grill to medium (350 to 375°F).

In a small bowl, combine the chili powder, salt, and pepper. Whisk in the olive oil and lime juice. Brush both sides of the pork chops with the oil mixture. Grill the chops, turning once, until the internal temperature is 145°F, 7 to 9 minutes. Let the chops rest for 3 to 5 minutes.

MAKE THE SALAD: In a medium bowl, combine the watermelon, onion, and cilantro. Drizzle with the olive oil and lime juice. Sprinkle with the salt and pepper; toss gently to coat.

Serve the grilled pork chops with the watermelon salad. If desired, serve with lime wedges and sprinkle with additional cilantro.

PORK AND TOMATILLO STEW

A topping of shredded cabbage and sliced radishes give freshness and crunch to this hearty Mexican-inspired stew. Substitute sweet potatoes for the Yukon Gold potatoes, if you like.

SERVES 4

PREP: 25 minutes   **COOK:** 35 minutes   **TOTAL:** 1 hour

8 ounces tomatillos (4 to 6), husked, rinsed, and dried

1 or 2 fresh jalapeños, halved and seeded, if desired

1 small fresh poblano pepper, seeded and halved

2 cups Chicken Bone Broth (page 284) or Whole30-compatible chicken broth

¼ cup chopped white onion

1 clove garlic, minced

½ teaspoon salt

1 tablespoon extra-virgin olive oil

1 pork tenderloin (1 pound), cut into 1-inch cubes

1 can (14.5 ounces) Whole30-compatible fire-roasted tomatoes, drained

2 medium Yukon Gold potatoes, peeled, if desired, and cut into 1-inch cubes

½ teaspoon ground cumin

½ teaspoon dried oregano, crushed

Black pepper

¼ cup roughly chopped fresh cilantro

Shredded cabbage

Sliced radishes

Lime wedges

Preheat the broiler. Line a large rimmed baking sheet with aluminum foil. Place the tomatillos, stem sides down, the jalapeños, and the poblano on the prepared baking sheet. Broil, turning once, until charred, 1 to 2 minutes per side for the chiles and 2 to 5 minutes per side for tomatillos. Let cool.

Remove the skins from the cooled chiles. Coarsely chop the tomatillos and chiles and transfer to a blender, along with any juices that accumulated on the foil. Add ¼ cup of the broth, the onion, garlic, and salt. Cover and blend until roughly chopped.

Heat the olive oil in a large pot over medium-high heat. Cook half the pork cubes until browned on all sides, 6 to 8 minutes. Transfer the meat to a plate and repeat with the remaining pork. Return all the pork and any accumulated juices to the pot. Add the tomatillo mixture, the remaining 1¾ cups broth, the tomatoes, potatoes, cumin, oregano, and black pepper to taste. Bring to a boil. Reduce the heat to medium-low. Cover and cook until the potatoes are tender and the pork is cooked through, about 20 minutes.

Stir in the cilantro. Divide the soup among four bowls. Top with shredded cabbage and sliced radishes and serve with lime wedges.

TIP The 20 minutes of cooking time is plenty to cook the potatoes, but the pork may vary a bit, depending on how evenly the pieces are cut. Check the pork after 20 minutes to see if it is tender enough for your taste. Larger pieces, especially, may need more cooking time.

SAUSAGE, POTATO, AND KALE SOUP

This is the perfect soup for warming up on a fall or winter evening. Leftovers hold really well and are wonderful for lunch—or even breakfast—the next day.

SERVES 4

PREP: 10 minutes   **COOK:** 30 minutes   **TOTAL:** 40 minutes

1 pound ground pork

2 teaspoons Italian seasoning, crushed

½ teaspoon salt, plus more as needed

½ teaspoon smoked paprika

¼ teaspoon fennel seeds

¼ teaspoon black pepper, plus more as needed

⅛ teaspoon red pepper flakes

1 tablespoon extra-virgin olive oil

½ cup chopped onion

3 cloves garlic, minced

4 cups Chicken Bone Broth (page 284) or Whole30-compatible chicken broth

1 can (14.5 ounces) diced tomatoes, undrained

1 pound red potatoes, cut into ¾-inch chunks

4 cups chopped fresh kale or Swiss chard leaves

2 teaspoons chopped fresh thyme leaves

In a large bowl, combine the ground pork, Italian seasoning, salt, paprika, fennel seeds, black pepper, and red pepper flakes; mix well.

Heat the olive oil in a large pot over medium heat. Add the pork mixture, the onion, and the garlic. Cook, stirring frequently, until the meat is browned.

Stir in the broth, tomatoes with their juices, and potatoes. Bring to a boil. Reduce the heat to low, cover, and simmer, stirring occasionally, until the potatoes are just tender, 15 to 20 minutes. Add the kale and thyme and cook, uncovered, until the kale is tender, 5 minutes more. Season with additional salt and black pepper and serve.

CLASSIC PORK MEATBALLS

FROM MELISSA JOULWAN OF *WELL FED*

Meatballs are the friendly result when the ground beef of a bunless burger is mashed up with the spices used in sausage. They're fun, easy to make, quick to cook, and extremely versatile—plus, they're delicious in both their original round form and when transformed into other recipes. This recipe uses classic seasonings, and the cream of tartar–baking soda combo creates meatballs that are crisp on the outside and tender on the inside. It's pretty much kitchen magic!

MAKES ABOUT 84 MEATBALLS

PREP: 45 minutes   **COOK:** 20 minutes   **TOTAL:** 1 hour 5 minutes

4 pounds ground pork

⅔ cup minced fresh parsley

4 cloves garlic, minced

1 tablespoon salt

1 teaspoon black pepper

1 teaspoon red pepper flakes

¼ cup warm water

2 teaspoons cream of tartar

1 teaspoon baking soda

Preheat the oven to 425°F. Line two rimmed baking sheets with parchment paper or aluminum foil.

In a large bowl, combine the pork, parsley, garlic, salt, black pepper, and red pepper flakes. In a small bowl, mix together the water, cream of tartar, and baking soda. Add the water mixture to the meat mixture and mix to combine. Shape the meat mixture into 1-inch balls (see Tip). Place the meatballs on the prepared baking sheets and bake for about 20 minutes, rotating the pans front to back and top to bottom halfway through the baking time, until the meatballs are browned. Let cool.

Divide the meatballs into three portions (about 28 meatballs each) to use in Italian Meatball Soup (page 105), Creamy Sesame Noodles (page 106), and Autumn Hash (page 108). Store in airtight containers or resealable plastic bags in the refrigerator for up to 3 days or freeze for up to 3 months. If frozen, thaw the meatballs in the refrigerator before using.

TIP A 1-inch cookie dough or ice cream scoop makes the job of shaping the meatballs go faster. They will also be more uniform in size. Keep a small bowl of cool water nearby and use it to slightly dampen your hands occasionally, which will help keep the meat from sticking to them.

MELISSA JOULWAN

Melissa Joulwan is the author of the best-selling Well Fed cookbook series. Her most recent title is *Well Fed Weeknights: Complete Paleo Meals in 45 Minutes or Less*. She also blogs at MelJoulwan.com, where she shares her triumphs and failures in the gym, in the kitchen, and in life. Melissa has been a featured chef for U.S. Wellness Meats and Lava Lake Lamb, as well as an instructor at Whole Foods, and she's a columnist for *Paleo Magazine*. After a lifetime of yo-yo dieting and food as the enemy, Melissa found the Paleo diet in 2009 and has been happily following it ever since. That year, she also underwent a thyroidectomy. In the aftermath, she became particularly interested in how diet affects hormones, body composition, mood, and motivation. These days, her workouts are just as likely to include yoga and meditation as lifting heavy things and sprinting to stay ahead of the stopwatch.

ITALIAN MEATBALL SOUP

FROM MELISSA JOULWAN OF *WELL FED*

My mom's heritage is Italian and Slovak, and as soon as I could reach the stove, I was learning my way around the spice rack and cooking with my family. This soup serves up all the bold, familiar tastes of pizza, without the food hangover! Don't be put off by the longish ingredients list, and don't skip the Swiss chard for extra micro-nutrition in every warm, comforting bowl. (Spinach, escarole, kale, or collard greens would also work well.)

SERVES 5

PREP: 20 minutes   **COOK:** 25 minutes   **TOTAL:** 45 minutes

1 tablespoon extra-virgin olive oil, plus more for drizzling

1 medium sweet onion, diced

1 tablespoon Whole30-compatible tomato paste

3 cloves garlic, minced

½ teaspoon dried oregano, crushed

½ teaspoon dried basil, crushed

½ teaspoon dried parsley

¼ teaspoon salt

⅛ teaspoon granulated garlic

⅛ teaspoon onion powder

Pinch of red pepper flakes

1 can (28 ounces) or 2 cans (14.5 ounces each) Whole30-compatible fire-roasted diced tomatoes, undrained

4 cups Chicken Bone Broth (page 284), Whole30-compatible chicken broth, or pork broth

1 bunch Swiss chard, stemmed and leaves cut into 1-inch strips (see Tip)

1 portion Classic Pork Meatballs (page 102; about 28 meatballs)

Handful of fresh basil leaves, minced

Heat the olive oil in a large stockpot over medium heat for 2 minutes. Add the onion and cook, stirring, until soft and translucent, 8 to 10 minutes. Add the tomato paste, minced garlic, oregano, dried basil, parsley, salt, granulated garlic, onion powder, and red pepper flakes to the pot. Cook until the tomato paste darkens, about 2 minutes. Add the tomatoes with their juices, broth, chard, and meatballs to the pot. Raise the heat to high and bring to a boil. Reduce the heat to medium and simmer until the soup is heated through and the chard is wilted and just tender, about 10 minutes.

To serve, ladle the soup into bowls and sprinkle with fresh basil and a drizzle of extra-virgin olive oil.

TIP To prepare chard for cooking, swish the leaves in several changes of cool water to remove sand and grit; shake to lightly dry. Remove and discard the center ribs and then slice the leaves.

CREAMY SESAME NOODLES

FROM MELISSA JOULWAN OF *WELL FED*

This recipe was inspired by one of my favorite Chinese takeout dishes, sesame noodles, eaten right out of the container. Now I eat this luscious sauce made from coconut aminos, rice vinegar, and the dreamy combination of sesame and almond butters instead. You'll love the tender zucchini noodles, those succulent meatballs, and crisp red bell peppers in this hearty dish.

SERVES 4

PREP: 30 minutes   **COOK:** 15 minutes   **TOTAL:** 45 minutes

4 medium zucchini

1 tablespoon salt

2 tablespoons tahini

2 tablespoons coconut aminos

2 tablespoons water

1 tablespoon unsweetened almond butter

1 tablespoon rice vinegar

1 teaspoon toasted sesame oil

½ teaspoon ground ginger

¼ teaspoon red pepper flakes

1 clove garlic, minced

1 tablespoon coconut oil

1 portion Classic Pork Meatballs (page 102; about 28 meatballs), thinly sliced

1 red bell pepper, seeded and cut into strips

4 green onions, white and green parts, thinly sliced

Minced fresh cilantro

Use a spiral slicer or julienne peeler to cut the zucchini lengthwise into long, thin noodles (or use a regular vegetable peeler to cut the zucchini lengthwise into thin ribbons). Place the zucchini noodles in a colander or wire strainer and toss with the salt. Allow the zucchini to drain for 20 minutes; discard any liquid that accumulates.

While the zucchini noodles are draining, in a food processor, combine the tahini, coconut aminos, water, almond butter, vinegar, sesame oil, ginger, red pepper flakes, and garlic and puree until smooth (or combine the ingredients in a 1-pint glass jar and puree with an immersion blender).

Rinse the zucchini noodles under cold running water, tossing lightly. Drain well and squeeze in a clean dishtowel over the sink to remove excess water.

Heat a large nonstick skillet over medium-high heat for 1 minute. Add 1 teaspoon of the coconut oil and allow it to get hot. Add the zucchini noodles and cook, stirring, until tender and hot, about 2 minutes. Divide among four serving plates. Add the remaining 2 teaspoons coconut oil to the skillet and let it get hot for 1 minute. Add the meatballs and bell pepper and cook, stirring, until the meatballs are sizzling and lightly browned and the peppers are tender, about 5 minutes. Reduce the heat to medium. Add the sauce and the green onions and toss to combine. Spoon the meatball mixture on top of the zucchini noodles and sprinkle with cilantro.

AUTUMN HASH

FROM MELISSA JOULWAN OF *WELL FED*

Nothing says autumn like apples, sweet potatoes, and cinnamon. With this recipe, you can enjoy the crisp flavors of fall any time of year. It's a sweet-savory-chewy-crunchy-hot-cold dish that tastes great at breakfast, lunch, or dinner. Feeling creative? You can fancy it up with a fried egg on top—or replace the apples and pecans with pears and almonds, or swap out the sweet potato for butternut squash.

SERVES 4

PREP: 15 minutes   **COOK:** 15 minutes   **TOTAL:** 30 minutes

2 tablespoons coconut oil, Clarified Butter (page 289), or ghee

1 apple, peeled, cored, and cut into ½-inch dice

½ sweet onion, diced

½ teaspoon salt

¼ teaspoon ground cinnamon

⅛ teaspoon black pepper

Pinch of ground nutmeg

Pinch of paprika

2 cups diced cooked sweet potatoes (see Tip)

1 portion Classic Pork Meatballs (page 102; about 28 meatballs), quartered

4 green onions, green parts only, thinly sliced

⅓ cup raw pecans, toasted (see Tip, page 19) and roughly chopped

1 bag (about 5 ounces) baby spinach

Heat 1 tablespoon of the coconut oil in a large nonstick skillet over medium heat for 2 minutes. Add the apple, sweet onion, and salt and cook, stirring, until the apple and onion are golden and tender, 7 to 10 minutes. Meanwhile, in a small bowl, stir together the cinnamon, pepper, nutmeg, and paprika.

Push the apple mixture to the side of the skillet and add the remaining 1 tablespoon coconut oil. Heat for 1 minute, then add the spice mixture, stirring it into the fat. When the spices are fragrant, after about 30 seconds, add the sweet potatoes and meatballs. Stir to combine all the ingredients and cook, stirring occasionally, until brown spots begin to appear on the sweet potatoes and the meatballs are heated through, 6 to 8 minutes.

Add the green onions and pecans and toss to combine. Divide the spinach among four shallow bowls. Top the spinach with the hash (the heat from the hash will wilt the spinach).

TIPS Be sure the sweet potatoes are cooked through but still firm enough to hold their shape without turning to mush. If you don't have leftovers, bake 2 medium sweet potatoes in a preheated 375°F oven for 40 or 45 minutes, until they can be pierced with a fork but are still slightly firm. Let cool completely before peeling and dicing.

SWEET-SPICY ITALIAN SAUSAGE AND GOLDEN POTATO HASH

A splash of fresh orange juice infuses the homemade Italian sausage with a touch of sweetness. The sausage is not hot—just nicely spiced with paprika, parsley, fennel, dried oregano, and pepper.

SERVES 4

PREP: 20 minutes   **COOK:** 20 minutes   **TOTAL:** 40 minutes

¼ cup fresh blood orange juice or orange juice

1 tablespoon sweet paprika

1 tablespoon chopped fresh parsley

2 teaspoons fennel seeds, lightly crushed

1 teaspoon dried oregano, crushed

1 teaspoon kosher salt

½ teaspoon black pepper

1 pound ground pork

1½ cups chopped onion

1 cup chopped red or yellow bell pepper

1 pound Yukon Gold potatoes, peeled, if desired, and diced

⅓ cup Beef Bone Broth (page 285) or Whole30-compatible beef broth

4 cups fresh baby spinach

In a large bowl, combine the orange juice, paprika, parsley, fennel seeds, oregano, salt, and black pepper. Add the pork and mix with your hands until thoroughly combined.

Cook the meat mixture in a large skillet over medium-high heat until browned, breaking it up into small pieces with a wooden spoon as it cooks. Add the onion and bell pepper and cook, stirring frequently, until the vegetables are just tender, about 5 minutes.

Stir in the potatoes. Cook, stirring, for 2 minutes. Add the broth and bring to a boil. Reduce the heat to medium-low, cover, and simmer, stirring occasionally, until the potatoes are very tender, 15 to 20 minutes. Gently stir in the spinach. Remove the skillet from the heat and let stand until the spinach is wilted, 4 to 5 minutes.

TIP You can crush the fennel seeds a number of ways. The simplest is to use a mortar and pestle or a spice grinder. But you also crush them under the flat side of a chef's knife or by putting them in a plastic bag and crushing them with a rolling pin.

SLOW-COOKER PORK LETTUCE WRAPS WITH SPICY PEACH SALSA

Make this dish in July or August, when peaches are at their sweetest and juiciest. The spicy-sweet salsa is lovely on the tender, aromatic pork.

SERVES 4

PREP: 30 minutes   **COOK:** 8 hours (low) or 4 hours (high)   **TOTAL:** 8 hours 30 minutes

FOR THE PORK

1 large sweet onion, cut into thin wedges

1 tablespoon chili powder

2 teaspoons ground cumin

2 teaspoons salt

1 teaspoon garlic powder

Pinch of cayenne pepper

2 pounds boneless pork shoulder

1 tablespoon extra-virgin olive oil

1 cup Chicken Bone Broth (page 284) or Whole30-compatible chicken broth

FOR THE SALSA

1 ripe medium peach, peeled, pitted, and chopped

¼ cup roughly chopped fresh cilantro

2 tablespoons finely chopped shallot

½ to 1 small jalapeño, seeded and finely chopped

1 tablespoon fresh lime juice

Pinch of salt

8 to 12 large butterhead or Bibb lettuce leaves

MAKE THE PORK: Place the onion wedges in a 3½- or 4-quart slow cooker. In a large bowl, combine the chili powder, cumin, salt, garlic powder, and cayenne. Trim the fat from the pork shoulder. Cut the pork into 2-inch pieces and add to the spice mixture. Toss gently to coat.

Heat the olive oil in a large skillet over medium-high heat. Cook the pork, in two batches, in the hot oil until browned on all sides. Using a slotted spoon, transfer the pork to the slow cooker. Pour the broth over the pork. Cover and cook on low for 8 to 10 hours or on high for 4 to 5 hours.

MAKE THE SALSA: Meanwhile, in a medium bowl, combine the peach, cilantro, shallot, jalapeño, lime juice, and salt. Cover and chill for up to 2 hours.

TO SERVE: Use a slotted spoon to transfer the pork to a cutting board and use two forks to shred the pork. Place the shredded pork in a bowl. Remove the onion from the cooking liquid and add to the pork. Skim off the fat from the cooking liquid. Add enough cooking liquid to the pork mixture to moisten. Spoon the shredded pork into the center of the lettuce leaves. Top with the salsa.

SPICY APRICOT-STUFFED BONELESS CHOPS WITH ARUGULA PESTO

The stuffing of celery, shallot, apricot, red pepper flakes, and parsley is so easy to put together but adds so much interest to these juicy chops. A peppery pesto of arugula, walnut, and garlic makes a beautiful, vibrant green, and flavorful finish on top. Serve with greens (such as collards or kale) sautéed in olive oil with a little garlic and red pepper flakes.

SERVES 2

PREP: 25 minutes   **COOK:** 15 minutes   **TOTAL:** 40 minutes

2 teaspoons Clarified Butter (page 289) or ghee

½ cup finely chopped celery

1 shallot, minced

6 unsulfured dried apricots, chopped

1 tablespoon Chicken Bone Broth (page 284) or Whole30-compatible chicken broth

⅛ teaspoon salt, plus more as needed

⅛ teaspoon red pepper flakes

2 teaspoons finely chopped fresh parsley

2 boneless pork chops, ¾ inch thick

Black pepper

1 tablespoon extra-virgin olive oil

Arugula, Walnut, and Garlic Pesto (page 256)

Preheat the oven to 350°F.

Melt the butter over medium heat in a small skillet. Add the celery and shallot and cook, stirring until the celery is crisp-tender, 3 minutes. Add the apricots and broth and cook, until the apricots are softened, about 1 minute. Season with the salt and red pepper flakes. Stir in the parsley. Remove the skillet from the heat.

Make a pocket in each chop with a small sharp knife, cutting almost through to the opposite side. Spoon the apricot mixture into the pockets, pressing lightly to close the opening as much as possible. Season the chops lightly with additional salt and black pepper.

Heat the olive oil over high heat in an oven-safe skillet. Sear the chops in the hot oil until browned, about 2 minutes per side. Transfer the skillet to the oven and bake for about 15 minutes or until the chops are cooked through and their internal temperature is 145°F. Let the chops rest for 5 minutes.

Serve the chops with Arugula, Walnut, and Garlic Pesto.

POULTRY

ORANGE CHICKEN SALAD

FROM NAN AND NICOLE OF *WHOLE SISTERS*

This salad takes us back to our childhood, when our mom would make it. We wanted a new version that omitted the sugar and soy sauce but still mimicked the yummy flavors we grew up loving. After many attempts, we got it. We love when food takes us back to happy memories.

SERVES 4

PREP: 20 minutes   **TOTAL:** 20 minutes

FOR THE VINAIGRETTE

¼ cup coconut aminos

¼ cup fresh orange juice

2 tablespoons extra-virgin olive oil

2 tablespoons toasted sesame oil

1 tablespoon minced garlic

1½ teaspoons minced fresh ginger

1 teaspoon salt

½ teaspoon black pepper

¼ teaspoon cayenne pepper

FOR THE SALAD

4 cups shredded napa cabbage

4 cups shredded green cabbage

1½ cups snow peas, trimmed

1 cup shredded red cabbage

1 cup shredded carrots

½ cup chopped fresh cilantro

3 green onions, sliced

2 cups shredded cooked chicken

½ cup sliced almonds, toasted (see Tip, page 19)

2 tablespoons black sesame seeds

2 tablespoons sesame seeds

MAKE THE VINAIGRETTE: In a small jar with a lid, combine the coconut aminos, orange juice, olive oil, sesame oil, garlic, ginger, salt, black pepper, and cayenne. Cover the jar and shake vigorously to blend.

FOR THE SALAD: In a very large bowl, combine the napa cabbage, green cabbage, snow peas, red cabbage, carrots, cilantro, and green onions. Add the chicken, almonds, and sesame seeds and toss to combine. Pour the vinaigrette over the salad and toss to coat. Serve immediately.

WHOLE SISTERS

Nan Jensen and Nicole Bangerter, the creators of *Whole Sisters*, are mothers who love to eat and cook with their families. They believe that eating healthy can still taste amazing, so their recipes incorporate nutritious ingredients with delicious, fresh flavors. While it's not always easy to cook healthy meals with a busy family, taking the time to prepare clean food has made a world of difference in their lives, and they hope to inspire others who want to find amazing tastes while maintaining good health.

BAKED CHICKEN WITH TARRAGON BUTTER OVER CHARRED LEEKS

In this dish, the leek "planks" act as a sort of edible roasting rack. The chicken juices drip down over the leeks as everything roasts, adding to the great flavor contributed by a lemon-tarragon-mustard-garlic compound butter that gets tucked under the skin of the chicken before cooking.

SERVES 2

PREP: 15 minutes   **COOK:** 35 minutes   **TOTAL:** 50 minutes

3 leeks

¼ teaspoon salt, plus more as needed

⅛ teaspoon black pepper, plus more as needed

¼ teaspoon grated lemon zest

1 tablespoon Clarified Butter (page 289), softened slightly, or ghee

½ to 1 teaspoon finely chopped fresh tarragon, or ¼ to ½ teaspoon dried tarragon

½ teaspoon Whole30-compatible whole-grain mustard

1 clove garlic, minced

2 chicken hindquarters (attached drumstick and thigh) (about 8 ounces each)

1 tablespoon lemon juice

2 cups button mushrooms, trimmed and quartered

Preheat the oven to 400°F.

Cut off and discard the dark green portions of the leeks and slice off the roots. Quarter the leeks lengthwise and rinse thoroughly under running water; pat dry. Place the leeks, cut sides down, in a single layer in the bottom of a square baking dish (see Tip). Sprinkle with the salt and pepper and set aside.

In a small bowl, stir together the lemon zest, butter, tarragon, mustard, garlic, and a pinch of salt. With your fingers, gently loosen the skin from the chicken. Spoon the butter mixture under the skin of each chicken piece and use your fingers to spread the mixture evenly. Place the chicken pieces, skin sides up, on the leeks in the baking dish. Brush the lemon juice over the chicken and season with salt and pepper.

Bake, uncovered, for 25 minutes. Remove the chicken from the baking dish. Add the mushrooms and toss to coat with the juices in the dish. Place the chicken on top of the vegetables. Bake for 10 minutes more, the spooning juices over the chicken twice, until the internal temperature of the chicken is 180°F and the meat is no longer pink. Check the leeks during the last 10 minutes of baking and cover loosely with aluminum foil if they are browning too quickly. Serve the chicken over the vegetables.

TIP For easier cleanup, line the baking dish with parchment paper before you add the leeks.

BBQ CHICKEN SALAD

FROM KENDRA CARDOZA OF *PALEO PAPARAZZI*

This is one of our favorite ways to eat salad; it's hearty and filling with a delicious crunch and wonderful smoky flavor. Instead of the usual refined sugar found in most BBQ sauces, this one is sweetened with pineapple juice. You can make the chicken the day before, giving it some time to marinate in the sauce.

SERVES 4

PREP: 5 minutes   **COOK:** 45 minutes   **TOTAL:** 50 minutes

FOR THE SAUCE

1 cup Whole30-compatible canned fire-roasted tomatoes

1 can (6 ounces) Whole30-compatible tomato paste

½ cup water

3½ tablespoons unsweetened pineapple juice

2 tablespoons plus ¾ teaspoon apple cider vinegar

1 tablespoon Whole30-compatible yellow mustard

1 tablespoon Red Boat fish sauce

1 tablespoon fresh lemon juice

1¾ teaspoons dehydrated onion

1½ teaspoons coconut aminos

½ teaspoon dry mustard

½ teaspoon garlic powder

½ teaspoon Whole30-compatible hot sauce

¼ teaspoon salt

⅛ teaspoon smoked paprika

FOR THE SALAD

4 cups shredded cooked chicken

2 heads romaine lettuce, chopped

2 large avocados, halved, pitted, peeled, and diced

2 fresh tomatoes, diced

1 large bell pepper, seeded and chopped

½ cup matchstick-size pieces jicama

⅓ cup diced red onion

¼ cup fresh cilantro leaves, roughly chopped

MAKE THE SAUCE: In a large saucepan, combine all the ingredients for the sauce. Whisk to mix well. Bring to a boil over medium-high heat. Reduce the heat to low and simmer, uncovered, until the sauce has reduced by about half, 40 to 45 minutes. Let cool slightly. Transfer the sauce to a blender and blend until smooth. Let cool completely.

MAKE THE SALAD: In a large bowl, toss the chicken with 1 cup (about half) of the barbecue sauce. Add the lettuce, avocados, diced tomatoes, bell pepper, jicama, red onion, and cilantro and toss gently to combine, adding more barbecue sauce as desired.

TIP Jicama (HEE-kah-mah) is a large, roundish, tuberous root with crisp, juicy flesh similar to a water chestnut. It is used both cooked and raw but most often raw. It can be found in the produce section of most supermarkets and at Mexican markets. It is easily peeled with a vegetable peeler.

SIMPLE ROASTED CHICKEN THIGHS

FROM MICHELLE TAM OF NOM NOM PALEO

Trust me: you need to make this chicken recipe a weeknight standard. The budget-friendly, flavor-packed marinade can be cobbled together from pantry staples in literally two minutes. Plus, when you roast a whole tray of thighs, you can eat half for supper and still have enough left to make both Chicken and Salsa Frittata Muffins and Chinese Chicken and Bok Choy Soup later in the week. Winner, winner, chicken dinner—times three!

SERVES 4, WITH 6 THIGHS LEFT OVER

PREP: 10 minutes   **MARINATING:** 30 minutes to 24 hours   **COOK:** 40 minutes   **TOTAL:** 50 minutes plus marinating

½ cup extra-virgin olive oil

3 tablespoons fresh lemon juice

2 tablespoons balsamic vinegar

6 cloves garlic, minced

2 teaspoons coarse kosher or sea salt

¾ teaspoon dried thyme, crushed

½ teaspoon red pepper flakes

½ teaspoon cracked black pepper

12 bone-in, skin-on chicken thighs (4 to 4½ pounds total)

In a large bowl, whisk together the olive oil, lemon juice, vinegar, garlic, salt, thyme, red pepper flakes, and black pepper. Add the chicken and turn to coat. Cover the bowl and marinate the chicken in the refrigerator for at least 30 minutes or up to 24 hours.

When you're ready to cook the chicken, preheat the oven to 425°F (see Tip). Line a rimmed baking sheet with aluminum foil and set an oven-safe wire rack on the baking sheet.

Remove the chicken thighs from the marinade and place them, skin side down, in a single layer on the baking sheet. Discard the marinade.

Roast the chicken thighs, turning once, for about 40 minutes, until the skin is browned and the internal temperature is 170°F. Serve four of the thighs. Let the remaining thighs cool, then pack in an airtight container or resealable plastic bags. Use to make Chinese Chicken and Bok Choy Soup (page 122) and Chicken and Salsa Frittata Muffins (page 125).

TIP If using a convection oven, preheat the oven to 400°F.

CHINESE CHICKEN AND BOK CHOY SOUP

FROM MICHELLE TAM OF NOM NOM PALEO

Hands down, the quickest and easiest leftover makeover is soup. Just chop up leftover cooked protein, combine it with broth and chopped vegetables, and *voilà:* dinner is served! This recipe reminds me of my mom's hearty chicken soup, filled with Asian greens, shiitake mushrooms, and diced chicken. Remember: Chicken broth will vary in salt content, so slurp up a spoonful of the final product and adjust the seasoning to taste.

SERVES 2

PREP: 10 minutes   **COOK:** 15 minutes   **TOTAL:** 25 minutes

4 cups Chicken Bone Broth (page 284) or Whole30-compatible chicken broth

1 teaspoon Red Boat fish sauce, plus more as needed

4 large shiitake mushrooms, thinly sliced

1 carrot, thinly sliced into coins

3 cups thinly sliced bok choy or napa cabbage

2 cups diced cooked chicken thigh meat from Simple Roasted Chicken Thighs (page 121; 4 leftover thighs)

Salt

½ teaspoon toasted sesame oil

¼ cup minced green onions

In a medium saucepan, bring the broth and fish sauce to a boil over high heat. Add the mushrooms and carrot and return to a boil. Reduce the heat to maintain a simmer and cook until the carrot slices are slightly softened, about 5 minutes. Carefully add the bok choy and cooked chicken to the pan and simmer until the bok choy is tender, about 10 minutes. Remove from the heat. Taste and adjust the seasoning with salt and additional fish sauce.

Add the sesame oil and the green onions. Ladle into two bowls.

MICHELLE TAM

New York Times best-selling author Michelle Tam is the food nerd behind *Nom Nom Paleo*, the *Saveur* award–winning food blog, with over three million visitors a month. Her cookbook, *Nom Nom Paleo: Food for Humans*, was nominated for a 2015 James Beard Foundation Award and named one of the best cookbooks of the year by *Serious Eats*, the *Wall Street Journal*, and *America's Test Kitchen*. Michelle is also the Webby Award–winning creator of the best-selling Nom Nom Paleo cooking app. She's an avid Instagrammer, occasional Periscoper and podcaster, and busy mom. With her husband and two young boys, she splits her time between Palo Alto, California, and Portland, Oregon.

CHICKEN AND SALSA FRITTATA MUFFINS

FROM MICHELLE TAM OF NOM NOM PALEO

Portable mini frittata muffins are my favorite protein-packed grab-and-go noms, which is why I make extra batches whenever I can. If you already have leftover chicken in the fridge, combine it with eggs, spinach, and your favorite Whole30-friendly salsa, and you can easily bake a dozen at a time. Mini frittatas do tend to stick to cupcake liners and muffin tins, so either grease the tins really well or line them with silicone or parchment paper liners.

SERVES 4

PREP: 5 minutes   **COOK:** 20 minutes   **TOTAL:** 25 minutes

1 cup diced cooked chicken thigh meat from Simple Roasted Chicken Thighs (page 121; 2 leftover thighs)

1 cup packed baby spinach, finely chopped

¼ cup Whole30-compatible roasted tomato salsa

8 large eggs

1½ tablespoons coconut flour

1 tablespoon chili powder

¾ teaspoon kosher salt

Preheat the oven to 375°F. Line a 12-cup muffin tin with parchment paper liners or silicone liners.

Combine the chicken, spinach, and salsa in a medium bowl and mix well. Divide the chicken mixture among the prepared muffin cups (about 2 tablespoons in each cup).

In a large bowl, whisk together the eggs, coconut flour, chili powder, and salt. Make sure there are no lumps in the batter. Pour the batter evenly into each muffin cup, leaving ¼ inch of space at the top.

Bake the muffins for about 20 minutes, rotating the muffin tin halfway through the baking time, until the tops spring back when you touch them and a toothpick inserted into the centers comes out clean.

Cool the muffins in the tin on a wire rack for 5 minutes. Remove the muffins from the tin and place them on the wire rack to cool completely. If you aren't eating them right away, pack the cooled muffins in a sealed container and store in the refrigerator for up to 4 days.

CHICKEN AND GREEN OLIVE MEATBALLS WITH SMOKED PAPRIKA TOMATO SAUCE

The sauce for these savory meatballs gets a double dose of smoky goodness from the smoked paprika and the fire-roasted tomatoes.

SERVES 4, OR 2 WITH LEFTOVERS

PREP: 20 minutes   **COOK:** 40 minutes   **TOTAL:** 45 minutes

FOR THE SAUCE

1 tablespoon extra-virgin olive oil

⅓ cup chopped onion

2 cloves garlic, minced

1 can (28 ounces) Whole30-compatible fire-roasted diced tomatoes, undrained

1 can (6 ounces) Whole30-compatible tomato paste

2 teaspoons dried oregano, crushed

1 teaspoon smoked paprika

Salt and black pepper

FOR THE MEATBALLS

1 pound ground chicken or turkey (see Tip)

¼ cup finely chopped onion

2 tablespoons chopped pitted green olives

1½ teaspoons Italian seasoning

1 teaspoon fennel seeds, crushed

½ teaspoon salt

¼ teaspoon garlic powder

¼ teaspoon red pepper flakes

1 spaghetti squash, cooked and shredded into noodles (see Tip, page 47)

Chopped fresh parsley (optional)

MAKE THE SAUCE: Heat the olive oil in a large saucepan over medium heat. Add the onion and cook, stirring occasionally, until tender, 6 to 8 minutes. Add the garlic and cook, stirring, for 2 minutes more. Stir in the tomatoes with their juices, tomato paste, oregano, and paprika and bring to a boil. Reduce the heat, cover, and simmer, stirring occasionally, for 20 minutes. Remove the lid and simmer for 10 minutes more. Season with salt and black pepper.

MAKE THE MEATBALLS: Meanwhile, preheat the oven to 375°F. Line a baking sheet with parchment paper. In a large bowl, combine the chicken, onion, olives, Italian seasoning, fennel seeds, salt, garlic powder, and red pepper flakes. Shape the mixture into twenty 1½-inch meatballs and place them on the prepared baking sheet. Bake the meatballs for 15 to 20 minutes, until the internal temperature is 160°F and no pink remains in the middle of the meatballs.

Serve the meatballs and sauce over spaghetti squash noodles. Garnish with parsley, if desired.

TIP Do not use extra-lean ground chicken or turkey made from breast meat only. The meatballs need a little fat to help them hold together and to keep them from drying out.

CHERRY-CHIPOTLE BBQ CHICKEN THIGHS

FROM MICHELLE SMITH OF *THE WHOLE SMITHS*

Gatherings and social events can sometimes seem daunting while you're on a Whole30, but you'll be the hit of the party with these Cherry-Chipotle BBQ Chicken Thighs. As cherry season starts in late spring, they're perfect for a summertime cookout or family dinner on the patio. Whether your guests are on a Whole30 or not, they're sure to appreciate the bold spiciness of the chipotle combined with the sweet, tartness of the cherries.

SERVES 3

PREP: 25 minutes   **MARINATING:** 1 to 4 hours   **COOK:** 20 minutes   **TOTAL:** 45 minutes plus marinating

4 cups frozen pitted dark sweet cherries (about two 12-ounce packages), thawed

3 tablespoons plus 1 teaspoon Clarified Butter (page 289) or ghee

⅓ cup finely chopped shallots (about 3)

Salt

½ cup coconut aminos

2 teaspoons white wine vinegar

1½ teaspoons ground chipotle chile pepper

½ teaspoon smoked paprika

6 bone-in, skin-on chicken thighs

Black pepper

In a large saucepan, combine the cherries and 3 tablespoons of the butter and bring to a simmer over medium heat. Cook, gently crushing the cherries, until tender, about 5 minutes.

Meanwhile, heat the remaining 1 teaspoon butter in a small saucepan over medium heat. Add the shallots and season with a pinch of salt. Cook, stirring, until the shallots are tender and lightly browned, 4 to 5 minutes. Add the shallots to the pan with the cherries. When the cherries are tender, add the coconut aminos, vinegar, chipotle, paprika, and ½ teaspoon salt. Cook over medium heat until slightly thickened, about 10 minutes.

Transfer 1 cup of the cherry mixture to a large bowl for the marinade and let cool to room temperature. Cook the remaining cherry mixture for 10 minutes more to make cherry sauce to serve with the chicken.

MICHELLE SMITH

Michelle Smith believes wellness begins with real food, and shares family-friendly, healthy recipes on her blog, *The Whole Smiths*, and two cookbooks. She is passionate about food, but not in an annoying way; she just wants to show people that eating wholesome doesn't have to be boring or pretentious, and that it's attainable for everyone. On any given weekend, you'll find her in the kitchen, mixing up a variety of old and new flavors, drinking kombucha, and holding impromptu hip-hop dance parties.

Combine the chicken and the reserved cherry marinade in a large resealable plastic bag. Turn the bag to coat the chicken. Place in a shallow dish and marinate in the refrigerator for 1 to 4 hours, turning occasionally.

Preheat a grill to medium (350 to 375°F).

Remove the chicken from the marinade and discard the marinade. Generously season the chicken thighs with salt and pepper.

Place the chicken, skin side down, on the grill over direct heat. Close the grill and cook for 10 minutes. Flip the chicken, cover, and grill until the internal temperature of the chicken is 175°F, 10 to 12 minutes more. Remove the chicken from the grill and let stand for 5 minutes.

Serve the chicken with the warm cherry sauce.

CHICKEN CUTLETS WITH BITTER GREENS, CARAMELIZED PEARS, AND SHALLOTS

Pairing the sweetness of fruit—in this case, pears—with mildly bitter greens such as radicchio and escarole creates a wonderful balance of flavors.

SERVES 2

PREP: 15 minutes   **COOK:** 20 minutes   **TOTAL:** 35 minutes

FOR THE PEARS

2 Bosc pears, peeled, cored, and cut lengthwise into 8 wedges each

1 tablespoon extra-virgin olive oil

Salt and black pepper

FOR THE CHICKEN

2 boneless, skinless chicken breast halves (6 to 8 ounces each)

¼ cup coconut flour

¼ cup almond flour

1 tablespoon Italian seasoning, crushed

½ teaspoon garlic powder

¼ teaspoon dried lemon peel

¼ teaspoon salt

1 large egg

1 tablespoon water

3 tablespoons extra-virgin olive oil, plus more if needed

FOR THE SALAD

¼ cup extra-virgin olive oil

3 tablespoons apple cider vinegar

2 teaspoons finely chopped shallot

1 teaspoon Whole30-compatible Dijon mustard

¼ teaspoon salt

⅛ teaspoon black pepper

½ small head radicchio, torn into bite-size pieces

½ small head escarole, torn into bite-size pieces

2 tablespoons chopped walnuts, toasted (see Tip, page 19)

MAKE THE PEARS: Preheat the oven to 425°F. Place the pears in a baking pan and drizzle with the olive oil. Lightly season with salt and pepper. Roast the pears for 20 to 25 minutes, turning once or twice, until tender and beginning to caramelize. Let cool.

MAKE THE CHICKEN: While the pears are baking, place the chicken breasts between two pieces of plastic wrap and use the flat side of a meat mallet to flatten them to ¼-inch thickness. In a shallow dish, combine the coconut flour, almond flour, Italian seasoning, garlic powder, lemon peel, and salt. In another shallow dish, whisk together the egg and water. Dip the chicken into the egg mixture, then into the seasoned flour to coat both sides.

Heat the olive oil in a large skillet over medium heat. Add the chicken and cook until golden, 2 to 3 minutes per side, adding more oil if needed.

MAKE THE SALAD: In a small bowl, whisk together the olive oil, vinegar, shallot, mustard, salt, and pepper. Place the radicchio and escarole in a large bowl; drizzle with some of the vinaigrette and toss to mix.

Serve the roasted pears on top of the salad and sprinkle with walnuts. If desired, drizzle with more of the vinaigrette. Serve the chicken with the salad.

CHICKEN MARBELLA WITH SAUTÉED KALE

This Jewish-American dish was made famous in *The Silver Palate Cookbook* by Sheila Lukins, and is often found on the table at Shabbat and Passover. There's a tradition of pairing fruit and meat in Jewish culinary history, and Sheila claims inspiration from the cuisine of Spain and the tagines of Morocco. It gets sweetness from dates, saltiness and piquancy from olives and capers, tang from vinegar—plus the piney astringency of rosemary.

SERVES 4

PREP: 15 minutes   **COOK:** 40 minutes   **TOTAL:** 55 minutes

FOR THE CHICKEN

4 large bone-in chicken thighs (1 to 1¼ pounds)

¼ teaspoon salt

⅛ teaspoon black pepper

1 tablespoon extra-virgin olive oil

1 cup pitted dates, halved

½ cup pitted Kalamata olives, drained

2 medium shallots, thinly sliced

½ cup Chicken Bone Broth (page 284) or Whole30-compatible chicken broth

2 tablespoons red wine vinegar

2 tablespoons capers, rinsed and drained

2 sprigs fresh rosemary

FOR THE KALE

1 tablespoon extra-virgin olive oil

2 cloves garlic, thinly sliced

2 bunches kale, stemmed and leaves chopped (about 16 cups)

½ cup Chicken Bone Broth (page 284) or Whole30-compatible chicken broth

Salt and black pepper

Chopped fresh parsley (optional)

MAKE THE CHICKEN: Preheat the oven to 400°F. Season the chicken with the salt and pepper. In a large ovenproof skillet, heat the olive oil over medium-high heat. Add the chicken and cook until the skin is browned, turning once, about 5 minutes. Remove the skillet from the heat. Add the dates, olives, shallots, broth, vinegar, capers, and rosemary and transfer the skillet to the oven. Roast, uncovered, 25 to 30 minutes, until the internal temperature of the chicken is 165°F and the meat is no longer pink.

MAKE THE KALE: Meanwhile, heat the olive oil in a large skillet over medium heat. Add the garlic and cook, stirring, until fragrant, about 30 seconds. Add the kale and broth and stir to combine. Cover and cook until wilted, about 5 minutes. Uncover and cook, stirring frequently, until all the liquid has evaporated, 2 to 3 minutes. Season with salt and pepper.

Place the sautéed kale on a serving platter. Arrange the chicken, olives, and dates on top of the kale. Drizzle the pan juices over all. Sprinkle with parsley, if desired.

CRISPY SPICY TURKEY WITH LEMON AND HERBS

This interesting cooking method for ground poultry (though it can also be used on beef, pork, or lamb) involves making two large patties and searing them in a hot skillet without moving them until the bottoms are browned and crispy. The patties are then carefully broken up into large chunks so that large pieces of the delicious crust are retained. The crisp, caramelized meat combined with the warm spices—smoked paprika, cumin seeds, and red pepper flakes—adds up to all kinds of deliciousness.

SERVES 3

PREP: 20 minutes   **COOK:** 10 minutes   **TOTAL:** 30 minutes

1 pound ground turkey (see Tip)

¾ teaspoon salt

Black pepper

2 teaspoons smoked paprika

1 teaspoon cumin seeds

¾ teaspoon red pepper flakes, plus more as needed

3 tablespoons coconut oil

2 cloves garlic, minced

1 medium head cauliflower, broken into florets

2 tablespoons coarsely chopped almonds, toasted (see Tip, page 19)

2 teaspoons grated lemon zest

⅓ cup snipped fresh mint

Lemon wedges

In a large bowl, mix together the turkey, ½ teaspoon of the salt, and black pepper to taste. Shape the turkey mixture into two ¼-inch-thick patties. In a small bowl, combine the paprika, cumin seeds, and red pepper flakes; stir well to blend.

Heat 1 tablespoon of the coconut oil in a very large skillet over medium-high heat. Very carefully place the patties in the skillet (they will be soft); cook the patties, undisturbed, until the bottoms are browned and crisp, about 3 minutes. Reduce the heat to medium. Break the patties into small pieces; sprinkle the spice mixture and the garlic over the meat. Cook, stirring, until the spices are fragrant and the meat is cooked through, 2 to 3 minutes more.

Meanwhile, in a food processor, pulse the cauliflower (in batches, if necessary) until the pieces are the size of rice. In a large skillet, heat the remaining 2 tablespoons coconut oil over medium heat. Add the cauliflower and the remaining ¼ teaspoon salt and cook, stirring occasionally, until tender and just beginning to brown, about 5 minutes. Stir in the almonds and lemon zest.

Serve the turkey over the cauliflower rice. Sprinkle with the mint and additional red pepper flakes, if desired. Pass lemon wedges alongside.

TIP Be sure to use regular ground turkey, which is a blend of white and dark meat—not extra-lean 100% breast meat. The fat in the meat is what helps it develop a delicious crunchy crust when cooked.

GINGER-COCONUT CHICKEN "NOODLE" BOWL

Cubes of sweet potato get crispy and caramelized in the oven. Their natural sweetness complements the slightly spicy coconut milk sauce. So good!

SERVES 2

PREP: 30 minutes   **CHILLING:** 30 to 60 minutes   **COOK:** 30 minutes   **TOTAL:** 1 hour plus chilling

1 tablespoon finely chopped fresh ginger

1 tablespoon extra-virgin olive oil

2 cloves garlic, minced

½ teaspoon plus ⅛ teaspoon coarse salt

⅛ teaspoon red pepper flakes

2 small boneless, skinless chicken breasts (5 to 6 ounces each)

1 medium orange sweet potato or Okinawan sweet potato, peeled and cut into 1-inch pieces

1 small onion, cut into thin wedges (about ¾ cup)

¼ teaspoon black pepper

1 tablespoon coconut oil

1 small zucchini (about 8 ounces), trimmed

½ cup canned coconut milk (see Tip)

½ cup Chicken Bone Broth (page 284) or Whole30-compatible chicken broth

1 cup lightly packed baby spinach leaves

1 tablespoon chopped fresh cilantro

1 tablespoon chopped fresh mint

Combine the ginger, olive oil, half the garlic, ¼ teaspoon of the salt, and the red pepper flakes in a medium bowl. Cut the chicken into bite-size strips. Add the chicken to the ginger mixture and toss to evenly coat. Cover and chill for 30 to 60 minutes.

Meanwhile, preheat the oven to 400°F. In a shallow roasting pan, combine the sweet potato and onion. Sprinkle with ⅛ teaspoon of the black pepper and ⅛ teaspoon of the salt. Add ½ tablespoon of the coconut oil. Bake, uncovered, for 2 to 3 minutes, until the coconut oil has melted. Toss the potato mixture to coat with the oil and spread it into an even layer in the pan. Bake for 25 to 30 minutes more, stirring twice, until the vegetables are tender and lightly browned.

Use a spiral slicer or julienne peeler to cut the zucchini lengthwise into long, thin noodles (or use a regular vegetable peeler to cut the zucchini lengthwise into thin ribbons). In a large skillet, heat the remaining ½ tablespoon coconut oil over medium-high heat. Add the zucchini, the remaining garlic, remaining ¼ teaspoon salt, and remaining ⅛ teaspoon black pepper. Cook, tossing gently with tongs, until the noodles are crisp-tender, 1 to 2 minutes. Remove the zucchini noodles from the skillet; keep warm.

Add the chicken mixture to the skillet. Cook, uncovered, over medium heat, stirring occasionally, until the chicken is no longer pink, 3 to 5 minutes. Add the coconut milk and broth. Bring just to a boil, stirring frequently. Remove from the heat. Stir in the spinach.

To serve, divide the chicken mixture between two shallow serving bowls. Top with zucchini noodles and roasted sweet potato. Sprinkle with the cilantro and mint.

TIP Canned coconut milk separates in the can, with the cream rising to the top. Make sure to whisk the coconut milk well before measuring the amount needed for the recipe.

HERB-ROASTED CHICKEN AND FINGERLINGS WITH CELERY ROOT–CARROT REMOULADE

A slice of prosciutto and a sage leaf tucked under the skin of the chicken breasts permeates the meat with flavor and looks beautiful too—a bit like stained glass—showing through the cooked skin. The chicken is served with a refreshing side of celery root remoulade—a French condiment (known as *céleri rémoulade*) of shredded raw celery root tossed with mayo and lemon juice that is served as an accompaniment to roasted meats. Our version has shredded carrot added for color and flavor.

SERVES 2

PREP: 15 minutes   **COOK:** 45 minutes   **TOTAL:** 1 hour

FOR THE CHICKEN

2 bone-in, skin-on chicken breasts
(about 10 ounces each)

2 slices Whole30-compatible prosciutto

2 fresh sage leaves

2 teaspoons extra-virgin olive oil

Coarse salt and black pepper

FOR THE POTATOES

1 tablespoon extra-virgin olive oil

1 clove garlic, minced

1 teaspoon minced fresh rosemary

¼ teaspoon salt

⅛ teaspoon black pepper

8 ounces fingerling potatoes, halved
lengthwise

FOR THE REMOULADE

¼ cup Basic Mayonnaise (page 287)

2 teaspoons fresh lemon juice

1 teaspoon Whole30-compatible Dijon mustard

¼ teaspoon salt

Black pepper

1 medium celery root (8 to 12 ounces) or jicama,
peeled and coarsely shredded

2 carrots, coarsely shredded

2 teaspoons minced fresh parsley

MAKE THE CHICKEN: Preheat the oven to 400°F. Line a large rimmed baking sheet with parchment paper. Gently pull back the skin on each breast half, leaving it attached on one side. Place a slice of prosciutto and a sage leaf on top of the meat on each breast half. Pull the skin back over the breast, pressing gently to adhere. Brush the chicken with the olive oil and season lightly with salt and pepper. Place on one side of the prepared baking sheet. Roast for 25 minutes.

MAKE THE POTATOES: In a medium bowl, combine the olive oil, garlic, rosemary, salt, and pepper. Add the potatoes and toss to coat.

Arrange the potatoes in a single layer on the baking sheet with the chicken. Return the baking sheet to oven. Roast chicken and potatoes for 20 to 25 minutes more, until the internal

temperature of chicken is 165°F, the chicken is no longer pink, and the potatoes are crisp on the outside and tender when pierced with a fork.

MAKE THE REMOULADE: While the chicken and potatoes are roasting, in a large bowl, whisk together the mayonnaise, lemon juice, mustard, salt, and pepper to taste. Add the celery root and carrots and toss to coat with the dressing. Add the parsley and toss again. Taste and adjust the seasonings, if desired.

Serve the chicken and potatoes with the celery root remoulade.

JAMAICAN JERK–INSPIRED RASPBERRY CHICKEN WITH SAUTÉED PLANTAINS

For such an incredibly simple dish, this island-inspired chicken has wonderful, complex flavor thanks to a spice blend of onion powder, thyme, allspice, pepper, nutmeg, cinnamon, cloves, and cayenne. And it looks so pretty on the plate thanks to the beautiful bright-red raspberry sauce.

SERVES 2

PREP: 5 minutes   **COOK:** 30 minutes   **TOTAL:** 35 minutes

4 bone-in, skin-on chicken thighs

Grated zest and juice of 1 navel orange

2 teaspoons Whole30-compatible Jamaican jerk seasoning (see Tip)

Salt

1 cup fresh raspberries

½ small jalapeño, seeded and finely chopped

2 teaspoons Clarified Butter (page 289) or coconut oil

2 ripe plantains, peeled and sliced crosswise (see Tip)

1 tablespoon sliced green onion

2 tablespoons white balsamic vinegar

Preheat the oven to 375°F. Line a baking sheet with parchment paper or aluminum foil.

Place the chicken thighs on the prepared pan and brush with 1 tablespoon of the orange juice (set aside the remaining juice and the zest). Rub the chicken with the jerk seasoning and season with salt. Roast the chicken thighs on the prepared baking sheet, skin sides down, for 20 minutes. Flip the chicken over and roast for about 10 minutes more, until the internal temperature is 180°F and the meat is no longer pink.

Meanwhile, in a small saucepan, heat the raspberries and 2 tablespoons of the orange juice over low heat to soften the berries. Press the berry mixture through a fine-mesh sieve. Stir in the jalapeño and ½ teaspoon of the orange zest.

Heat the butter in a large nonstick skillet over medium heat. Add the plantains and green onion and cook, stirring occasionally, until the plantains are golden and slightly softened, 2 to 3 minutes. Stir in the vinegar and cook for 1 minute more.

Serve the chicken with raspberry sauce and plantains.

TIPS If you can't find a compatible Jamaican jerk seasoning, make your own: In a small bowl, stir together 1 tablespoon onion powder, 1 tablespoon dried thyme, 1½ teaspoons ground allspice, 1 teaspoon black pepper, ½ teaspoon ground nutmeg, ½ teaspoon ground cinnamon, ½ teaspoon ground cloves, and ¼ teaspoon cayenne pepper. Store tightly sealed in a cool dry place for up to 6 months. Give it a shake or stir before using. Makes about ¼ cup.

The peels of the plantains should be almost black.

SPICE MARKET CHICKEN WITH CARROT-PISTACHIO SLAW

The spice combination that flavors this dish is classic in Morocco, where spice merchants tout their *ras el hanout,* or "head of the shop." The phrase refers to a proprietary blend of their very best spices. Some versions of ras el hanout can contain up to 50 ingredients.

SERVES 4

PREP: 1 hour   **COOK:** 50 minutes   **TOTAL:** 1 hour 50 minutes

FOR THE SPICE MIXTURE

2 teaspoons sweet paprika

1 teaspoon ground cumin

1 teaspoon ground coriander

1 teaspoon ground ginger

1 teaspoon ground turmeric

½ teaspoon ground cinnamon

¼ teaspoon black pepper

1 whole chicken (3 to 4 pounds), cut into serving pieces and skin removed (optional; see Tip)

FOR THE SLAW

2 cups coarsely grated carrots

½ cup chopped pitted unsweetened dates

½ teaspoon grated lemon zest

¼ cup sliced green onions

¼ cup snipped fresh parsley

¼ cup fresh lemon juice

2 tablespoons extra-virgin olive oil

¼ teaspoon ground cumin

¼ teaspoon ground cinnamon

¼ teaspoon smoked paprika

¼ teaspoon red pepper flakes

2 tablespoons extra-virgin olive oil

1 teaspoon salt

1 medium yellow onion, chopped

3 cloves garlic, minced

1 lemon, thinly sliced

1 cup pitted green olives, halved lengthwise

½ cup organic sulfite-free golden raisins or dark raisins (see Tip)

½ cup water

¼ cup chopped fresh cilantro

¼ cup chopped fresh parsley

¼ cup roughly chopped raw unsalted pistachios

MAKE THE SPICE MIXTURE: Combine the paprika, cumin, coriander, ginger, turmeric, cinnamon, and black pepper in a small bowl.

Pat the chicken dry with a paper towel. Place the chicken in a large bowl. Sprinkle the spice mixture over the chicken and toss to coat with the spice mixture. Cover and let stand for 1 hour at room temperature.

(Continued)

MAKE THE SLAW: In a large bowl, combine the carrots, dates, green onions, parsley, lemon zest, lemon juice, olive oil, cumin, cinnamon, paprika, and red pepper flakes. Cover and chill until serving time.

Heat the olive oil in a large, heavy-bottomed sauté pan or skillet with a lid over medium-high heat. Season the chicken with the salt and place the pieces, skin sides down, in the pan. Cook, without moving, until lightly browned, 4 to 5 minutes.

Reduce the heat to medium-low. Sprinkle with the onion and garlic. Cover and cook for 15 minutes.

Turn the chicken pieces over. Add the lemon slices, olives, raisins, and water. Bring to a simmer over medium heat. Cover and reduce the heat to low. Cook until the chicken is cooked through and tender, about 30 minutes.

Sprinkle the chicken with the cilantro and parsley. Stir the pistachios into the slaw and serve alongside the chicken.

TIPS Whole, cut-up chickens are generally available in the poultry department of most supermarkets and natural- and whole-foods stores. They may not be skinned. You can do that yourself at home or ask a butcher to do it for you. If you can't find a whole cut-up chicken, ask the butcher to cut one up for you.

Many golden raisins are treated with sulfur dioxide or other forms of sulfites, but sulfite-free golden raisins are available at natural- and whole-foods stores. If you can't find them, substitute regular raisins.

TURKEY AND MUSTARD GREENS SOUP WITH PARSNIP NOODLES

Scorching the aromatics—onion, ginger, cinnamon sticks, and cloves—before covering them with the warm chicken broth intensifies their flavors. As the name implies, the aromatics are what give the soup great taste and a wonderful smell as it bubbles on the stovetop.

SERVES 4

PREP: 20 minutes   **COOK:** 20 minutes   **TOTAL:** 40 minutes

6 cups Chicken Bone Broth (page 284) or Whole30-compatible chicken broth

1 tablespoon coconut oil

1 medium onion, quartered

1 (1-inch) piece fresh ginger, unpeeled, halved

2 cinnamon sticks

4 whole cloves

1 pound parsnips, peeled, trimmed, and cut into noodles (see Tip)

1 portion Turkey Base (page 146)

3 cups lightly packed torn mustard greens (center stems removed) or stemmed spinach leaves

4 teaspoons Red Boat fish sauce

1 jalapeño, thinly sliced

½ cup loosely packed chopped fresh cilantro

½ cup loosely packed chopped fresh basil

1 lime, cut into wedges

Heat the broth in a large saucepan, covered, over medium heat.

Meanwhile, melt the coconut oil in a Dutch oven or large pot over medium heat. Add the onion, ginger, cinnamon sticks, and cloves (these are the aromatics). Raise the heat to high and scorch the aromatics, stirring occasionally, until darkened, about 5 minutes.

Pour the warmed broth over the aromatics. Bring to a boil. Reduce the heat to low, cover, and simmer for 8 minutes. Use a slotted spoon to remove and discard the aromatics. Add the parsnip noodles, Turkey Base, mustard greens, and fish sauce. Cook, covered, until the mustard greens are tender, about 5 minutes.

Serve the soup topped with the jalapeño slices, cilantro, and basil, with lime wedges alongside.

TIP To cut the parsnips into noodles, trim off the ends and use a spiral slicer, julienne peeler, or mandoline to cut them into long, thin noodles. One pound parsnips will yield about 4 cups noodles.

THAI-INSPIRED TURKEY "NOODLE" BOWL

There is a lot going on in this colorful curried noodle bowl, but it comes together super-fast, especially if the Turkey Base—flavored with Thai chiles, garlic, lemongrass, and fresh lime—is made ahead.

SERVES 4

PREP: 15 minutes   **COOK:** 20 minutes   **TOTAL:** 35 minutes

1 spaghetti squash (2 pounds), halved and seeded

1 cup chopped red bell pepper

½ cup julienne-cut carrot

1 tablespoon minced fresh ginger

1 portion Turkey Base (recipe follows)

1 head baby bok choy, sliced

1 can (14.5 ounces) Whole30-compatible fire-roasted tomatoes, drained

1 can (13.5 ounces) full-fat coconut milk

½ cup Chicken Bone Broth (page 284) or Whole30-compatible chicken broth

1 to 2 tablespoons Whole30-compatible red curry paste

1 tablespoon coconut aminos

½ teaspoon salt

1 cup chopped fresh pineapple

Fresh mint, cilantro, and/or basil leaves

Lime wedges

Place the squash halves, cut sides down, in a microwave-safe baking dish. Cover with vented plastic wrap. Microwave for 12 to 15 minutes, until tender. (See Tip, page 47, for roasting directions.)

Meanwhile, in an extra-large skillet, heat the coconut oil over medium heat. Add the bell peppers, carrot, and ginger. Cook until the vegetables are crisp-tender, about 3 minutes. Add the Turkey Base; stir in the bok choy, tomatoes, coconut milk, broth, curry paste, coconut aminos, and salt. Bring to a boil. Reduce the heat to medium-low, add the pineapple, and simmer, uncovered, until heated through.

Use a fork to remove the squash pulp from the shell. Serve the turkey mixture over spaghetti squash. Sprinkle with fresh herbs and serve with lime wedges.

TURKEY BASE

MAKES THREE 2⅓-CUP PORTIONS

PREP: 10 minutes   **COOK:** 15 minutes   **TOTAL:** 25 minutes

3 pounds ground turkey breast

1 cup finely chopped mushrooms

1 cup finely chopped yellow onion

2 fresh Thai chiles, thinly sliced (see Tip)

12 cloves garlic, minced

3 tablespoons minced lemongrass

⅓ cup fresh lime juice

1½ teaspoons coarse salt

Black pepper

3 tablespoons coconut oil

In a very large bowl, combine the turkey, mushrooms, onion, chiles, garlic, lemongrass, lime juice, salt, and black pepper to taste and mix well.

Heat the coconut oil in a very large skillet over medium heat. Add the turkey mixture and cook, stirring, until the turkey is no longer pink, about 15 minutes. Divide the turkey base into three portions (about 2⅓ cups each). Use immediately to make Thai-Inspired Turkey "Noodle" Bowl

(above), Turkey Larb (page 150), and Turkey and Mustard Greens Soup with Parsnip Noodles (page 145) or store in airtight containers in the refrigerator for up to 3 days or freeze for up to 3 months.

TIP You will sometimes see the fresh version of Thai chile—red or green and 1 to 1½ inches in length—labeled "Thai bird chiles." In fact, the bird chile is the dried form of the fresh chile. You want it in its fresh form for this recipe.

OLIVE-STUFFED TURKEY PICCATA

In Italian cooking, the term *piccata* indicates the presence of lemon, butter, and capers—usually in a sauce for a thin scallop of chicken that is coated in flour and panfried. This dish features a take on the classic sauce, but with the bonus of a stuffing of olives, green onion, oregano, lemon zest, and minced garlic.

SERVES 2

PREP: 30 minutes   **COOK:** 30 minutes   **TOTAL:** 1 hour

3 tablespoons chopped pitted green and/or Kalamata olives

1 tablespoon finely chopped green onion (white part only)

2 teaspoons snipped fresh oregano, or ½ teaspoon dried oregano, crushed

1 teaspoon grated lemon zest

2 cloves garlic: 1 minced, 1 thinly sliced

1 small turkey breast tenderloin (10 to 12 ounces)

1 tablespoon plus 2 teaspoons extra-virgin olive oil

6 small Roma (plum) tomatoes, halved lengthwise

¼ teaspoon coarse salt

Black pepper

¼ cup Chicken Bone Broth (page 284) or Whole30-compatible chicken broth

2 tablespoons fresh lemon juice

1 tablespoon capers

1 tablespoon Clarified Butter (page 289) or ghee

2 tablespoons roughly chopped fresh parsley

2 tablespoons thinly sliced green onion tops (green parts only)

Preheat the oven to 375°F.

In a small bowl, combine the olives, green onion whites, oregano, lemon zest, and minced garlic. Using a sharp knife, cut a long pocket in the side of the turkey tenderloin, cutting horizontally to, but not through, the opposite side. Spoon the olive mixture into the pocket. Seal the pocket closed with wooden toothpicks or tie the tenderloin in several places with 100% cotton kitchen string, if desired.

Heat 1 tablespoon of the olive oil in a medium skillet over medium heat. Add the stuffed turkey. Cook, turning once, until browned, 6 to 8 minutes. Remove the skillet from the heat.

In a 3-quart rectangular baking dish or au gratin dish, toss together the tomato halves, remaining 2 teaspoons olive oil, and the salt. Arrange the tomatoes around the perimeter of the dish. Remove the turkey from the skillet, reserving the drippings, and place the turkey in the center of the dish. Sprinkle all with pepper. Set the skillet with the drippings aside.

Bake the turkey and tomatoes for 20 to 25 minutes, until the internal temperature of the turkey is 165°F, the turkey is no longer pink, and the tomatoes are tender and starting to brown. Remove from the oven and let rest while making the sauce.

Add the sliced garlic to the reserved drippings in the skillet and cook over medium heat until fragrant, about 30 seconds. Carefully add the broth and lemon juice. Bring to a boil, scraping up any browned bits from the bottom of the skillet. Reduce the heat and simmer, uncovered, until the liquid has reduced slightly, 3 to 4 minutes. Stir in the capers and butter. Cook, whisking, until the butter has completely melted and the sauce is well combined.

Remove the toothpicks or string, if necessary, and thinly slice the turkey crosswise. Divide the turkey slices and tomatoes between two plates. Spoon the sauce over the turkey and sprinkle with the parsley and green onion tops.

TURKEY LARB

Larb—sometimes spelled *laap* or *laab*—is essentially a highly seasoned minced meat salad served in crisp lettuce leaves. It's popular in both Thailand and Laos, and—by swapping coconut aminos for soy sauce and using Red Boat fish sauce—is naturally Whole30 compatible.

SERVES 2

PREP: 5 minutes   **COOK:** 5 minutes   **TOTAL:** 10 minutes

¼ cup lime juice (from 2 limes)

1 portion Turkey Base (page 146)

1 tablespoon Red Boat fish sauce

1 tablespoon coconut aminos

½ teaspoon red pepper flakes

¼ cup chopped fresh mint

¼ cup chopped fresh cilantro

2 tablespoons chopped fresh basil

1 tablespoon grated lime zest

1 head Bibb lettuce, separated into leaves

In a large skillet, combine the lime juice, Turkey Base, fish sauce, coconut aminos, and red pepper flakes and cook, stirring, over medium-high heat, until heated through. Let cool until slightly warmer than room temperature.

Stir in the mint, cilantro, basil, and lime zest. Serve in the lettuce leaves.

ONE-PAN NORTH AFRICAN–SPICED CHICKEN WITH ROASTED CARROTS

As the chicken roasts, it bathes the carrots in aromatic spices and cooking juices. Look for smaller chicken leg quarters—8 ounces is a perfect-size portion per person.

SERVES 2

PREP: 25 minutes   **COOK:** 40 minutes   **TOTAL:** 1 hour 5 minutes

1 dried ancho chile, cut into ½-inch pieces

2 teaspoons caraway seeds

2 teaspoons coriander seeds

1½ teaspoons cumin seeds

1 teaspoon whole black peppercorns

1½ teaspoons kosher salt

1 tablespoon extra-virgin olive oil

2 chicken hindquarters (attached drumstick and thigh) (about 8 ounces each)

1 pound carrots, cut into sticks

Grated zest and juice of 1 navel orange

¼ cup fresh cilantro leaves

Heat a small skillet over medium heat. Add the ancho chile, caraway seeds, coriander seeds, cumin seeds, and peppercorns. Cook, shaking the skillet often, until fragrant, about 5 minutes. Let cool slightly. Use a spice grinder or mortar and pestle to finely grind the chile and seeds. Combine the spice mixture with the salt and rub it evenly over the chicken.

Preheat the oven to 400°F. Heat a large ovenproof skillet over medium-high heat. Add the olive oil and swirl to coat the bottom of the skillet. Add the chicken and cook until browned, turning once, about 10 minutes.

Meanwhile, remove the chicken from the skillet and set aside on a plate. Add the carrots and 1 to 2 tablespoons of the orange juice to the skillet, scraping up any browned bits stuck to the pan. Place the chicken in the skillet. Transfer the skillet to the oven and roast for about 30 minutes, or until the internal temperature of the chicken is 180°F and the carrots are just tender.

Drizzle the remaining orange juice over the chicken and carrots. Sprinkle with the orange zest and the cilantro just before serving.

PIQUILLO PEPPER CHICKEN PATTIES ON GRILLED EGGPLANT WITH CARAMELIZED FENNEL MAYO

Spanish piquillo peppers are sweet, with very little to no heat, but they take on a wonderfully smoky flavor when they are roasted over hot embers before being peeled, seeded, and packed in jars. The flecks of minced red peppers and chopped fresh basil give the patties a colorful confetti interior.

SERVES 4

PREP: 10 minutes   **COOK:** 25 minutes   **TOTAL:** 45 minutes

FOR THE MAYO

1 tablespoon extra-virgin olive oil

1 fennel bulb, trimmed, cored, thinly sliced, and chopped

2 cloves garlic, minced

½ cup Basic Mayonnaise (page 287)

FOR THE PATTIES

⅓ cup chopped fresh basil

4 piquillo peppers or roasted red peppers, minced

1 teaspoon dried oregano, crushed

1 teaspoon kosher salt

½ teaspoon ground fennel seeds

1½ pounds ground chicken (light and dark meat)

1 medium eggplant, cut into eight ½-inch-thick slices

1 tablespoon extra-virgin olive oil

Black pepper

4 cups baby arugula

MAKE THE MAYO: In a medium skillet, heat the olive oil over medium heat. Add the fennel and cook, stirring occasionally, until soft and golden brown, 10 to 12 minutes. Add the garlic and cook, stirring, for 1 minute more. Transfer to a small bowl and let cool completely. Stir in the mayonnaise. Cover and chill until needed.

Preheat a grill to medium-high (375 to 400°F).

MAKE THE PATTIES: In a large bowl, combine the basil, piquillo peppers, oregano, salt, and fennel seeds. Add the ground chicken. Mix with your hands until thoroughly combined. Form the chicken mixture into four ¾-inch-thick patties.

Place the patties on the grill rack directly over medium-high heat. Grill the patties for 12 to 16 minutes, turning once, until they are cooked through and their internal temperature is 165°F.

Brush the eggplant slices with the olive oil. Sprinkle with salt and black pepper. Grill the eggplant, turning once, until tender, 4 to 6 minutes.

Divide the arugula among four plates. Top each serving with two grilled eggplant slices. Place one patty on top of the eggplant slices. Top with some of the mayo.

PLANK-SMOKED BACON-WRAPPED CHICKEN WITH PINEAPPLE

There's something about the combination of smoky, salty pork and the sweetness and acidity of pineapple. Before being wrapped in bacon and grilled, the chicken gets a rub-down with a blend of chili powder, coriander, garlic powder, onion powder, coarse salt, and ground chipotle chile pepper.

SERVES 2

PREP: 10 minutes   **SOAKING:** 1 hour   **COOK:** 15 minutes   **TOTAL:** 25 minutes plus soaking

½ teaspoon chili powder

½ teaspoon ground coriander

¼ teaspoon garlic powder

¼ teaspoon onion powder

⅛ teaspoon coarse salt

Dash to ⅛ teaspoon ground chipotle chile pepper

2 boneless, skinless chicken breast halves (6 to 8 ounces each)

4 to 6 slices Whole30-compatible bacon

¼ cup Whole30 Ketchup (page 288) or Whole30-compatible ketchup

4 fresh pineapple rings (½ inch thick)

Soak a 6½ x 14-inch hickory or oak grilling plank in water for at least 1 hour before grilling (top the plank with a heavy dish to keep it submerged).

Preheat a grill to medium (350 to 375°F).

Combine the chili powder, coriander, garlic powder, onion powder, salt, and chipotle in a small bowl. Sprinkle the spice mixture evenly over both sides of the chicken breast halves. Wrap 2 to 3 bacon slices around each breast half. Secure with toothpicks if necessary.

Place the plank on the grill rack over direct heat until the plank begins to crackle and smoke. Place the chicken on the plank. Cover and grill the chicken until it is no longer pink and the internal temperature registers 175°F, 15 to 20 minutes. The last 5 minutes of grilling, brush the chicken once with the ketchup. Grill the pineapple until browned, turning once halfway through grilling, 5 minutes.

If you used toothpicks for the chicken, remove them before serving. Serve the chicken with the pineapple.

PULLED TURKEY TENDERLOIN WITH SWEET & SPICY CASHEW SAUCE

This dish features a creamy, sweet, and spicy Thai-inspired sauce with cashew butter and coconut milk, reminiscent of the satay and noodle dishes you eat at your favorite restaurant, but perfectly Whole30 compatible.

SERVES 2

PREP: 10 minutes   **COOK:** 25 minutes   **TOTAL:** 35 minutes

FOR THE TURKEY

2 cups Chicken Bone Broth (page 284) or Whole30-compatible chicken broth

1 bay leaf

1 turkey breast tenderloin (about 1 pound)

¼ cup coconut milk

3 tablespoons Whole30-compatible cashew butter

2 tablespoons coconut aminos or Red Boat fish sauce

1 clove garlic, minced

½ Thai chile or jalapeño, seeded and finely chopped

FOR THE NOODLES

2 medium zucchini

1 tablespoon coconut oil

¼ teaspoon salt

⅛ teaspoon black pepper

2 teaspoons chopped fresh cilantro

Raw or toasted cashews, chopped (optional)

MAKE THE TURKEY: Combine the broth and bay leaf in a medium saucepan. Bring to a boil and add the turkey. Reduce the heat to low and simmer, covered, until tender, about 20 minutes. Transfer the turkey to a cutting board, reserving ¼ cup of the cooking liquid in the saucepan. Let the turkey cool slightly. Use two forks to shred the turkey.

Whisk the coconut milk, cashew butter, coconut aminos, garlic, and chile into the broth in the saucepan. Cook, stirring, over medium-low heat until heated through and slightly thickened. Stir the shredded turkey into the sauce. Keep warm while you make the noodles.

MAKE THE NOODLES: Use a vegetable peeler or sharp knife to cut the zucchini lengthwise into long, thin strips. Heat the coconut oil in a large skillet over medium heat. Add the zucchini noodles and cook, stirring occasionally, until lightly browned and tender, 3 to 4 minutes. Season with the salt and black pepper.

Serve the turkey and sauce over the zucchini noodles. Garnish with the cilantro and cashews, if desired.

ROASTED ROOTS WITH CHICKEN

This is a great dish to make in the fall, when root vegetables are in season and at their sweetest. A squeeze of fresh lemon right before serving brightens up the rich flavors.

SERVES 2

PREP: 10 minutes **COOK:** 40 minutes **TOTAL:** 50 minutes

1 cup cubed peeled sweet potato (1-inch cubes)

1 cup cubed peeled rutabaga (1-inch cubes)

2 medium carrots, cut into ½-inch-thick slices

1 medium parsnip, peeled and cut into ½-inch-thick slices

½ small onion, cut into thin wedges

2 ounces pancetta, chopped

½ teaspoon coarse salt

½ teaspoon freshly ground black pepper

4 small bone-in, skin-on chicken thighs

2 teaspoons snipped fresh rosemary

2 teaspoons grated lemon zest

1 clove garlic, minced

1 tablespoon extra-virgin olive oil

Lemon wedges, for serving

Preheat the oven to 400°F.

Combine the sweet potato, rutabaga, carrots, parsnip, onion, and pancetta in a shallow roasting pan. Sprinkle with ¼ teaspoon each of the salt and pepper. Toss to coat the vegetables and spread in an even layer. Cover with aluminum foil and bake for 10 minutes.

Meanwhile, use your fingers to loosen the skin from the meat of the chicken, but do not remove the skin. In a small bowl, combine the rosemary, lemon zest, garlic, and remaining ¼ teaspoon each salt and pepper. Spoon the rosemary mixture evenly under the skin of the thighs and rub it evenly over the meat with your fingers.

Heat the olive oil in a medium skillet over medium heat. Add the chicken thighs, skin side down, and cook, turning once, until browned, 6 to 8 minutes.

Remove the foil from the vegetables. Stir the vegetables and spread into an even layer. Place the chicken thighs on the vegetables, skin side up. Roast, uncovered, for 30 to 40 minutes, until the chicken is no longer pink and its internal temperature is 180°F, and the vegetables are tender.

Serve the chicken and vegetables with lemon wedges for squeezing.

SKEWERED GINGER-MANGO CHICKEN WITH CURRIED GRILLED BOK CHOY

Efficiency can be a great friend to flavor. The zesty mixture of pureed mango, orange juice, lime zest and juice, basil, cilantro, ginger, chile, and garlic is used as both a marinade and a sauce. It takes all of 15 minutes to put together and the results are divine.

SERVES 2

PREP: 15 minutes   **MARINATING:** 2 to 4 hours   **COOK:** 10 minutes   **TOTAL:** 25 minutes plus marinating

1 mango, pitted, peeled, and chopped

2 tablespoons fresh orange juice

½ teaspoon grated lime zest

2 tablespoons fresh lime juice

2 tablespoons chopped fresh basil

2 tablespoons chopped fresh cilantro, plus more for serving

2 teaspoons minced fresh ginger

1 serrano chile pepper, seeded and minced

1 clove garlic, minced

1 teaspoon salt

4 tablespoons walnut oil or avocado oil

2 tablespoons rice vinegar

2 boneless, skinless chicken breast halves (6 to 8 ounces each), thinly sliced lengthwise

3 heads baby bok choy

2 teaspoons Whole30-compatible green curry paste

Combine the mango, orange juice, lime zest, 1 tablespoon of the lime juice, the basil, cilantro, ginger, chile, garlic, and salt in a small food processor. Cover and pulse until smooth. Measure 2 tablespoons of the mango sauce into a medium bowl (cover and chill the remaining sauce until needed). Whisk 2 tablespoons of the walnut oil and the rice vinegar into the sauce in the bowl. Add the sliced chicken and toss to coat. Cover and marinate in the refrigerator for 2 to 4 hours.

Meanwhile, soak eight to ten 8-inch wooden skewers in water for at least 30 minutes.

Preheat a grill to medium (350 to 375°F). Drain the chicken and discard the marinade. Thread the chicken onto skewers, accordion-style, using two or three pieces of chicken per skewer.

Slice each head of bok choy in half lengthwise. In a small bowl, whisk together the remaining 1 tablespoon lime juice, remaining 2 tablespoons walnut oil, and the green curry paste. Brush the curry mixture on the bok choy.

Grill the chicken and the bok choy over direct heat, turning once, until the chicken is no longer pink and the bok choy is lightly charred, 8 to 10 minutes. Transfer the bok choy to a serving dish. Place a small amount of the reserved mango sauce in a small bowl. Brush the chicken on both sides with the sauce from the bowl, adding more sauce if necessary, and grill the chicken, turning once, just until the sauce caramelizes, 2 to 3 minutes more.

Sprinkle the chicken with cilantro, if using, and serve with the grilled bok choy and any remaining mango sauce (see Tip).

TIP Discard any mango sauce that has had a brush dipped into it, as it has had contact with raw chicken and is not safe to eat.

ROASTED TURKEY BREAST WITH BRUSSELS SPROUTS AND SQUASH

This is a great recipe to make on a weekend. It takes a bit of time in the oven, filling the air with yummy smells, so you can putter around the house while it cooks—and it yields leftovers for later in the week.

SERVES 4 WITH LEFTOVERS

PREP: 30 minutes   **COOK:** 1 hour 15 minutes   **TOTAL:** 1 hour 45 minutes

FOR THE TURKEY

2 bone-in, skin-on turkey breast halves
(3 to 3½ pounds each)

2 tablespoons Clarified Butter (page 289)
or ghee, melted

2 cloves garlic, minced

2 teaspoons chopped fresh rosemary

2 teaspoons chopped fresh thyme

1 teaspoon salt

½ teaspoon black pepper

FOR THE VEGETABLES

1 pound Brussels sprouts, trimmed and halved

1 medium delicata squash, halved lengthwise,
seeded, and sliced

2 tablespoons extra-virgin olive oil

½ teaspoon salt

¼ teaspoon black pepper

MAKE THE TURKEY: Preheat the oven to 350°F. Place the turkey breast halves, bone sides down, on a rack in a roasting pan. Brush with the butter. Sprinkle with the garlic, rosemary, thyme, salt, and pepper. Roast, uncovered, for 1 hour 15 minutes to 1 hour 30 minutes, until the internal temperature in the thickest part of the breast is 165°F. If necessary, cover the turkey with aluminum foil for the last 30 minutes to prevent overbrowning. Let stand, covered with foil, for 10 minutes before slicing.

MAKE THE VEGETABLES: Line a large rimmed baking sheet with parchment paper. In a large bowl, combine the Brussels sprouts and squash and drizzle with the olive oil; mix well to coat. Add the salt and pepper and mix well. Spread the vegetables evenly on the prepared baking sheet. Roast for 30 minutes alongside the turkey; stir. Roast for 25 to 30 minutes more, until the vegetables are tender and browned.

Remove the meat from the bones on the turkey breasts, leaving the meat in one piece. Discard the bones. Slice one-third of the turkey (about 1 pound). Divide the remaining turkey into two equal portions to use in Turkey Avocado Collard Wraps (page 166) and Turkey-Sweet Potato Hash (page 168). Wrap tightly in plastic wrap and place in airtight containers or resealable plastic bags. Store in the refrigerator for up to 4 days.

Serve the sliced turkey with the roasted vegetables.

TIP If you can't find delicata squash, substitute a small butternut squash (1 to 1½ pounds). Instead of slicing it, cut it into 1-inch cubes.

TURKEY-AVOCADO COLLARD WRAPS

Roll these up before you leave for work and you will look forward to lunch all morning. The combination of oven-roasted turkey breast, avocado, juicy tomato, crispy bacon, mayo, and green onion is positively yummy!

SERVES 2

PREP: 15 minutes   **TOTAL:** 15 minutes

2 large collard green leaves

1 ripe medium avocado, halved, pitted, peeled, and mashed

2 teaspoons fresh lemon juice

1 clove garlic, minced

⅛ teaspoon salt

Dash of cayenne pepper

1 portion Roasted Turkey Breast (page 165), sliced

1 Roma (plum) tomato, thinly sliced

2 slices Whole30-compatible bacon, cooked until crisp and crumbled

2 tablespoons Basic Mayonnaise (page 287)

2 tablespoons sliced green onion

Remove and discard the stems from the collard leaves. Use a sharp knife to shave down the tough spine on the back side of each leaf until the spine is almost even with the leaf (this will make the leaves easier to roll).

Fill a large pot with water and bring to a boil. Fill a large bowl with ice water. Blanch the collard leaves in the boiling water until just softened, 30 seconds. Immediately plunge the leaves into the ice water to cool. Drain the leaves and pat dry.

Place the collard leaves on a work surface, top sides up. In a small bowl, stir together the mashed avocado, lemon juice, garlic, salt, and cayenne. Spread the avocado mixture vertically on one side of each leaf; layer with the turkey, tomato, and bacon. Drizzle with the mayonnaise and sprinkle with the green onion. Wrap burrito-style; secure with toothpicks and cut each wrap in half to serve.

TURKEY–SWEET POTATO HASH

This veggie-packed turkey hash is served with fried eggs. If you're fond of a crispy-edged egg white (called "frizzling"), turn the heat to medium-high and let the pan get good and hot. Carefully crack the eggs into the pan and cook until the whites are opaque and the edges are lacy and browned. Turn the heat to medium before carefully turning the eggs.

SERVES 2

PREP: 10 minutes   **COOK:** 15 minutes   **TOTAL:** 25 minutes

4 tablespoons extra-virgin olive oil

1 medium sweet potato, peeled and cut into ½-inch pieces

½ cup chopped onion

½ teaspoon salt

¼ teaspoon black pepper

½ cup roughly chopped red bell pepper

2 cloves garlic, minced

1 portion coarsely chopped Roasted Turkey Breast (page 165)

1 teaspoon smoked paprika

½ teaspoon chopped fresh thyme, plus more if needed

4 large eggs

Heat 2 tablespoons of the olive oil in a large skillet over medium heat. Add the sweet potato, onion, salt, and black pepper. Cover and cook, stirring occasionally, until the potatoes are tender, 8 to 10 minutes. Add the bell pepper and garlic and cook, stirring, for 2 minutes. Add the turkey, paprika, and thyme and cook, stirring frequently, until heated through, 3 to 5 minutes more.

Meanwhile, heat the remaining 2 tablespoons olive oil in a large skillet over medium heat. Crack the eggs into the pan. When the egg whites are opaque, carefully turn the eggs, if desired. Cook for 1 to 2 minutes for over easy, 3 to 4 minutes for over medium.

Serve the hash with the fried eggs. If desired, garnish with additional thyme.

SLOW-COOKER SHREDDED CHICKEN

FROM NAN AND NICOLE OF *WHOLE SISTERS*

We love the ease of making slow-cooker chicken and using the shredded chicken for salads, tacos, soups, lettuce wraps—let's just say the possibilities are endless. It's simple to place a whole chicken in your slow cooker, head out to run errands, and then come home to a perfectly cooked chicken that shreds easily.

SERVES 3 OR 4 (4 TO 4½ CUPS MEAT)

PREP: 15 minutes   **COOK:** 3 to 4 hours   **TOTAL:** 3 hours 15 minutes

---

1 whole chicken (3 to 3½ pounds)

1 tablespoon extra-virgin olive oil

Salt

Black pepper

Onion powder

Garlic powder

Drizzle the chicken with the olive oil and rub it all over the skin. Season the chicken all over, including in the cavity, with salt, pepper, onion powder, and garlic powder.

Tear four or five sheets of aluminum foil and roll them into balls. Place the foil balls in the bottom of a 5- to 6-quart slow cooker. Set the chicken on top of the foil balls, adjusting them as necessary to support the chicken and keep it above the cooking juices that will accumulate in the bottom of the slow cooker as the chicken cooks.

Cover and cook on high for 3 to 4 hours or until the juices run clear and an instant-read meat thermometer inserted into the thickest part of a thigh registers 180°F.

Remove the chicken from the cooker and place on a large plate or platter. Let cool completely. Remove the meat from the bones and use two forks to shred it. (Reserve bones for making Chicken Bone Broth, page 284, if desired.)

TOM KHA GAI–STYLE CHICKEN SOUP

At a Thai restaurant this might also be called *tom kha kai*. Like many Thai dishes, it satisfies multiple tastes all at once with a brilliant and balanced combination of ingredients: sweet (coconut milk), sour (lime juice), salty (fish sauce), and hot (chiles).

SERVES 4

PREP: 10 minutes   **COOK:** 20 minutes   **TOTAL:** 30 minutes

2 tablespoons coconut oil

1 bunch green onions, thinly sliced

4 cloves garlic, minced

2 tablespoons grated fresh ginger

2 stalks lemongrass (see Tip), chopped

1 Thai red chile or jalapeño, seeded and finely chopped

4 cups Chicken Bone Broth (page 284) or Whole30-compatible chicken broth

1 can (15 ounces) Whole30-compatible straw mushrooms, drained and rinsed

1 can (13.5 ounces) full-fat coconut milk

2 teaspoons Red Boat fish sauce

1 tablespoon fresh lime juice

½ teaspoon sea salt

1 pound boneless, skinless chicken breast

Snipped fresh cilantro

Lime wedges

Melt the coconut oil in a large saucepan over medium-low heat. Add green onions, garlic, ginger, lemongrass, and chile. Cook, stirring continuously to avoid burning the garlic and ginger, for 2 minutes. Raise the heat to medium and stir in the broth, mushrooms, coconut milk, fish sauce, lime juice, and salt. Add the chicken and bring to a boil. Reduce the heat and simmer, uncovered, until the chicken is no longer pink and the internal temperature registers 165°F, about 15 minutes.

Remove the chicken from the soup and let it rest for 2 minutes. Use two forks to shred the chicken into chunks, then return the chicken to the soup. Serve the soup with fresh cilantro and lime wedges.

TIP To prepare the lemongrass, cut off the woody root tip of each stalk until the purplish-tinted rings begin to show. Remove the loose, dry outer layers and use only the faintly colored, dense inner stalk that holds together when cut into shorter segments or rings.

TOMATO-COCONUT CURRY WITH CHICKEN

You'll have warm thoughts of your favorite Indian restaurant when you tuck into this classic curry. It makes a big pot—which is just fine, because it reheats beautifully. If you'd like more heat, use 1 teaspoon hot curry powder and 1 teaspoon mild curry powder.

SERVES 4 GENEROUSLY

PREP: 25 minutes   **COOK:** 25 minutes   **TOTAL:** 50 minutes

FOR THE SAUCE

2 tablespoons Clarified Butter (page 289) or ghee

1 medium yellow onion, halved and thinly sliced

2 cloves garlic, minced

1 jalapeño, seeded and minced

2 teaspoons minced fresh ginger

2 tablespoons mild curry powder

1 can (28 ounces) crushed tomatoes

1 can (13.5 ounces) full-fat coconut milk

¾ teaspoon salt

Black pepper

FOR THE CAULIFLOWER RICE

1 large head cauliflower, cut into florets

2 tablespoons Clarified Butter (page 289) or ghee

⅓ cup Chicken Bone Broth (page 284) or Whole30-compatible chicken broth

¾ teaspoon salt

½ teaspoon black pepper

1¼ pounds boneless, skinless chicken breast, cut into bite-size pieces

¼ cup chopped fresh cilantro, plus more for serving

MAKE THE SAUCE: Melt the butter in a large skillet or sauté pan over medium heat. Add the onion, garlic, jalapeño, and ginger and cook, stirring, until the vegetables have softened, about 5 minutes. Add the curry powder and cook, stirring, until fragrant, about 1 minute. Add the tomatoes and coconut milk and bring to a boil. Add the salt and black pepper to taste. Reduce the heat to low and simmer until slightly thickened and reduced, 15 to 20 minutes.

MAKE THE CAULIFLOWER RICE: Place half the cauliflower florets in a food processor and pulse until they have broken down to a rice-like consistency, 15 to 20 pulses. (Don't overcrowd the cauliflower in the food processor, and don't overpulse or the "rice" will get mushy.) Transfer to a bowl and rice the remaining cauliflower.

In a large skillet, melt the butter over medium heat and swirl to coat the bottom of the pan. When the butter is hot, add the riced cauliflower to the skillet. Stir to coat. Add the broth, salt, and pepper. Cover the pan and steam the cauliflower until tender, but not mushy or wet, 10 to 12 minutes. Remove the pan from the heat. Cover to keep warm until ready to serve.

Stir the chicken into the sauce. Reduce the heat to medium. Simmer, stirring occasionally and adjusting the heat if necessary, until the chicken is cooked through, 5 to 6 minutes. Stir in the cilantro. Serve the chicken and sauce over the cauliflower rice, topped with additional cilantro, if desired.

TURKEY CURRY MEATBALLS WITH ROASTED VEGETABLES AND LEMONGRASS CREAM SAUCE

This dish borrows from a wide swath of Asia (both India and Vietnam), and the result is truly intriguing. The kale is added to the vegetables at the very end of the roasting time so that it gets crisp and stays that way.

SERVES 2

PREP: 15 minutes   **COOK:** 40 minutes   **TOTAL:** 55 minutes

FOR THE VEGETABLES

2 medium red potatoes, scrubbed and cut into ½-inch-thick wedges

2 cups cauliflower florets

1 tablespoon coconut oil, melted

¼ teaspoon coarse salt

⅛ teaspoon black pepper

2 cups torn kale leaves

FOR THE MEATBALLS

1 large egg, lightly beaten

¼ cup almond meal (see Tip)

1 teaspoon curry powder

¼ teaspoon coarse salt

⅛ to ¼ teaspoon black pepper

12 ounces ground turkey (breast or a blend of light and dark meat)

FOR THE SAUCE

2 teaspoons coconut oil

2 tablespoons chopped shallot

2 to 3 teaspoons finely chopped fresh lemongrass

½ cup full-fat coconut milk (see Tip)

½ teaspoon arrowroot

⅛ teaspoon coarse salt

⅛ teaspoon red pepper flakes

2 tablespoons chopped fresh basil

MAKE THE VEGETABLES: Preheat the oven to 425°F. In a shallow roasting pan, combine the potatoes and cauliflower. Drizzle with the melted coconut oil and sprinkle with the salt and black pepper. Toss to coat the vegetables. Roast for 35 minutes, until just tender and browned. Add the kale to the roasting pan and gently stir the vegetables. Spread in an even layer. Roast for 5 to 10 minutes more, until the kale is lightly browned and crisp.

MAKE THE MEATBALLS: While the vegetables roast, line a small baking sheet with aluminum foil. In a medium bowl, whisk together the egg, almond meal, curry powder, salt, and black pepper. Add the turkey and mix well. Shape the mixture into six meatballs (see Tip). Place the meatballs on the prepared baking sheet. Bake the meatballs alongside the vegetables for 20 to 25 minutes, until the meatballs are cooked through and their internal temperature is 165°F.

MAKE THE SAUCE: Heat the coconut oil in a small skillet over medium-low heat. Add the shallot and lemongrass and cook, stirring occasionally, until just tender, 5 to 7 minutes. In a small bowl, whisk together the coconut milk, arrowroot, salt, and red pepper flakes. Add the coconut milk mixture all at once to the shallot mixture. Cook, stirring, until the sauce has thickened. Remove from the heat. Stir in the basil.

Divide the meatballs and roasted vegetables between two plates. Drizzle the sauce over the meatballs (keep sauce off the vegetables so the kale stays crisp).

TIPS Canned coconut milk separates in the can, with the cream rising to the top. Make sure to whisk the coconut milk well before measuring the ½ cup.

To prevent the meat mixture from sticking to your hands when forming the meatballs, dip your hands in a small bowl of cool water to dampen them slightly.

Almond meal and almond flour are both made from ground almonds. Almond meal is coarser and is usually made from skin-on almonds. Almond flour is finer and is most often made from blanched (skinless) almonds. In most Whole30 recipes—such as being mixed into a ground meat mixture or used as a coating to panfry or bake fish or poultry—they can be used interchangeably.

FISH AND SHELLFISH

ALMOND-CRUSTED SOLE WITH CHIVE-GARLIC MASHED POTATOES AND SAUTÉED SPINACH

A combination of chopped toasted almonds and coconut flour seasoned with lemon zest, paprika, salt, black pepper, thyme, and cayenne creates a crisp, flavorful coating for this oven-baked fish.

SERVES 2

PREP: 30 minutes   **COOK:** 30 minutes   **TOTAL:** 60 minutes

FOR THE POTATOES

2 medium russet potatoes, peeled and quartered

1 clove garlic

⅓ cup Chicken Bone Broth (page 284) or Whole30-compatible chicken broth, hot

1 tablespoon Clarified Butter (page 289) or ghee, melted

2 teaspoons chopped fresh chives

¼ teaspoon salt

Black pepper

FOR THE FISH

½ cup almonds, toasted (see Tip, page 19)

1 teaspoon grated lemon zest

½ teaspoon sweet paprika

½ teaspoon salt

¼ teaspoon dried thyme, crushed

Pinch of cayenne pepper

Black pepper

2 large eggs

1 tablespoon water

½ cup coconut flour

4 tablespoons Clarified Butter (page 289) or ghee, melted

12 ounces fillet of sole

FOR THE SPINACH

1 tablespoon extra-virgin olive oil

1 clove garlic, sliced

8 cups baby spinach

⅛ teaspoon salt

Black pepper

Lemon wedges

MAKE THE POTATOES: Place the potatoes and garlic in a large saucepan and add water to cover by 1 inch. Bring to a boil. Reduce the heat and simmer until the potatoes are fork-tender, 20 to 25 minutes. Drain the potatoes and return to the pan. Add the hot broth and butter. Mash to the desired consistency with a potato masher. Stir in the chives, salt, and black pepper to taste. Cover and keep warm.

MAKE THE FISH: While the potatoes are cooking, preheat the oven to 375°F. In a food processor, chop the almonds to a medium-fine texture. Transfer the almonds to a shallow dish and stir in the lemon zest, paprika, salt, thyme, cayenne, and black pepper to taste. In a medium bowl, beat the eggs with the water and pour into a large shallow plate or dish. Spread the coconut flour on a sheet of waxed paper. Pour 2 tablespoons of the butter into a 9 x 13-inch baking dish and swirl to coat.

Dip pieces of the fish in the coconut flour, one at a time, coating both sides. Shake off the excess. Dip in the egg, allowing the excess to drip back into the dish. Dip both sides in the almond mixture and place in the dish with the butter. Drizzle the remaining 2 tablespoons butter over the coated fish. Bake for about 15 minutes, until the fish just barely starts to flake when pulled apart with a fork.

MAKE THE SPINACH: Heat the olive oil in a large skillet over medium heat. Add the garlic and cook, stirring, until fragrant, about 1 minute. Add the spinach and salt. Cook, tossing, until just wilted, 2 to 3 minutes. Season with black pepper.

Serve the fish with the potatoes, spinach, and lemon wedges.

BROILED SHRIMP WITH GREMOLATA

Gremolata is a mixture of chopped fresh parsley, lemon peel, and garlic that is traditionally sprinkled over osso buco—an Italian dish of braised veal shanks—to give it a burst of freshness and flavor. Those same elements, along with pine nuts, spark up these simple broiled shrimp.

SERVES 2

PREP: 15 minutes   **COOK:** 5 minutes   **TOTAL:** 20 minutes

12 ounces shrimp (medium or jumbo size), peeled and deveined, tails removed

Extra-virgin olive oil

⅛ teaspoon coarse salt

⅛ teaspoon black pepper

⅓ cup pine nuts, chopped

2 cloves garlic, minced

1 teaspoon grated lemon zest

2 tablespoons snipped fresh parsley

Lemon wedges

Preheat the broiler to high. Line a large rimmed baking sheet with aluminum foil.

Rinse the shrimp and pat them dry with paper towels. Use a sharp knife to split the shrimp horizontally, cutting almost through to the opposite sides, but leaving the shrimp halves attached.

Open the shrimp so they lay flat. Arrange the shrimp, flat sides down, on the prepared baking sheet and brush lightly with olive oil. Sprinkle with the salt and pepper.

In a small bowl, combine the pine nuts, garlic, lemon zest, and 1 tablespoon olive oil.

Broil the shrimp, 4 to 5 inches from the heat, until almost completely opaque, 4 to 5 minutes for jumbo shrimp or 2 to 3 minutes for medium shrimp. Carefully flip each shrimp. Spoon the pine nut mixture evenly on the shrimp. Broil for 1 minute more.

To serve, divide the shrimp between two serving plates. Sprinkle with the parsley and serve with lemon wedges for squeezing over the shrimp.

CITRUSY MUSSELS WITH SPICED SWEET POTATO "FRIES"

Be sure to dip the sweet potato fries in the savory and aromatic cooking liquid for the mussels—a combination of fresh orange juice, tomato, garlic, red pepper flakes, clarified butter, and parsley. Delicious!

SERVES 4

PREP: 15 minutes   **COOK:** 35 minutes   **TOTAL:** 50 minutes

3 medium sweet potatoes, peeled and cut lengthwise into ½-inch-thick wedges

2 tablespoons extra-virgin olive oil

1 teaspoon smoked paprika

1 teaspoon dried oregano, crushed

1 teaspoon salt

½ teaspoon garlic powder

½ teaspoon black pepper

¾ cup fresh orange juice

1 ripe tomato, seeded and chopped

3 cloves garlic, minced

½ teaspoon red pepper flakes

2 pounds mussels, scrubbed and debearded

1 small Meyer lemon, cut into 6 wedges

¼ cup finely chopped fresh parsley

2 tablespoons Clarified Butter (page 289) or ghee

Preheat the oven to 425°F.

Place the sweet potatoes in a large roasting pan or on a baking sheet. Drizzle the sweet potatoes with the olive oil and sprinkle with the paprika, oregano, salt, garlic powder, and black pepper. Toss to coat. Arrange the sweet potatoes in a single layer. Roast for 35 to 40 minutes, turning once halfway through the cooking time, until golden brown.

About 10 minutes before the sweet potatoes are done, in a Dutch oven or large saucepan, combine the orange juice, tomato, minced garlic, and red pepper flakes. Bring to a boil over high heat. Add the mussels. Top with the lemon wedges. Cover and cook just until the mussels open, about 4 minutes. Discard any mussels that do not open. Stir in the parsley and butter.

Ladle the mussels and cooking liquid into serving bowls. Serve with the sweet potato fries.

TIP Meyer lemon is thought to be a cross between a lemon and a mandarin orange. They taste much sweeter than a lemon, with an almost spicy-smelling rind. The Meyer is only available seasonally (between December and May), so if you can't find them, substitute a regular lemon.

FISH EN PAPILLOTE

The aroma that wafts out of the parchment packets when they are opened after cooking is just heavenly. While this recipe calls for halibut or cod, tilapia, sole, and salmon are all wonderful cooked this way.

SERVES 2

PREP: 15 minutes   **COOK:** 15 minutes   **TOTAL:** 30 minutes

1 cup chopped seeded tomato

1 small shallot, thinly sliced

2 cloves garlic, minced

2 tablespoons extra-virgin olive oil

1½ teaspoons herbes de Provence

¼ teaspoon salt

2 halibut or cod fillets (5 to 6 ounces each)

⅛ teaspoon black pepper

8 Kalamata or oil-cured black olives, pitted and halved

1 tablespoon chopped fresh parsley

Lemon wedges

Preheat the oven to 425°F.

Combine the tomato, shallot, garlic, 1 tablespoon of the olive oil, herbes de Provence, and ⅛ teaspoon of the salt in a medium bowl; mix well.

Cut two 12 x 15-inch squares of parchment paper. Rinse the fish and pat dry with paper towels. Place a fillet on each piece of parchment about 4 inches from the edge of the shorter sides. Sprinkle the fish with the remaining ⅛ teaspoon salt and the pepper. Spoon the tomato mixture on top of the fish and drizzle with the remaining 1 tablespoon olive oil.

Working with one packet at a time, fold the parchment over the fish, making the edges of the parchment even with each other. Starting at the bottom of the fold, tightly crimp the edges of the parchment to seal, making a half-moon-shaped packet.

Arrange the packets on a large baking sheet. Bake for about 12 minutes, until the fish just barely starts to flake when pulled apart with a fork (carefully open the packets to check doneness).

To serve, place each packet on a dinner plate; carefully open the packets. Top with the olives and parsley. Serve with lemon wedges.

TIP Baking fish in parchment paper creates a steamy compartment, which leaves your fish moist, tender, and flaky. (It also makes cleanup a snap.) The key is creating a tight seal to trap in the heat and juice. It may help to fold the paper in half, draw half a heart, then cut along the lines to form a half-moon shape before you even start folding. If you can't get the very last edges of the paper to seal tight, twist them instead of folding.

COCONUT-CRUSTED FISH WITH STIR-FRIED VEGGIES

Big flakes of coconut turn golden and toasty in the oven to form a delicious, crunchy crust on top of meaty cod fillets. While the fish bakes, make a quick ginger-garlic-sesame-infused veggie stir fry on top of the stove—and dinner is done in a flash.

SERVES 2

PREP: 15 minutes   **COOK:** 10 minutes   **TOTAL:** 25 minutes

FOR THE FISH

2 skinless cod or sea bass fillets, cut about ½ inch thick (5 to 6 ounces each)

⅛ teaspoon coarse salt

⅛ teaspoon black pepper

¼ cup almond meal

¼ cup unsweetened flaked coconut

¼ cup finely chopped shallots

1 tablespoon coconut oil, melted

FOR THE VEGETABLES

1 tablespoon coconut oil

1 bunch fresh broccolini, trimmed, or 1 cup fresh broccoli florets

¾ cup halved and thinly sliced yellow summer squash

¼ cup sliced quartered onion

1 cup coarsely shredded napa cabbage

8 snow peas, trimmed and halved lengthwise

2 teaspoons minced fresh ginger

1 clove garlic, minced

1 tablespoon toasted sesame oil

1 tablespoon coconut aminos

1 tablespoon Whole30-compatible rice vinegar

2 teaspoons sesame seeds, toasted (see Tip, page 19; optional)

Preheat the oven to 425°F.

MAKE THE FISH: Line a baking sheet with parchment paper. Rinse the fish; pat dry with paper towels. Place the fish on the prepared baking sheet. Sprinkle the fish with the salt and pepper. In a small bowl, combine the almond meal, flaked coconut, and shallots. Add the coconut oil to the coconut mixture and mix well. Spoon the coconut mixture evenly on top of the fish fillets.

Bake the fish for 8 to 11 minutes, until the topping is browned and the fish just barely starts to flake when pulled apart with a fork.

MAKE THE VEGETABLES: Heat the coconut oil in a wok or large nonstick skillet over medium heat. Add the broccolini; cover and cook for 2 minutes. Uncover and cook, stirring, for 2 minutes more. Add the squash and onion. Cook, stirring, until the vegetables are crisp-tender, 3 to 5 minutes. Add the cabbage, snow peas, ginger, and garlic. Cook, stirring, for 2 minutes. Add the sesame oil, coconut aminos, and rice vinegar. Cook, stirring, for 1 minute.

Divide the vegetable stir-fry between two serving plates. Top with the fish. Sprinkle with sesame seeds, if desired.

TIP Toasted sesame oil is widely available. Look for it in the Asian section of your supermarket.

COD FILLETS WITH OLIVE-ANCHO RELISH AND CAULIFLOWER-POBLANO PILAF

The relish comes together in a flash but adds amazing depth to this simple baked fish dish. It's a combination of piquant olives, orange zest and juice, fresh thyme, and ancho chile powder, which has mild heat and a wonderfully sweet and fruity flavor.

SERVES 4

PREP: 10 minutes   **COOK:** 20 minutes   **TOTAL:** 30 minutes

FOR THE RELISH

½ cup pitted green olives

½ cup extra-virgin olive oil

1 shallot, minced

2 tablespoons fresh orange juice

2 teaspoons fresh thyme leaves

1 teaspoon ground ancho chile

½ teaspoon grated orange zest

FOR THE FISH

4 cod fillets (5 to 6 ounces each)

2 tablespoons extra-virgin olive oil

½ teaspoon dried thyme

½ teaspoon salt

½ teaspoon black pepper

FOR THE PILAF

1 head cauliflower, cut into florets

2 tablespoons olive oil

1 small poblano pepper, seeded and finely chopped

1 shallot, minced

½ teaspoon salt

½ teaspoon black pepper

¼ cup sliced almonds, toasted (see Tip, page 19)

2 tablespoons fresh lemon juice

FOR THE RELISH: In a food processor, combine all the ingredients for the relish. Pulse until the mixture is very finely chopped and forms a loose paste. Transfer the olive relish to a bowl and set aside.

FOR THE FISH: Preheat the oven to 400°F. Arrange the fish on a rimmed baking sheet. Drizzle with the olive oil. Sprinkle with the dried thyme, salt, and black pepper. Roast for 20 minutes, until the fish just barely starts to flake when pulled apart with a fork.

FOR THE PILAF: Place half the cauliflower in a food processor and pulse into a rice-like consistency, 15 to 20 pulses. Transfer to a bowl and repeat with the remaining cauliflower. In a large skillet, heat the olive oil over medium heat. Add the poblano and shallot and cook, stirring, until just tender, about 5 minutes. Add the cauliflower, salt, and black pepper. Cook, stirring frequently, until the cauliflower is just tender and beginning to brown, about 5 minutes. Stir in the almonds and lemon juice.

Serve the fish over the pilaf and top with the olive relish. Store leftover relish in an airtight container in the refrigerator for up to 3 days.

TIP Your local Mexican market is the perfect place to stock up on unique spices and blends. Just make sure to read the labels on your spices, to ensure there isn't any added sugar or other off-plan ingredients.

GINGER-POACHED SNAPPER WITH SHIITAKE MUSHROOMS AND SESAME BOK CHOY

Toasted sesame oil is powerful—a little goes a long way. Its nutty flavor infuses this dish of meltingly tender poached fish served over crisp sautéed bok choy and topped with sautéed shiitake mushrooms.

SERVES 2

PREP: 10 minutes   **COOK:** 15 minutes   **TOTAL:** 25 minutes

1½ teaspoons toasted sesame oil

1¼ cups sliced shiitake mushroom caps (3 to 4 ounces)

2½ teaspoons grated lemon zest

Salt and black pepper

1 cup Chicken Bone Broth (page 284), Whole30-compatible chicken broth, or water

2 teaspoons coconut aminos

2 red snapper fillets (6 ounces each)

1 tablespoon thinly sliced fresh ginger

2 teaspoons avocado oil

1 clove garlic

½ teaspoon black or white sesame seeds

4 cups sliced bok choy

Lemon wedges

Fresh chives, snipped (optional)

Heat 1 teaspoon of the sesame oil in a large skillet over medium heat. Add 1 cup of the mushrooms and cook, stirring, until tender, 3 to 4 minutes. Stir in ½ teaspoon of the lemon zest. Season with salt and pepper. Remove the mushroom mixture from the pan and keep warm.

Combine the remaining ¼ cup mushrooms, the broth, remaining 2 teaspoons lemon zest, the coconut aminos, and ¼ teaspoon of the sesame oil in the same skillet. Bring to a boil. Reduce the heat to keep the liquid at a low simmer. Carefully add the fish. Sprinkle the fish lightly with salt and place the ginger slices on top. Cover and cook until the fish barely starts to flake when pulled apart with a fork, 4 to 5 minutes. Remove the fish from the skillet and cover to keep warm. Discard the poaching liquid and wipe out the skillet with a paper towel.

Heat the avocado oil in the skillet over medium heat. Add the garlic and sesame seeds and cook, stirring, for 1 minute. Stir in the bok choy and cook, covered, stirring occasionally, until the stems are crisp-tender and the leaves are wilted, 3 to 5 minutes. Remove the skillet from the heat and lightly season the bok choy with salt; drizzle with the remaining ¼ teaspoon sesame oil.

Spoon the bok choy onto two dinner plates. Top each with a fish fillet and spoon sautéed mushrooms onto the fish. Serve with lemon wedges and sprinkle with chives, if desired.

TIP If you can't find red snapper, you can substitute flounder, black sea bass, or branzino.

GRILLED HALIBUT WITH ASPARAGUS

When you have Compound Butter ready and waiting in the fridge, throwing together a fabulous dinner takes no time at all. Not counting salt and olive oil, this recipe requires only five ingredients and a mere 15 minutes. Although our recipe for Compound Butter features hazelnuts and thyme, you can switch up the ingredients. Try toasted walnuts and basil; almonds, chives, and dill; or minced garlic or shallot and lemon zest.

SERVES 2

PREP: 5 minutes   **COOK:** 10 minutes   **TOTAL:** 15 minutes

2 halibut fillets (5 to 6 ounces each), about 1 inch thick

2 tablespoons extra-virgin olive oil

1 pound asparagus spears, trimmed

½ teaspoon salt

⅛ teaspoon red pepper flakes

2 tablespoons Compound Butter (page 290)

Lemon wedges

Fresh thyme (optional)

Grease a grill rack and preheat the grill to medium (350 to 375°F).

Brush both sides of the fish with 1 tablespoon of the olive oil. Drizzle the remaining 1 tablespoon oil over the asparagus. Sprinkle the fish and asparagus with the salt and red pepper flakes.

Place the fish and asparagus on the greased grill rack. Grill the fish for 8 to 12 minutes, turning once, until it just barely starts to flake when pulled apart with a fork. Grill the asparagus for 7 to 10 minutes, turning occasionally, until tender.

To serve, top the grilled fish with the butter. Serve with the grilled asparagus and lemon wedges. Garnish with fresh thyme, if desired.

TIP Halibut can be expensive, but any firm white fish would work here. Try cod, striped bass, fluke, or flounder if you're cooking for a larger group or on a budget.

JAMAICAN JERK–INSPIRED SALMON WITH FRESH MANGO SALSA

If mango is not in season or you can't find it, you can substitute fresh pineapple.

SERVES 4

PREP: 10 minutes   **COOK:** 10 minutes   **TOTAL:** 20 minutes

FOR THE SALSA

1 ripe mango, pitted, peeled, and chopped

1 ripe avocado, halved, pitted, peeled, and chopped

½ cup chopped red bell pepper

½ cup roughly chopped fresh cilantro leaves

1 small fresh jalapeño, seeded and finely chopped

1 tablespoon fresh lime juice

Salt

FOR THE FISH

1½ teaspoons dried thyme, crushed

½ teaspoon garlic powder

½ teaspoon salt

½ teaspoon ground allspice

¼ teaspoon cayenne pepper

¼ teaspoon ground cinnamon

4 skinless salmon fillets (6 to 8 ounces each), about 1 inch thick

1 tablespoon extra-virgin olive oil

6 cups fresh baby spinach

MAKE THE SALSA: In a medium bowl, gently combine the mango, avocado, bell pepper, cilantro, jalapeño, and lime juice. Season with salt. Cover and refrigerate for up to 2 hours.

MAKE THE FISH: Grease the grill rack (see Tip). Preheat the grill to medium (350 to 375°F). In a small bowl, combine the thyme, garlic powder, salt, allspice, cayenne, and cinnamon; set aside. Rinse the fish; pat dry with paper towels. Brush both sides of the fish with the olive oil. Sprinkle with the spice blend and rub it in with your fingers. Grill the fish over direct heat for 8 to 12 minutes, turning once, until it barely starts to flake when pulled apart with a fork.

To serve, divide the spinach leaves between two plates. Top with the grilled salmon and mango salsa.

TIP To broil the salmon instead of grilling it, preheat the broiler. Prepare the salmon as directed and place it on the unheated greased rack of a broiler pan. Broil 4 to 5 inches from the heat for 8 to 12 minutes, turning once, until the fish barely starts to flake when pulled apart with a fork.

GRILLED SALMON WITH CAULIFLOWER COUSCOUS–SPINACH SALAD

The salad that accompanies this seared, crisp-crusted salmon is a riot of color and textures. Tossed with spinach, tomatoes, basil, and crunchy toasted almonds, you would never know the "couscous," composed of tiny pieces of cauliflower, isn't the real thing.

SERVES 4

PREP: 30 minutes **COOK:** 15 minutes **TOTAL:** 45 minutes

FOR THE SALAD

1 small head cauliflower, broken into large florets

2 tablespoons extra-virgin olive oil

2 cups baby spinach or kale (not packed)

1 cup grape tomatoes, halved

⅓ cup thinly sliced fresh basil leaves

⅓ cup sliced almonds, toasted (see Tip, page 19)

FOR THE VINAIGRETTE

⅓ cup extra-virgin olive oil

3 tablespoons champagne vinegar, white wine vinegar, or apple cider vinegar

1 tablespoon finely chopped shallots

1 teaspoon Whole30-compatible Dijon mustard

¼ teaspoon salt

¼ teaspoon black pepper

FOR THE FISH

4 skinless salmon fillets (6 to 8 ounces each)

Extra-virgin olive oil

Salt and black pepper

2 tablespoons chopped fresh chives

Lemon wedges

Grease a grill rack and preheat the grill to medium (350 to 375°F).

MAKE THE SALAD: In a food processor, pulse the cauliflower (in batches) until the pieces are the size of couscous. In a large skillet, cook the cauliflower couscous in the olive oil, stirring occasionally, until tender and just beginning to brown, about 5 minutes. Transfer to a large bowl. Add the spinach, tomatoes, basil, and almonds and toss to combine.

MAKE THE VINAIGRETTE: In a small bowl, whisk together the olive oil, vinegar, shallots, and mustard. Season with the salt and pepper. Drizzle the couscous salad with the vinaigrette and toss to coat.

MAKE THE SALMON: Brush the salmon with olive oil and season with salt and pepper. Close the grill lid and grill the salmon until it is nicely seared, crispy, and releases easily from the grill, about 6 minutes. Turn the salmon and grill until it barely starts to flake when pulled apart with a fork, about 2 minutes. Remove the salmon from the grill and let rest for 3 minutes.

Sprinkle the salmon with the chives and serve with the cauliflower couscous salad and lemon wedges.

HARISSA SALMON WITH WARM TUNISIAN SALAD

Harissa is a Tunisian condiment, usually made with hot chiles, garlic, cumin, coriander, caraway, and olive oil, that is traditionally served with couscous or used to flavor soups and stews. It is often fiery-hot, but there are milder varieties as well. Choose one according to your taste and sample a tiny bit before you cook with it so you can adjust the amount you use, if necessary.

SERVES 2

PREP: 10 minutes   **COOK:** 10 minutes   **TOTAL:** 20 minutes

2 tablespoons Whole30-compatible harissa paste

2 teaspoons coriander seeds, crushed

2 teaspoons grated lemon zest

2 skin-on salmon fillets (6 to 8 ounces each)

2 tablespoons extra-virgin olive oil

1 small yellow onion, cut into slivers

1 small red bell pepper, seeded and cut into matchsticks

1 small green bell pepper, seeded and cut into matchsticks

1 tablespoon fresh lemon juice

1 large ripe tomato, seeded and chopped

1 clove garlic, thinly sliced

¼ teaspoon sea salt, plus more as needed

Black pepper

¼ cup snipped fresh cilantro

Preheat the oven to 450°F.

In a small bowl, mix together the harissa, coriander, and lemon zest. Place the salmon fillets, skin side down, in a shallow baking pan. Wearing plastic or rubber gloves, spoon the harissa mixture on top of the salmon and rub it in with your fingers. Let the salmon stand while you prepare the salad.

Heat the olive oil in a large skillet over medium heat. Add the onion and bell peppers and cook, stirring, for 5 minutes. Add the lemon juice, tomato, garlic, salt, and black pepper to taste and cook, stirring, until the tomato begins to soften, about 3 minutes. Remove the skillet from the heat and top with the cilantro. Let the salad stand while you roast the salmon.

Roast the salmon for 4 to 6 minutes per ½-inch thickness, until the fish just barely starts to flake when pulled apart with a fork. Season with salt. Serve the salmon with the warm salad.

SALMON CAKES WITH MANGO RELISH

FROM JENN BUMB OF *PRETEND IT'S A DONUT*

Do you even know the level of deliciousness that you are about to embark on with this recipe?! This is one of my family's favorite meals, and the spices can easily be adapted to what you like. Need to spice up your life? Add some diced jalapeño to the relish or some cayenne to the salmon cakes. Also, these freeze pretty well. Cook them up, let cool, place a piece of parchment paper between each patty, and stick them in the freezer until you are ready to consume again. Mangoes not in season? Try peaches, strawberries, or pineapple. You won't be disappointed. I promise.

SERVES 3

PREP: 10 minutes   **COOK:** 10 minutes   **TOTAL:** 20 minutes

4 teaspoons extra-virgin olive oil

¼ cup finely chopped red bell pepper

3 cans (6 ounces each) wild-caught salmon, drained

¼ cup Basic Mayonnaise (page 287)

1 teaspoon ground cumin

1 teaspoon minced yellow onion

1 teaspoon garlic powder

1 teaspoon sweet paprika

1 teaspoon dried oregano, crushed

¼ teaspoon cayenne pepper (optional)

Salt and black pepper

1 cup diced fresh mango or pineapple

1 cup diced avocado

⅓ cup diced red onion

¼ cup snipped fresh cilantro

1 jalapeño, seeded and finely chopped (optional)

1 tablespoon fresh lime juice

Heat 1 teaspoon of the olive oil in a large nonstick skillet over medium heat. Add the bell pepper and cook, stirring, until tender, 2 to 3 minutes.

In a large bowl, combine the bell pepper, salmon, mayonnaise, cumin, yellow onion, garlic powder, paprika, oregano, cayenne (if using), and salt and black pepper to taste. Stir until combined. Shape the fish mixture into nine ¼-inch-thick patties, using a scant ¼ cup per patty.

Add the remaining 3 teaspoons oil to the same skillet and heat over medium heat. Cook the patties, four or five at a time, in the hot oil, turning once, until browned on both sides, 7 to 9 minutes.

Meanwhile, in a medium bowl, combine the mango, avocado, red onion, cilantro, jalapeño (if using), and lime juice.

Serve the patties topped with some of the relish.

ONE-PAN HERB-CRUSTED ROASTED SALMON WITH ROASTED BROCCOLI STEAKS

A head of broccoli sliced lengthwise is transformed into gorgeous green "steaks" with which the salmon is roasted—all together in one pan for easy cleanup. As you are slicing the broccoli, save any florets that fall away for a stir-fry or salad—or simply eat them as a snack dipped in a little Dump Ranch dressing (page 261).

SERVES 2

PREP: 15 minutes   COOK: 25 minutes   TOTAL: 40 minutes

½ cup fresh basil leaves

½ cup fresh parsley leaves

6 tablespoons extra-virgin olive oil

1 tablespoon fresh lemon juice

1 teaspoon salt

1 teaspoon black pepper

½ teaspoon grated lemon zest

¼ cup almond flour

2 salmon fillets (6 ounces each)

3 small heads broccoli with the stems attached (about 1 pound total)

½ cup sliced almonds, toasted (see Tip, page 19)

Preheat the oven to 400°F.

Combine the basil, parsley, 4 tablespoons of the oil, lemon juice, ½ teaspoon of the salt, ½ teaspoon of the pepper, and the lemon zest in a blender or food processor. Cover and pulse until smooth. Pour the herb mixture into a bowl and stir in the almond flour.

Place the salmon fillets in a large roasting pan or on a rimmed baking sheet. Pack the herb mixture on the top of each fillet.

Trim the broccoli stems to about 3 inches below the florets. Slice the broccoli heads lengthwise into 1-inch-thick slabs (two or three slabs per head), cutting from the bottom of the stems through the crown to preserve the shape of the broccoli. Brush both sides of each broccoli slice with the remaining 2 tablespoons olive oil and sprinkle with the remaining ½ teaspoon salt and ½ teaspoon pepper. Arrange the broccoli in a single layer in the pan around the salmon.

Roast the broccoli and salmon for 25 minutes, until the salmon just barely starts to flake when pulled apart with a fork and the broccoli is lightly browned, turning the broccoli once halfway through roasting. Sprinkle the broccoli with the toasted almonds before serving.

PAN-SEARED SCALLOPS WITH BACON OVER BRAISED SWISS CHARD

You can either go Indian or Cajun with these scallops, depending on the seasoning blend you choose to use in the almond flour coating. There are nearly as many versions of garam masala as there are Indian cooks, but most commercial versions contain some combination of black pepper, cinnamon, cloves, coriander, cumin, cardamom, chiles, fennel, mace, and nutmeg. It is usually warmly flavored but not hot.

SERVES 2

PREP: 10 minutes   **COOK:** 15 minutes   **TOTAL:** 25 minutes

12 ounces Swiss chard

8 ounces fresh sea scallops

1 tablespoon almond flour

1 teaspoon garam masala or Cajun seasoning

½ teaspoon dried thyme, crushed

Pinch of salt

2 slices Whole30-compatible bacon, chopped

1 tablespoon extra-virgin olive oil

1 clove garlic, minced

1 tablespoon water, Chicken Bone Broth (page 284), or Whole30-compatible chicken broth

1 tablespoon balsamic or apple cider vinegar

Cut the stems and center ribs from the Swiss chard, discarding tough areas near the base of the stems. Cut the stems into 1-inch pieces and tear the leaves into two or three pieces each. Set aside.

Rinse the scallops and pat them dry. In a medium bowl, combine the almond flour, garam masala, thyme, and salt. Add the scallops and toss to coat. Set the scallops aside.

Cook the bacon in a large skillet over medium heat until just brown and crispy, about 5 minutes. Use a slotted spoon to transfer the bacon to a paper towel–lined plate to drain, reserving the drippings in the skillet. Add the scallops to the drippings in the hot skillet and cook over medium-high heat, turning once, until browned and opaque, about 6 minutes. Remove the scallops from the skillet.

Heat the olive oil in the skillet over medium heat. Add the chard stems and the garlic and cook, stirring, for 2 minutes. Add the chard leaves and the water. Cook over medium-high heat, covered, until the chard stems are tender and the leaves have wilted, 2 minutes more. Add the vinegar and toss to coat evenly. Return the scallops and bacon to the skillet and cook just to heat through.

ROASTED SALMON CAESAR SALAD WITH PARSNIP "CROUTONS"

The tangy Caesar dressing and sweetness of the roasted parsnip "croutons" complement each other beautifully in this Whole30 take on the classic salad. Try it with other proteins as well—sliced grilled steak, shrimp, and chicken are equally delicious.

SERVES 4

PREP: 20 minutes   **COOK:** 15 minutes   **TOTAL:** 35 minutes

FOR THE PARSNIP CROUTONS

1 pound parsnips, peeled and diced

3 tablespoons extra-virgin olive oil

1½ teaspoons Italian seasoning, crushed

½ teaspoon salt

FOR THE SALMON

4 salmon fillets (6 ounces each)

1 tablespoon extra-virgin olive oil

½ teaspoon Italian seasoning, crushed

½ teaspoon salt

FOR THE DRESSING

6 Whole30-compatible anchovies

1 large egg yolk

2 tablespoons fresh lemon juice

2 teaspoons Whole30-compatible Dijon or coarse-grain mustard

1 teaspoon nutritional yeast

1 clove garlic, minced

½ teaspoon black pepper

⅓ cup extra-virgin olive oil

1 head romaine lettuce, cut or torn into bite-size pieces (about 8 cups)

Preheat the oven to 450°F.

MAKE THE PARSNIP CROUTONS: Place the parsnips in a large roasting pan. Drizzle with the oil, sprinkle with the Italian seasoning and salt, and toss to coat. Spread the parsnips into a single layer.

MAKE THE SALMON: Arrange the salmon fillets, skin sides down, on a medium baking sheet or in a roasting pan. Brush the salmon with the olive oil and sprinkle with the Italian seasoning and salt.

Roast the parsnips and salmon together for 15 to 20 minutes, stirring the parsnips once, until the parsnips are lightly browned and the salmon just barely starts to flake when pulled apart with a fork.

MAKE THE DRESSING: In a blender, combine the anchovies, egg yolk, lemon juice, mustard, nutritional yeast, garlic, and pepper. Blend until smooth. With the blender running, slowly add the olive oil and blend until emulsified.

Arrange the romaine lettuce on a plate. Drizzle with some of the dressing. (Refrigerate any leftover dressing.) Top with the salmon and the parsnip croutons.

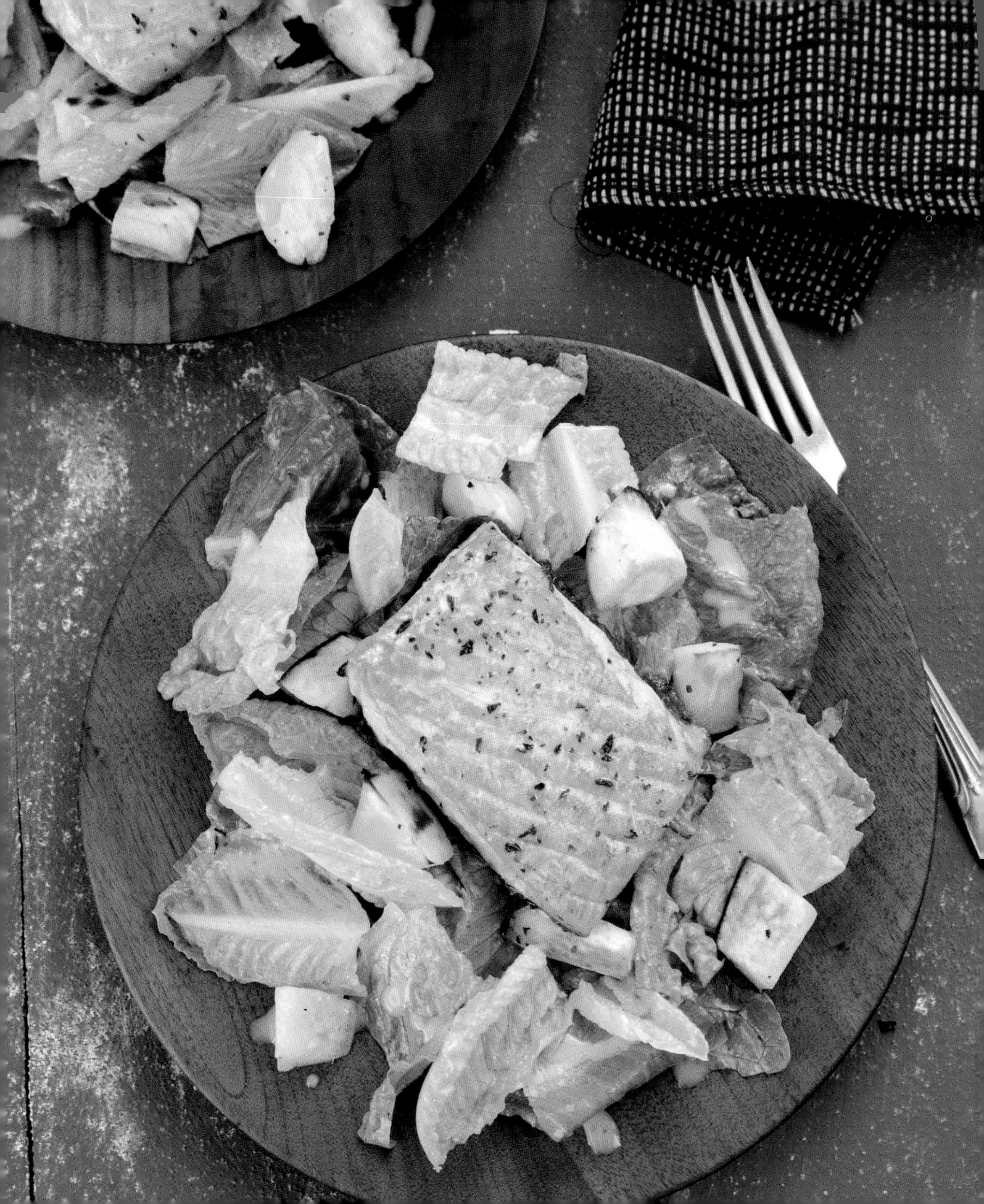

PAN-SEARED SCALLOP SALAD

The key to perfectly seared scallops is a really hot pan that quickly caramelizes their natural sugars and creates a tantalizing golden crust on both sides. The scallops are ready to turn when they easily release from the pan. Cast iron is terrific but not necessary, as long as the skillet is fairly heavy.

SERVES 2

PREP: 15 minutes   **COOK:** 5 minutes   **TOTAL:** 20 minutes

FOR THE VINAIGRETTE

½ cup avocado oil or extra-virgin olive oil

¼ cup fresh lime juice

2 tablespoons apple cider vinegar

1 tablespoon coconut aminos

1 tablespoon grated fresh ginger

1 teaspoon Red Boat fish sauce

1 clove garlic, minced

1 red or green jalapeño, chopped

FOR THE SALAD

4 cups shredded napa cabbage

½ cup coarsely shredded carrots (2 medium)

½ cup snipped fresh cilantro and/or mint

¼ cup thinly sliced green onions

FOR THE SCALLOPS

8 large sea scallops

Salt and black pepper

3 tablespoons coconut oil

2 teaspoons sesame seeds, toasted
(see Tip, page 19)

MAKE THE VINAIGRETTE: In a small bowl, whisk together the avocado oil, lime juice, vinegar, coconut aminos, ginger, fish sauce, garlic, and jalapeño.

MAKE THE SALAD: In a large bowl, toss together the napa cabbage, carrots, cilantro, and green onions. Drizzle with the desired amount of the vinaigrette.

MAKE THE SCALLOPS: Rinse the scallops; pat dry with paper towels. Lightly season with salt and black pepper. In a large skillet, melt the coconut oil over high heat. When the oil is very hot, carefully add the scallops, making sure the scallops are not touching. Sear the scallops, turning once, until each side develops a ¼-inch-thick crust and the centers are translucent.

Divide the salad between two plates. Place the scallops on top of the salads. Sprinkle with the toasted sesame seeds.

SEARED FRESH TUNA WITH FENNEL SLAW

A marinade of balsamic vinegar, olive oil, garlic, salt, and red pepper flakes infuses the fish with a hint of spicy sweetness. A quick turn on a hot grill gives it a beautiful brown crust and tender pink interior.

SERVES 2

PREP: 25 minutes   **MARINATING:** 2 to 4 hours   **COOK:** 5 minutes   **TOTAL:** 30 minutes plus marinating

2 tuna steaks (6 ounces each), about 1 inch thick

¼ cup balsamic vinegar

¼ cup extra-virgin olive oil

2 cloves garlic, minced

¼ teaspoon plus ⅛ teaspoon coarse salt

¼ teaspoon red pepper flakes

1 small fennel bulb

⅓ cup coarsely shredded carrot

⅓ cup thin bite-size strips red bell pepper

¼ cup thinly sliced green onions

¼ cup Basic Mayonnaise (page 287)

1 tablespoon white wine vinegar

1 teaspoon snipped fresh dill

⅛ teaspoon black pepper

Place the tuna steaks in a resealable plastic bag set in a shallow dish. In a small bowl, whisk together the balsamic vinegar, olive oil, garlic, ¼ teaspoon of the salt, and the red pepper flakes. Pour the marinade over the tuna in the bag; seal the bag. Turn gently to coat the tuna. Marinate in the refrigerator for 2 to 4 hours, turning the bag occasionally.

Trim the fennel bulb, reserving the feathery tops (fronds). Snip enough of the feathery tops to make 1 teaspoon; set aside. Core the fennel bulb and then coarsely shred it. In a medium bowl, combine the shredded fennel, carrot, bell pepper, and green onions. In a small bowl, whisk together the mayonnaise, white wine vinegar, dill, remaining ⅛ teaspoon salt, the black pepper, and the reserved fennel fronds. Pour over the fennel slaw; toss to coat. Cover and chill until ready to serve.

Grease a grill rack. Preheat the grill to medium-high (375 to 400°F).

Drain the tuna and discard the marinade. Grill the tuna over direct heat, turning once, for 4 to 6 minutes, until the tuna steaks are well browned on the outside but pink in the center. Transfer the tuna to a cutting board. Cut the steaks into ¼-inch-thick slices.

Divide the tuna and fennel slaw between two plates and serve.

TIP To panfry the tuna, drain the tuna and discard the marinade. Heat 2 tablespoons coconut oil in a large skillet over medium-high heat. Reduce the heat to medium. Add the tuna steaks. Cook, turning once, until the steaks are well browned on the outside but still pink in the center, 4 to 6 minutes. Remove the tuna from the skillet and continue as directed.

SALMON-AVOCADO SALAD

This riff on classic tuna salad calls for salmon instead of tuna and avocado to add creaminess in place of mayonnaise. Celery adds a pleasant crunch. Use leftover baked, grilled, or poached salmon if you have it—or bake some just for use in this recipe.

SERVES 3

PREP: 15 minutes   **TOTAL:** 15 minutes

3 tablespoons finely chopped sun-dried tomatoes

4 teaspoons white wine vinegar

4 teaspoons extra-virgin olive oil

1 tablespoon plus 1 teaspoon chopped fresh chives

¾ teaspoon Whole30-compatible coarse-grain mustard

¼ teaspoon coarse salt

10 to 12 ounces flaked cooked salmon (see Tip)

1 medium avocado, halved, pitted, peeled, and roughly chopped

½ cup thinly sliced celery

6 cups arugula or watercress

In a medium bowl, combine the sun-dried tomatoes, vinegar, olive oil, 1 tablespoon of the chives, the mustard, and the salt. Remove 2 tablespoons of the tomato mixture from the bowl and set aside.

Add the salmon, avocado, and celery to the tomato mixture remaining in the bowl and toss gently to combine.

In a large bowl, toss the arugula with the reserved tomato mixture. Divide the arugula between two plates. Top with the salmon-avocado mixture. Sprinkle with the remaining 1 teaspoon chives.

TIP Preheat the oven to 425°F. Line a small baking pan with aluminum foil. Rinse a salmon fillet (10 to 12 ounces) and pat dry with paper towels. Place the salmon, skin side down, in the prepared pan. Season lightly with salt and pepper. Bake for 8 to 12 minutes, until the salmon just barely starts to flake when pulled apart with a fork. Use a spatula to lift the salmon meat off the skin; discard the skin. Use two forks to gently flake the salmon. Let cool completely.

SEARED SCALLOPS WITH CAULIFLOWER-PARSNIP PUREE

FROM KIRSTEN BUCK OF *BUCK NAKED KITCHEN*

This recipe is one that I've been making for years. It was inspired by a Spanish tapas dish I had while traveling. It is simple, yet so rich in flavor—it truly melts in your mouth. If you want to impress dinner guests, this is how you do it—just double the recipe.

SERVES 2

PREP: 15 minutes   **COOK:** 20 minutes   **TOTAL:** 35 minutes

FOR THE PUREE

3 cups cauliflower florets

2 medium parsnips, peeled, trimmed, and chopped (about 1 cup)

½ cup Chicken Bone Broth (page 284) or Whole30-compatible chicken broth

¼ cup full-fat coconut milk

2 tablespoons ghee or Clarified Butter (page 289)

Salt and black pepper

FOR THE SCALLOPS

10 large scallops

Salt and black pepper

1 tablespoon extra-virgin olive oil

1 tablespoon ghee or Clarified Butter (page 289)

Chopped fresh dill

Capers, rinsed and drained (optional)

2 to 3 slices crisp-cooked prosciutto

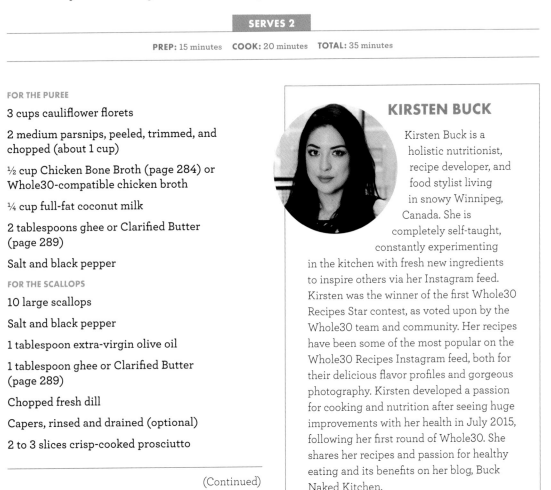

KIRSTEN BUCK

Kirsten Buck is a holistic nutritionist, recipe developer, and food stylist living in snowy Winnipeg, Canada. She is completely self-taught, constantly experimenting in the kitchen with fresh new ingredients to inspire others via her Instagram feed. Kirsten was the winner of the first Whole30 Recipes Star contest, as voted upon by the Whole30 team and community. Her recipes have been some of the most popular on the Whole30 Recipes Instagram feed, both for their delicious flavor profiles and gorgeous photography. Kirsten developed a passion for cooking and nutrition after seeing huge improvements with her health in July 2015, following her first round of Whole30. She shares her recipes and passion for healthy eating and its benefits on her blog, Buck Naked Kitchen.

(Continued)

MAKE THE PUREE: Pour 1 inch of water into a pot fitted with a steamer basket. Place the cauliflower florets and parsnips in the steamer basket. Cover the pot and bring to a boil. Reduce the heat and steam until the vegetables are fall-apart soft, about 15 minutes. Transfer the vegetables to a blender. Add the broth, coconut milk, and ghee. Blend until smooth. Season with salt and pepper.

MAKE THE SCALLOPS: Rinse the scallops; pat dry with paper towels. Lightly season the scallops with salt and pepper. Heat a large cast-iron skillet or other heavy skillet over high heat for 1 minute. Add the olive oil and ghee and heat until barely smoking, about 30 seconds. Using tongs, place the scallops in the skillet, seasoned side down, making sure the scallops are not touching. Sear the scallops, turning once, until each side develops a ¼-inch-thick golden crust and the centers are translucent, about 90 seconds per side.

Divide the puree between two shallow bowls. Top with the scallops and garnish with dill, capers (if using), and crisp-cooked prosciutto.

SEARED SEA BASS WITH WASABI BUTTER, GREEN ONIONS, AND PEACHES

Sea bass is the non-fish-lover's fish. Its mild-flavored flesh is firm but tender and buttery. The combination of sweet, juicy, ripe peaches with nose-tingling wasabi and a splash of rice vinegar in this dish is just fabulous. It's simple enough for a weeknight meal but fancy enough for company.

SERVES 2

PREP: 15 minutes   **COOK:** 10 minutes   **TOTAL:** 25 minutes

FOR THE FISH

3 teaspoons Clarified Butter (page 289) or ghee

2 sea bass fillets (5 to 6 ounces each), pin bones removed

Salt

1 ripe large peach, pitted, peeled, and cut into ½-inch slices

¼ cup sliced green onions

1 teaspoon rice vinegar

¼ to ½ teaspoon Whole-30-compatible wasabi paste or powder

FOR THE SALAD

2 tablespoons avocado oil

1 tablespoon rice vinegar

1 tablespoon chopped fresh parsley or cilantro

1 clove garlic, minced

Salt and black pepper

4 cups torn butterhead lettuce

½ cup thinly sliced cucumber

¼ cup thinly sliced radishes

MAKE THE FISH: Heat 1 teaspoon of the butter in a large nonstick skillet over medium-high heat. Add the fish and cook, turning once, until the fish just barely starts to flake when pulled apart. Remove the fish from the skillet and cover to keep warm. Season with salt.

Cook the peach slices in the same skillet over medium-high heat, turning once, until golden, 2 to 4 minutes. Add the green onions and vinegar and cook for 1 minute more. Remove from the heat.

Melt the remaining 2 teaspoons butter in a small saucepan over medium heat. Stir in the wasabi and remove from the heat.

MAKE THE SALAD: In a small jar with a lid, combine the avocado oil, rice vinegar, parsley, garlic, and salt and pepper to taste. Shake vigorously to blend. In a large bowl, combine the lettuce, cucumber, and radishes. Drizzle the salad with the vinaigrette and toss to coat.

To serve, spoon the peach mixture over the fish and drizzle with the wasabi butter. Serve the salad alongside.

SHRIMP, SNOW PEA, AND SHIITAKE STIR-FRY

The flavor and combination of crisp vegetables in this dish is so delicious, you will not miss your go-to Chinese takeout at all. Shiitake mushrooms are native to East Asia, and have a softer texture and smokier flavor than their portobello counterparts.

SERVES 2

PREP: 20 minutes   **COOK:** 10 minutes   **TOTAL:** 30 minutes

3 tablespoons rice vinegar

2 tablespoons coconut aminos

2 cloves garlic, thinly sliced

1 teaspoon minced fresh ginger

¼ teaspoon red pepper flakes

¼ teaspoon salt

2 tablespoons coconut oil

8 ounces shiitake mushrooms, stemmed and sliced

1 pound medium shrimp, peeled and deveined

2 cups snow peas, trimmed

2 stalks celery, sliced on an angle

1 tablespoon toasted sesame oil

½ cup unsalted cashews, roasted (see Tip), and coarsely chopped

2 green onions, sliced

In a small bowl, mix the vinegar, coconut aminos, garlic, ginger, red pepper flakes, and salt; set aside.

Heat the coconut oil in a large skillet or wok over medium-high heat. Add the mushrooms and cook, stirring, until just starting to become tender, about 3 minutes.

Stir in the vinegar mixture and cook until slightly reduced, about 1 minute. Add the shrimp, snow peas, and celery and cook, stirring, until the shrimp are opaque throughout, 3 to 4 minutes. Stir in the sesame oil and cashews. Top with the green onions.

TIP If you can't find roasted unsalted cashews, buy raw unsalted cashews and roast them in a 375°F oven for 6 to 7 minutes or until golden brown, stirring once.

TUNA NIÇOISE SALAD

This classic south-of-France dish is what's called a composed salad because rather than tossing everything together, it's beautifully arranged on a platter or plate. This version is super simple to make because it uses canned tuna. Be sure to get tuna packed without broth (which often contains soy).

SERVES 2

PREP: 20 minutes   **COOK:** 10 minutes   **TOTAL:** 30 minutes

FOR THE VINAIGRETTE

¼ cup white wine vinegar

10 pitted Kalamata olives, finely chopped

1 anchovy fillet, minced

1 clove garlic, minced

1 teaspoon Whole30-compatible Dijon mustard

½ cup extra-virgin olive oil

Black pepper

FOR THE VEGETABLES

4 small Yukon Gold potatoes

Salt

6 to 8 asparagus spears, trimmed

FOR THE SALAD

4 cups baby arugula

2 hard-cooked eggs, quartered (see Tip, page 270)

1 ripe large tomato, cut into wedges

2 cans (5 ounces each) water-packed wild albacore tuna, drained and broken into chunks

Small fresh basil leaves (optional)

MAKE THE VINAIGRETTE: In a medium bowl, whisk together the vinegar, olives, anchovy, garlic, and mustard. While whisking, slowly drizzle in the oil until emulsified. Season with pepper.

MAKE THE VEGETABLES: Place the potatoes in a large saucepan with lightly salted water to cover. Bring to a boil and reduce the heat to medium-low. Simmer, uncovered, just until tender, about 10 minutes. Drain, halve the potatoes, and drizzle with some of the vinaigrette. (Refrigerate the remaining vinaigrette.) Steam the asparagus until crisp-tender, about 3 minutes. Immediately place in ice water to cool. Drain.

MAKE THE SALAD: Divide the arugula between two plates. Arrange the potatoes, asparagus, eggs, tomato, and tuna on the arugula. Drizzle with the remaining vinaigrette and sprinkle with basil, if desired.

SIDE DISHES

CURRIED CARROT AND SWEET POTATO SOUP

FROM ARSY VARTANIAN OF *RUBIES & RADISHES*

The sweet potato makes for a naturally sweet and luxuriously creamy soup, while the curry powder and cayenne balance out the flavors with some added heat. Pair this elegant yet simple-to-make soup with your favorite protein for a perfect weeknight meal.

SERVES 4

PREP: 20 minutes   **COOK:** 4 to 5 hours (on low)   **TOTAL:** 4 to 5 hours + 20 minutes

1 tablespoon coconut oil

1 large leek, white and light green parts only, thinly sliced

½ pound carrots, sliced

1 tablespoon Madras curry powder

½ teaspoon sea salt

1 teaspoon grated fresh ginger

3 cloves garlic, minced

Pinch of cayenne pepper

2 Japanese sweet potatoes, peeled and chopped (see Tip)

3 cups Chicken Bone Broth (page 284) or Whole30-compatible chicken broth

2 cups full-fat coconut milk

Chopped fresh chives

Red pepper flakes

Heat the coconut oil in a large skillet over medium heat. Add the leek and carrots and cook, stirring frequently, until the leek is soft, 5 to 7 minutes.

Add the curry powder, salt, ginger, garlic, and cayenne to the skillet. Cook, stirring, until the garlic is fragrant, about 1 minute. Transfer the leek mixture to a 3½- or 4-quart slow cooker. Add the sweet potatoes, broth, and coconut milk to the slow cooker. Cover and cook on low for 4 to 5 hours.

Turn off the slow cooker and remove the lid; let the soup cool slightly. Using an immersion blender, puree the soup until smooth. Ladle the soup into bowls and top with chives and red pepper flakes.

TIP Japanese sweet potatoes have purple-red skin and pale butter-colored flesh that is drier and starchier than orange-fleshed sweet potatoes. If you can't find Japanese sweet potatoes, you can substitute regular sweet potatoes. The soup will be slightly sweeter and darker in color.

DUKKAH-CRUSTED BRUSSELS SPROUTS

Dukkah (DOO-kah), or duqqa, is an Egyptian spice blend made of toasted nuts, seeds, and spices that are ground to a coarse powder. It gives these simple roasted sprouts incredible flavor and aroma and a crunchy coating to boot. Sprinkle it over vegetables and meats, or, for a fantastic appetizer, dip raw vegetables first in extra-virgin olive oil and then the dukkah.

SERVES 4

PREP: 5 minutes   **COOK:** 20 minutes   **TOTAL:** 25 minutes

FOR THE DUKKAH

½ cup shelled pistachios

¼ cup sesame seeds

3 tablespoons coriander seeds

2 tablespoons cumin seeds

1 teaspoon kosher salt

½ teaspoon cracked black pepper

FOR THE BRUSSELS SPROUTS

1½ pounds Brussels sprouts

3 tablespoons extra-virgin olive oil

MAKE THE DUKKAH: Preheat the oven to 350°F. Place the pistachios on a rimmed baking sheet and toast for 5 minutes; add the sesame seeds, coriander, and cumin and toast for 5 minutes more, until the nuts are golden and the spices are fragrant. Remove from the oven and let cool (keep the oven on). Place the pistachio mixture in a food processor and add the salt and pepper. Pulse just until roughly chopped (do not overprocess). Let cool completely. Store the dukkah in an airtight container at room temperature for up to 1 week. (Makes about 1 cup.)

MAKE THE BRUSSELS SPROUTS: Increase the oven temperature to 400°F. Trim the ends from the Brussels sprouts and remove any yellow outer leaves. Cut each sprout in half lengthwise and place them in a 10 x 15-inch baking pan. Drizzle with the olive oil and toss to coat. Sprinkle with 3 tablespoons of the dukkah and stir to coat. Roast for 20 minutes, stirring after 15 minutes, until the Brussels sprouts are golden brown and crisp on the outside and tender inside.

EASY GREEK-STYLE LEMON POTATOES

FROM KIRSTEN BUCK OF *BUCK NAKED KITCHEN*

This recipe was inspired by my love of Greek food. My sister was a server at a Greek restaurant known for their lemon potatoes. I asked her how they were made and all she knew was "they put them in a pool of chicken stock and lemons and bake them for hours!" I knew there had to be more to it than that. I figured out an easier way. Here they are, an almost exact replica.

SERVES 6

PREP: 15 minutes   **COOK:** 1 hour 30 minutes   **TOTAL:** 1 hour 45 minutes

½ cup Chicken Bone Broth (page 284) or Whole30-compatible chicken broth

½ cup fresh lemon juice

⅓ cup extra-virgin olive oil

1 tablespoon dried thyme, crushed

1 tablespoon dried oregano, crushed

3 cloves garlic, minced

½ teaspoon sea salt

6 medium russet potatoes, peeled, if desired, and cut into ½-inch-thick wedges

Preheat the oven to 400°F.

Combine the broth, lemon juice, olive oil, thyme, oregano, garlic, and salt in a large bowl. Mix well.

Arrange the potato wedges in a single layer in a large baking dish. Pour the broth mixture over the potatoes. Cover with aluminum foil and bake, stirring once, for 1 hour 30 minutes.

GRILLED ROMAINE WITH SPICY TAHINI DRIZZLE

Romaine is the only lettuce sturdy enough to stand up to the grill, which gives it a wonderfully smoky flavor and delicious charring on the edges of the leaves. A drizzle of spicy sesame dressing provides the finishing touch.

SERVES 2

PREP: 10 minutes   **TOTAL:** 10 minutes

1 tablespoon fresh lemon juice

1 teaspoon tahini

½ to 1 teaspoon coconut aminos

¼ teaspoon hot chili sesame oil

1 clove garlic, minced

Pinch of salt

4 teaspoons avocado oil

1 romaine heart, halved lengthwise

Fresh cilantro leaves (optional)

Chopped toasted almonds (see Tip, page 19; optional)

Preheat a grill to medium (350 to 375°F).

In a small bowl, whisk together the lemon juice, tahini, coconut aminos, sesame oil, garlic, and salt. Slowly whisk in 3 teaspoons of the avocado oil.

Brush the romaine halves with the remaining 1 teaspoon avocado oil.

Grill the romaine, cut sides down, over direct heat for 4 to 6 minutes, until slightly charred. Place the romaine on salad plates, cut sides up. Drizzle with the dressing. Sprinkle with cilantro and almonds, if desired.

KALE CAESAR SALAD WITH ROASTED PISTACHIOS

The heartiness of kale means that even if there are leftovers of this salad (and there likely won't be), the leaves will stay crisp and fresh until the next day without getting limp. The dressing can be made and chilled up to 24 hours ahead. Let it stand at room temperature for 30 minutes before using.

SERVES 2 OR 3

PREP: 10 minutes   **CHILLING:** 30 minutes   **TOTAL:** 40 minutes

FOR THE DRESSING

3 tablespoons extra-virgin olive oil

2 anchovy fillets

2 teaspoons fresh lemon juice

2 cloves garlic

1 teaspoon Whole30-compatible Dijon mustard

⅛ teaspoon cayenne pepper

1 hard-cooked egg (page 270), yolk and white separated

Salt and black pepper

FOR THE SALAD

1 bunch curly leafed or Tuscan kale, stemmed and leaves sliced

⅓ cup roasted salted pistachios, chopped

MAKE THE DRESSING: In a blender, combine the olive oil, anchovy fillets, lemon juice, garlic, mustard, cayenne, and the hard-cooked egg yolk (reserve the egg white for another use or chop it and add it to the finished salad). Cover and blend until smooth. (Alternatively, place the ingredients in a bowl and use an immersion blender.) Season with salt and black pepper.

MAKE THE SALAD: Place the kale in a large bowl; add the dressing. Using your hands, work the dressing into the kale for 15 seconds. Chill for 30 minutes or up to 2 hours. Sprinkle the pistachios over the salad just before serving.

HERBED RUTABAGA OVEN FRIES WITH SPICY GARLIC KETCHUP

For a steakhouse-style meal at home, serve these crispy fries (and very zippy ketchup!) with roast chicken or grilled steak.

SERVES 4

PREP: 15 minutes **COOK:** 20 minutes **TOTAL:** 35 minutes

2 medium rutabagas or 1 large rutabaga (about 1½ pounds)

3 tablespoons extra-virgin olive oil

1 tablespoon chopped fresh rosemary

1 teaspoon salt

½ teaspoon dried oregano, crushed

½ teaspoon garlic powder

½ teaspoon black pepper

1 tablespoon finely chopped fresh parsley

1 teaspoon fresh thyme leaves

2 teaspoons Clarified Butter (page 289) or ghee

1 clove garlic, minced

½ cup Whole30 Ketchup (page 288) or Whole30-compatible ketchup

1 to 2 teaspoons Whole30-compatible hot sauce

Preheat the oven to 450°F.

Cut the rutabagas into ½-inch-thick sticks. Pat the sticks dry with paper towels and place them in a bowl. Add the olive oil, rosemary, salt, oregano, garlic powder, and pepper. Gently toss to coat the rutabaga with the oil and seasonings. Arrange in a single layer on a large baking sheet. Roast for 20 to 25 minutes, until golden and crisp. Sprinkle with the parsley and thyme.

Meanwhile, in a small skillet, combine the butter and the minced garlic. Cook over medium heat, stirring, for 1 minute. Whisk in the ketchup and hot sauce; cook until just heated through. Transfer to a small bowl and serve alongside the fries for dipping.

KALE AND SHAVED BUTTERNUT SQUASH SALAD WITH COCONUT-LIME DRESSING

FROM MICHELLE SMITH OF *THE WHOLE SMITHS*

I love the versatility and ease a salad offers. You choose your salad, prep the ingredients, and have an easy go-to lunch for the week. Between the variety of greens, toppings, and dressings, you really can't get bored. This coconut-lime dressing makes things really interesting, and I love adding some roasted chicken or grilled salmon to it to make it a complete meal.

SERVES 4

PREP: 20 minutes   TOTAL: 20 minutes

1 teaspoon grated lime zest

1 tablespoon fresh lime juice

¾ cup full-fat coconut milk

2 tablespoons fresh orange juice

1 teaspoon white wine vinegar

Salt

½ butternut squash (8 ounces), peeled and seeded

1 bunch curly leafed or Tuscan kale, stemmed and leaves cut into bite-size pieces (2 cups lightly packed)

¾ cup pomegranate seeds

⅓ cup slivered almonds

⅓ cup roasted unsalted pepitas (pumpkin seeds)

In a small bowl, combine lime zest, lime juice, coconut milk, orange juice, vinegar, and salt to taste. Set the dressing aside.

Use a vegetable peeler to shave the squash into thin strips (you should have 4 cups lightly packed). In a large bowl, combine the squash, kale, pomegranate seeds, almonds, and pepitas. Drizzle with ½ cup of the dressing and gently toss to coat. Season with salt. Store the remaining dressing in the refrigerator for up to 1 week.

TIP If fresh pomegranate seeds aren't available, you can use dehydrated pomegranate seeds. They add tartness and crunch to this salad.

SHREDDED SPROUT SLAW

A mustard-thyme vinaigrette flavors this crunchy slaw made with sliced Brussels sprouts, crisp and sweet apple, toasted walnuts, and green onions. Try it with a chicken or pork.

SERVES 2

PREP: 30 minutes (see Tip)   **TOTAL:** 30 minutes

2 pounds Brussels sprouts, trimmed

1 small apple, cored and chopped

¼ cup chopped walnuts, toasted (see Tip, page 19)

¼ cup thinly sliced green onions

2 tablespoons extra-virgin olive oil

1 tablespoon white wine vinegar

2 teaspoons snipped fresh thyme

1 teaspoon Whole30-compatible coarse-grain mustard

¼ teaspoon coarse salt

Cut the Brussels sprouts in half lengthwise. Place the halves, cut sides down, on a cutting board and thinly slice the halves. (You should have about 10 cups sliced sprouts.) Transfer 1½ cups of the sliced sprouts to a medium bowl. Place the remaining sprouts in an airtight container or plastic bag; seal and store in the refrigerator for up to 3 days. Use the sliced spouts to make Pan-Roasted Brussels Sprouts with Bacon (page 236).

Add the apple, walnuts, and green onions to the bowl with the Brussels sprouts and toss to combine. In a small bowl, whisk together the oil, vinegar, thyme, mustard, and salt. Drizzle the dressing over the slaw and toss to coat. Let stand for 5 to 10 minutes before serving; toss again before serving.

TIP Most of the prep time involves trimming and slicing the Brussels sprouts. It may seem lengthy, but you will have enough sprouts to make two more side dishes.

PAN-ROASTED BRUSSELS SPROUTS WITH BACON

Roasting—in the oven or on the stovetop—transforms Brussels sprouts into crisp, caramelized bite-size treats. Here they're browned with leeks in bacon fat and spiked with a little bit of vinegar.

SERVES 2

PREP: 5 minutes   **COOK:** 20 minutes   **TOTAL:** 25 minutes

4 slices Whole30-compatible bacon, chopped

2 medium leeks, halved, rinsed well, and thinly sliced crosswise

1 portion Brussels sprouts from Shredded Sprout Slaw (page 235)

2 tablespoons apple cider vinegar

½ teaspoon coarse salt

¼ teaspoon black pepper

In a very large skillet, cook the bacon until crisp, 6 to 8 minutes. Remove the bacon from the skillet with a slotted spoon and drain on paper towels. Add the leeks and Brussels sprouts to the bacon drippings in the skillet. Cook over medium heat, stirring occasionally, until the vegetables are tender and browned, 8 to 10 minutes. Add the vinegar and sprinkle with the salt and pepper. Add the bacon and toss well to combine.

Transfer half the sprouts mixture to a large bowl. Let stand until cool. Cover and chill for up to 3 days and use to make the Sprout-Spud Cakes (page 238).

Serve the sprouts remaining in the skillet.

SPROUT-SPUD CAKES

These crisp veggie cakes made with leftover Pan-Roasted Brussels Sprouts with Bacon and shredded Yukon Gold potatoes are the perfect accompaniment to a grilled steak—especially when topped with garlicky mayonnaise.

SERVES 3

PREP: 20 minutes **COOK:** 15 minutes **TOTAL:** 35 minutes

1 large or 2 small Yukon Gold potatoes, peeled and coarsely shredded (about 8 ounces)

Hot water

2 large eggs

¼ cup almond meal

½ teaspoon coarse salt

⅛ teaspoon black pepper

Reserved portion Pan-Roasted Brussels Sprouts with Bacon (page 236)

Extra-virgin olive oil

¼ cup Basic Mayonnaise (page 287; optional)

1 clove garlic, minced (optional)

Preheat the oven to 200°F.

Place the shredded potatoes in a medium bowl and add hot water to cover. Let stand for 10 minutes. Drain the potatoes in a colander. Rinse with cold water and drain well. Use paper towels to squeeze as much liquid as you can from the potatoes.

In a medium bowl, whisk together the eggs, almond meal, salt, and pepper. Place the Brussels sprouts mixture in a large bowl. Stir the egg mixture into the sprouts mixture. Add the potatoes and mix well.

Heat a lightly oiled nonstick griddle or very large ceramic nonstick skillet over medium heat. For each cake, spoon about ½ cup of the sprout mixture onto the griddle (you should have enough for six cakes). Evenly press and round the edges with the back of a spatula or spoon to form a cake that's about ½ inch thick. Cook the cakes, three at a time, turning them once, until golden brown and heated through, 3 to 4 minutes per side. Keep the finished cakes warm in the oven while cooking the remaining three cakes.

If desired, stir together the mayonnaise and the garlic and serve with the warm cakes.

NAPA SLAW

A sharp chef's knife is the only tool you need to transform an assortment of fresh vegetables into this tasty Asian-style slaw studded with crunchy cashews. It goes equally well with grilled chicken, fish, or steak.

SERVES 4

PREP: 15 minutes   TOTAL: 15 minutes

4 cups shredded napa cabbage

1 cup sugar snap peas, sliced crosswise

1 small red bell pepper, seeded and cut into bite-size strips

¼ cup sliced green onions

1 tablespoon chopped fresh cilantro

1 tablespoon rice vinegar

2 teaspoons coconut aminos

1 teaspoon toasted sesame oil

¼ teaspoon salt

⅛ teaspoon red pepper flakes

3 tablespoons extra-virgin olive oil

¼ cup chopped cashews

In a large bowl, toss the cabbage, peas, bell pepper, green onions, and cilantro to combine.

In a small bowl, whisk together the vinegar, coconut aminos, sesame oil, salt, and red pepper flakes. While whisking, drizzle in the olive oil to emulsify.

Pour the dressing over the cabbage mixture and toss to coat. Sprinkle with the cashews.

RED CURRY ROASTED CAULIFLOWER

This crisp roasted cauliflower is positively addictive! The Thai-style red curry powder will leave your lips tingling just a bit and your mouth wanting more. If you can't find red curry powder locally, there is an excellent blend available online at thespicehouse.com.

SERVES 4

PREP: 5 minutes   **COOK:** 35 minutes   **TOTAL:** 40 minutes

6 cups cauliflower florets

3 tablespoons Clarified Butter (page 289) or ghee, melted

2 teaspoons Whole30-compatible red curry powder

½ teaspoon salt

¼ teaspoon black pepper

2 tablespoons chopped fresh cilantro

Lime wedges

Preheat the oven to 400°F. Line a large rimmed baking sheet with parchment paper.

Place the cauliflower in a large bowl and drizzle it with the melted butter; mix well. Add the curry powder, salt, and pepper and toss to evenly coat the cauliflower. Spread the cauliflower evenly on the prepared baking sheet.

Roast for 20 minutes, then stir. Roast for 15 to 20 minutes more, until the cauliflower is tender and browned. Transfer to a serving bowl. Sprinkle with the cilantro and serve with lime wedges.

ROASTED ROOT VEGGIES WITH BALSAMIC-SHALLOT VINAIGRETTE

Once the vegetables are in the oven, you can pretty much walk away and do other things while they sizzle and turn incredibly sweet and tender. This is a perfect side to pork roast or pork chops.

SERVES 2

PREP: 15 minutes   **COOK:** 35 minutes   **TOTAL:** 50 minutes

FOR THE VEGETABLES

1 medium red, golden, or Chioggia beet, peeled and cut into 1-inch pieces (8 ounces)

1 small turnip, peeled and cut into 1-inch pieces (8 ounces)

1 bunch radishes, trimmed and halved lengthwise (8 ounces)

1 small onion, cut into 1-inch pieces

3 tablespoons extra-virgin olive oil

½ teaspoon salt

¼ teaspoon black pepper

FOR THE VINAIGRETTE

2 tablespoons extra-virgin olive oil

1 tablespoon balsamic vinegar

1 tablespoon minced shallot

¼ teaspoon salt

⅛ teaspoon black pepper

½ cup roughly chopped fresh parsley

MAKE THE VEGETABLES: Preheat the oven to 425°F. In a large bowl, combine the beet, turnip, radishes, onion, olive oil, salt, and pepper; toss to coat. Transfer the vegetables to a large rimmed baking sheet and spread them into a single layer. Roast for 35 to 45 minutes, stirring once and rotating the baking sheet halfway through the cooking time, until all the vegetables are tender and browned.

MAKE THE VINAIGRETTE: In a small bowl, whisk together the olive oil, vinegar, shallot, salt, and pepper.

Transfer the roasted vegetables to a large bowl. Drizzle with the vinaigrette and sprinkle with the parsley. Gently toss to coat.

SKILLET MUSHROOMS AND GREENS

Try this juicy combo of sautéed mushrooms and greens flavored with shallot, garlic, red pepper, and balsamic vinegar with a grilled steak. Perfection!

SERVES 2

PREP: 10 minutes   **COOK:** 5 minutes   **TOTAL:** 15 minutes

2 tablespoons Clarified Butter (page 289) or ghee

1 package (8 ounces) fresh cremini mushrooms, sliced

1 medium shallot, chopped

¼ teaspoon salt

⅛ teaspoon red pepper flakes

1 clove garlic, minced

6 cups fresh baby spinach or arugula

Balsamic vinegar (optional)

Heat the butter in a large skillet over medium heat. Add the mushrooms, shallot, salt, and red pepper flakes. Cook, stirring frequently, until the mushrooms are tender, 4 to 6 minutes. Add the garlic; cook, stirring, until fragrant, 30 seconds. Stir in the spinach and cook until wilted, about 1 minute. Drizzle with balsamic vinegar, if desired.

SKIN-ON GARLIC SMASHED POTATOES WITH CRISPY PROSCIUTTO, ONIONS, AND PINE NUTS

Garlicky potatoes are made creamy with ghee and coconut milk and topped with caramelized onion, crisped prosciutto and toasted pine nuts. They're fancy enough for a dinner party or a holiday, but simple enough for a weeknight dinner.

SERVES 3

PREP: 20 minutes   **COOK:** 20 minutes   **TOTAL:** 40 minutes

2 large russet potatoes (½ pound)

2 cloves garlic, sliced

1 tablespoon Clarified Butter (page 289) or ghee, melted

½ teaspoon salt

2 tablespoons full-fat coconut milk

4 thin slices prosciutto, or 3 slices Whole30-compatible bacon, chopped

1 sweet onion, quartered lengthwise and thinly sliced

1 tablespoon balsamic vinegar, Chicken Bone Broth (page 284), or Whole30-compatible chicken broth

1 tablespoon pine nuts, toasted (see Tip, page 19)

Bring a pot of lightly salted water to a boil. Add the potatoes and garlic and cook until tender, 20 to 25 minutes. Drain. Mash with a potato masher or hand mixer. Stir in the butter and salt. With a wooden spoon or hand mixer, beat in the coconut milk. Cover and keep warm.

Meanwhile, in a large skillet, cook the prosciutto over medium heat, stirring occasionally, for about 3 minutes. Add the onion and cook, stirring frequently, until the prosciutto is crispy and the onion is tender and brown on some of the edges, about 8 minutes more. Add the vinegar to the pan and stir to scrape up the browned bits on the bottom.

Spoon the onion mixture over the mashed potatoes and sprinkle with the pine nuts.

SPICED CARROT-PARSNIP SLAW

Crisp and colorful, this intensely flavored slaw is infused with warm North African spices such as cinnamon, cumin, coriander, and smoked paprika. Dates add a touch of sweetness and toasted almonds add crunch.

SERVES 6

PREP: 20 minutes   **TOTAL:** 20 minutes

¼ cup sliced almonds

¼ teaspoon ground cinnamon

¼ teaspoon ground cumin

¼ teaspoon ground coriander

¼ teaspoon smoked paprika

¼ cup extra-virgin olive oil

2 tablespoons fresh lemon juice

¼ teaspoon sea salt

¼ teaspoon red pepper flakes (optional)

2 cups coarsely shredded carrots

1 cup coarsely shredded parsnips

⅓ cup chopped fresh cilantro

¼ cup chopped pitted unsweetened dates

In a small skillet, toast the almonds over medium-low heat, stirring, until lightly toasted, about 2 minutes. Place in a large bowl. In the same skillet, toast the cinnamon, cumin, coriander, and paprika until fragrant, 1 to 2 minutes. Place the spices in the bowl with the almonds.

Stir in the olive oil, lemon juice, salt, and red pepper flakes (if using). Add the carrots and parsnips and stir to coat. Add the cilantro and dates and toss to combine.

SPINACH–RED GRAPEFRUIT SALAD WITH MASHED AVOCADO "DRESSING"

This riff on the classic avocado-grapefruit-red onion salad features the avocado as a rich, creamy dressing punched up with lemon, while a seeded seasoning blend adds flavor and crunch. Try it with grilled or broiled salmon.

SERVES 2

PREP: 10 minutes   TOTAL: 10 minutes

FOR THE SEASONING BLEND

1 tablespoon toasted sesame seeds
(see Tip, page 19)

1 teaspoon nutritional yeast

½ teaspoon chia seeds

½ teaspoon cumin seeds, crushed

¼ to ½ teaspoon ground chipotle chile

FOR THE SALAD

1 small ripe avocado, halved, pitted, and peeled

1 tablespoon fresh lemon juice

¼ teaspoon sea salt

4 cups torn fresh spinach leaves

¼ cup slivered red onion

1 large or 2 small red grapefruit, peeled and cut into segments

MAKE THE SEASONING BLEND: In a small jar with a lid, combine the sesame seeds, nutritional yeast, chia seeds, cumin seeds, and chipotle. Cover and shake well to mix.

MAKE THE SALAD: In a large bowl, mash the avocado using your fingers or a potato masher. Stir in the lemon juice and salt. Using your hands, add the spinach and red onion and toss until coated with the avocado mixture. Sprinkle with some of the seasoning blend. Gently fold in the grapefruit segments.

Divide the salad between two salad plates. Sprinkle with additional seasoning blend, reserving any remaining blend for another use.

STEAMED CABBAGE WEDGES IN SPICY CITRUS BUTTER

The humble cabbage is vastly underappreciated, but there are so many wonderful things you can do with it. Here, wedges are steamed until tender and drizzled with a fabulous butter infused with lemon, orange, garlic and Thai chile—and then sprinkled with fresh chives.

SERVES 6

PREP: 10 minutes **COOK:** 10 minutes **TOTAL:** 20 minutes

1 medium head cabbage (about 2 pounds)

3 tablespoons ghee or Clarified Butter (page 289)

1 fresh Thai chile, minced, or 1 teaspoon red pepper flakes

1 clove garlic, minced

½ teaspoon salt

½ teaspoon lemon zest

1 tablespoon fresh lemon juice

1 tablespoon fresh orange juice

2 tablespoons chopped fresh chives

Cut the cabbage lengthwise into six wedges; remove most of the core from each wedge but leaving enough to keep the leaves intact. Place a steamer basket in a large saucepan or Dutch oven. Add enough water to reach just below the basket. Bring the water to a boil; add the cabbage wedges to the basket. Cover and steam until the cabbage is tender, 8 to 10 minutes.

Meanwhile, melt the ghee in a small saucepan over medium heat. Add the chile, garlic, and salt. Cook, stirring, for 1 minute. Remove from the heat. Transfer to a small bowl and let cool slightly. Stir in the lemon zest, lemon juice, and orange juice.

Transfer the cabbage wedges to a serving platter. Drizzle the citrus butter over the cabbage and sprinkle with the chives.

SAUCES
AND
DRESSINGS

ARUGULA, WALNUT, AND GARLIC PESTO

PREP: 15 minutes   **TOTAL:** 15 minutes

1½ cups packed arugula

¾ cup packed fresh basil leaves

½ cup chopped walnuts, toasted (see Tip, page 19)

1 tablespoon fresh lemon juice

1 clove garlic, minced

¼ teaspoon salt

⅓ cup extra-virgin olive oil

In a food processor or blender, combine the arugula, basil, walnuts, lemon juice, garlic, and salt and process or blend until combined. With the motor running, add the olive oil through the opening in the lid in a thin, steady stream until the pesto is smooth and reaches the desired consistency.

CAESAR-STYLE DRESSING

MAKES ABOUT 2 CUPS

PREP: 15 minutes   **STAND:** 8 hours   **CHILLING:** 2 hours   **TOTAL:** 15 minutes plus standing and chilling

1 cup cashews

2 cups plus 6 tablespoons water

¼ cup fresh lemon juice

2 cloves garlic, minced

4 anchovy fillets

2 teaspoons coconut aminos

1 teaspoon Whole30-compatible Dijon mustard

½ teaspoon salt

¼ teaspoon black pepper

½ cup extra-virgin olive oil

Place the cashews in a medium bowl; cover with 2 cups of the water and soak for 8 hours or overnight. Drain and rinse the cashews. In a high-speed blender, combine the cashews, lemon juice, remaining 6 tablespoons water, the garlic, anchovy fillets, coconut aminos, mustard, salt, and pepper. Blend on low, then increase the speed to high and blend until smooth. With the blender running, slowly add the olive oil and blend until the dressing is smooth.

Refrigerate the dressing for at least 2 hours before using. If the dressing becomes too thick after chilling, whisk in water, 1 teaspoon at a time, until it reaches the desired consistency.

CHILE-GRAPEFRUIT VINAIGRETTE

MAKES ABOUT 1 CUP

PREP: 10 minutes   TOTAL: 10 minutes

1 teaspoon grated grapefruit zest

½ cup fresh grapefruit juice

1 serrano chile pepper, seeded, if desired, and minced

3 tablespoons finely chopped fresh cilantro

1 clove garlic, minced

1 teaspoon Whole30-compatible Dijon mustard

½ teaspoon salt

¼ cup avocado oil

¼ cup extra-virgin olive oil

In a bowl, whisk together the grapefruit zest and juice, the serrano pepper, cilantro, garlic, mustard, and salt. While whisking, drizzle in the avocado oil and olive oil in a steady stream until emulsified.

Transfer the vinaigrette to a bottle, jar, or storage container. Store in the refrigerator for up to 3 days.

CREAMY CARAMELIZED ONION SAUCE

MAKES ABOUT ½ CUP

PREP: 20 minutes   **COOK:** 10 minutes   **TOTAL:** 30 minutes

1 tablespoon coconut oil

2 green onions, thinly sliced, white and green parts kept separate

¾ cup thinly sliced quartered red onion

2 medium shallots, thinly sliced

2 cloves garlic, minced

¼ cup white wine vinegar

1 teaspoon Whole30-compatible coarse-grain mustard

¼ teaspoon coarse salt

⅛ teaspoon black pepper

⅓ cup extra-virgin olive oil

Heat the coconut oil in a medium skillet over medium heat. Add the white parts of the green onions, the red onion, and the shallots and cook, stirring occasionally, until tender and golden brown, 10 to 15 minutes. If the onions start to brown too quickly, reduce the heat. Add the garlic and cook, stirring, for 1 minute. Remove the skillet from the heat. Add the vinegar and stir to scrape up any browned bits from the bottom of the skillet.

Transfer the onion mixture to a blender. Add the mustard, salt, and pepper. Cover and blend until nearly smooth. With the blender running, slowly add the olive oil through the opening in the lid and blend until the sauce is well combined and smooth. Transfer to a small bowl. Stir in some of the green onion tops. Use immediately or cover and store the sauce in the refrigerator for up to 1 week.

CREMINI MUSHROOM, CAPER, AND PEARL ONION SAUCE

PREP: 20 minutes   TOTAL: 20 minutes

2 tablespoons extra-virgin olive oil

1 package (8 ounces) frozen pearl onions, thawed and patted dry

2 cloves garlic, minced

½ teaspoon dried thyme, crushed

12 ounces cremini or button mushrooms, cleaned and sliced

1 cup Beef Bone Broth (page 285) or Whole30-compatible beef or vegetable broth

2 teaspoons arrowroot powder

1 tablespoon capers, drained

¼ to ½ teaspoon black pepper

Salt

Heat 1 tablespoon of the olive oil in a large non-stick skillet over medium heat. Add the pearl onions and cook, stirring occasionally, until golden, 6 to 8 minutes. Add the garlic and thyme and cook, stirring, for 1 minute. Move the onions to the edge of the skillet and add the remaining 1 tablespoon olive oil to the center of the skillet. Raise the heat to medium-high. Add the mushrooms and cook, stirring occasionally, until tender, 5 to 8 minutes.

Meanwhile, in a small bowl, whisk together 1 tablespoon of the broth and the arrowroot powder; set aside. Stir the remaining broth into the mushroom mixture; raise the heat and bring to a boil. Reduce the heat and simmer for 3 minutes. Stir in the arrowroot mixture, capers, and pepper. Cook, stirring, for 1 minute. Season with additional pepper and salt to taste.

Serve the sauce over steak, pork, cooked vegetables, or mashed potatoes. To serve with chicken, prepare as directed except substitute chicken broth for the beef broth.

DUMP RANCH

FROM NAN AND NICOLE OF *WHOLE SISTERS*

Dump Ranch was created when we wanted a clean ranch dressing recipe that resembled the real thing without sacrificing flavor. It was also important that it be easy to make, hence you can just "dump" all the ingredients and blend. It has quickly become our signature recipe. It makes us so happy to see others enjoying it.

MAKES 2 CUPS

PREP: 15 minutes   **TOTAL:** 15 minutes

1 large egg, at room temperature

1 cup light olive oil

½ cup full-fat coconut milk

½ cup packed fresh cilantro, parsley, and/or other herbs

2 tablespoons red wine vinegar

1 tablespoon fresh lemon juice

1 teaspoon salt

¾ teaspoon onion powder

¾ teaspoon garlic powder

½ teaspoon black pepper

In a wide-mouth quart-size jar, combine the egg, olive oil, coconut milk, fresh herbs, vinegar, lemon juice, salt, onion powder, garlic powder, and pepper. Blend with an immersion blender for 1 minute. Store in the refrigerator for up to 1 week.

FIERY COCKTAIL SAUCE

MAKES 1 ¼ CUPS

PREP: 25 minutes   **COOK:** 25 minutes   **TOTAL:** 50 minutes

1 large red bell pepper, quartered, stemmed, and seeded

1 small head garlic

2 tablespoons plus ½ teaspoon extra-virgin olive oil

2 dried ancho chiles

3 dates, pitted

Boiling water

3 tablespoons fresh lemon juice

¾ teaspoon coarse salt

¼ teaspoon cayenne pepper

Preheat the oven to 425°F. Line a baking pan with aluminum foil.

Place the bell pepper quarters, skin side up, in the baking pan. Cut a thin slice off the top of the head of garlic to reveal the individual cloves. Leave the outer peel around the garlic head. Place the garlic head on a small square of foil, cut side up. Drizzle with ½ teaspoon of the olive oil. Enclose the garlic in the foil and place it in the pan with the peppers. Roast for 25 to 30 minutes, until the pepper skins are charred and the garlic cloves are tender. Wrap the foil up around the pepper quarters to fully enclose. Let the peppers and garlic cool. When the peppers are cool enough to handle, use a sharp knife to peel off and discard the pepper skin.

Combine the chiles and dates in a medium bowl. Add enough boiling water to cover by about 1 inch. Cover and let stand for 15 minutes. Drain the chiles and dates, reserving the water. Remove and discard the stems and seeds from the chiles. Chop the chiles.

Use your fingers to squeeze the garlic cloves from their peels. Place the garlic cloves in a blender. Add the roasted bell pepper, chiles, and dates. Add ½ cup of the reserved soaking liquid, the lemon juice, the remaining 2 tablespoons olive oil, the salt, and cayenne. Blend until smooth.

Serve the sauce warm or cold with cooked shrimp, fish, or meat. Store the sauce in an airtight container in the refrigerator for up to 1 week.

FIRE-ROASTED JALAPEÑO HARISSA SAUCE

MAKES ABOUT 1 CUP

PREP: 30 minutes   **COOK:** 10 minutes   **TOTAL:** 40 minutes

8 ounces jalapeños, halved and seeded

1 medium red bell pepper, halved and seeded

1½ teaspoons cumin seeds

1 teaspoon coriander seeds

1 teaspoon caraway seeds

1 tablespoon fresh lemon juice

2 cloves garlic, minced

1 teaspoon salt

½ teaspoon smoked paprika

¼ cup extra-virgin olive oil

Preheat the broiler. Line a large baking sheet with aluminum foil. Lightly grease the foil.

Arrange the jalapeños and bell pepper halves, cut sides down, on the prepared baking sheet. Broil 3 to 4 inches from the heat for 5 to 10 minutes,

until the skins are very charred. (If the jalapeño halves char before the bell pepper, transfer them to a bowl and continue broiling the bell pepper.) Let the peppers cool until easy to handle.

Toast the cumin, coriander, and caraway seeds in a small skillet over medium heat, shaking the skillet often, until fragrant, about 5 minutes.

Use a sharp knife to peel off the charred skin from the peppers (you do not need to remove every bit of the skins). Roughly chop the peppers. In a food processor, combine the peppers, toasted spices, lemon juice, garlic, salt, and paprika. Pulse until the peppers are chopped. With the food processor running, drizzle the olive oil through the opening in the lid to form a thick paste.

Store the sauce in an airtight container in the refrigerator for up to 1 month.

LEMONY TAHINI SAUCE

PREP: 10 minutes **CHILLING:** 1 hour **TOTAL:** 10 minutes plus chilling

¼ cup tahini

3 tablespoons fresh lemon juice

2 to 3 tablespoons warm water

¼ teaspoon grated lemon zest

1 garlic clove, minced

¼ teaspoon salt

Dash of cayenne pepper

1 tablespoon chopped fresh parsley

In a small bowl, whisk together the tahini and lemon juice until combined. (The mixture will be thick.) Whisk in the warm water, 1 tablespoon at a time, until the mixture is smooth and pourable. Add the lemon zest, garlic, salt, and cayenne; mix well.

Cover and refrigerate for at least 1 hour, allowing the flavors to blend. Stir in the parsley before serving.

SHERRY-ORANGE VINAIGRETTE

PREP: 10 minutes **TOTAL:** 10 minutes

1 teaspoon grated orange zest

2 tablespoons fresh orange juice

2 tablespoons sherry vinegar

1 teaspoon dry mustard

1 clove garlic, minced

¾ cup extra-virgin olive oil

1 teaspoon chopped fresh thyme

½ teaspoon salt

¼ teaspoon black pepper

In a small bowl, combine the orange zest, orange juice, vinegar, mustard, and garlic. While whisking, drizzle in the olive oil until emulsified. Add the thyme, salt, and pepper and whisk until blended.

Store the vinaigrette in an airtight container in the refrigerator for up to 3 days.

STEAK SAUCE

This tastes so much better than the bottled stuff. It's spicy, tangy, and sweet—without the addition of any processed sugars of any kind. It's great on steak—but on pork and chicken, too.

MAKES 2 CUPS

PREP: 15 minutes   **COOK:** 10 minutes   **COOLING:** 10 minutes   **TOTAL:** 35 minutes

¾ cup water

½ cup balsamic vinegar

2 cloves garlic, smashed

1 teaspoon grated orange zest

⅓ cup fresh orange juice

⅓ cup unsulfured black or golden raisins

¼ cup finely chopped yellow onion

¼ cup Whole30 Ketchup (page 288)

¼ cup Whole30-compatible Dijon or brown mustard

2 tablespoons coconut aminos

2 tablespoons fresh lemon juice

½ teaspoon celery seeds

½ teaspoon salt

¼ teaspoon black pepper

⅛ teaspoon ground cinnamon

⅛ teaspoon ground cloves

⅛ teaspoon ground ginger

Dash of cayenne pepper

Combine all the ingredients in a medium saucepan. Bring to a boil. Reduce the heat and simmer, uncovered, until the garlic is tender, 10 to 12 minutes. Let cool for 10 minutes.

Transfer the cooled mixture to a blender. Cover and blend until completely smooth.

Store in an airtight container in the refrigerator for up to 2 weeks.

NIBBLES AND DRINKS

CRISPY ANGRY CHICKEN DRUMMIES

Is there any better party food than fiery chicken wings and drummies dipped in cool ranch? Steaming the chicken pieces before roasting may seem counterintuitive, but it helps render excess fat from under the skin so that the skin itself gets lighter and crispier in the oven, much like that of a deep-fried wing—without plunging them into a vat of hot oil.

SERVES 8

PREP: 20 minutes   **CHILLING:** 1 hour   **COOK:** 50 minutes   **TOTAL:** 1 hour 10 minutes plus chilling

2 pounds chicken wings

¼ cup Whole30-compatible hot sauce

2 tablespoons Clarified Butter (page 289) or ghee, melted

1 tablespoon coconut aminos

1 clove garlic, minced

¼ teaspoon salt

Black pepper

Dump Ranch dressing (page 261)

Use kitchen shears or a very sharp chef's knife to remove the tips of the wings (discard the tips or save them for making stock). Cut along the edge of the drumette through the joint to separate the wingette and the drumette (you should have 8 drumettes and 8 wingettes).

Pour 1 inch of water into a 6-quart stockpot fitted with a steamer basket. Cover and bring to a boil. Place the chicken in the steamer basket and reduce the heat to medium. Steam, covered, for 10 minutes. Line a rimmed baking sheet with paper towels. Place a wire rack on the baking sheet. Place the chicken on the rack and pat dry with a paper towel. Chill in the refrigerator for 1 hour.

Preheat the oven to 425°F. Replace the paper towels under the rack with parchment paper. Roast the chicken for 20 minutes; turn over and roast for 20 minutes more, or until the chicken is cooked through and the skin is golden brown.

Meanwhile, in a large bowl, combine the hot sauce, butter, coconut aminos, garlic, salt, and black pepper to taste. Add the chicken and toss to coat with the sauce. Serve with Dump Ranch dressing for dipping.

BAJA-STYLE DEVILED EGGS

Deviled eggs may be old school, but a surprising number of people harbor a profound love for this humble snack. Hard-cooked eggs are a blank slate for all kinds of flavor profiles. This version features a creamy yolk blended with avocado, tomato, lime zest and juice, and garlic studded with homemade pickled jalapeños. To make enough for a party, triple or quadruple the recipe.

SERVES 2

PREP: 30 minutes   **COOK:** 5 minutes   **STAND:** 3 to 4 hours   **TOTAL:** 35 minutes plus standing

1 cup water

½ apple, cored and thinly sliced

1 small jalapeño, stemmed and thinly sliced crosswise

2 teaspoons plus ⅛ teaspoon coarse salt

⅓ cup white vinegar

3 hard-cooked eggs (see Tip)

¼ small avocado, peeled

¼ teaspoon grated lime zest

2 teaspoons fresh lime juice

1 clove garlic, minced

6 grape tomatoes, chopped

⅛ teaspoon black pepper

In a small saucepan, combine the water, apple, jalapeño, and 2 teaspoons of the salt. Bring to a boil. Reduce the heat to medium-low, cover, and simmer until the jalapeño slices are just tender, 3 to 5 minutes. Remove the saucepan from the heat and stir in the vinegar. Cover and let stand for 3 to 4 hours. Drain off the liquid and discard the apple slices. Set aside 4 of the jalapeno slices for garnish. Finely chop the remaining jalapeño.

Peel the eggs and halve them lengthwise. Scoop the yolks into a medium bowl. Add the chopped jalapeño, avocado, lime zest, lime juice, garlic, and the remaining ⅛ teaspoon salt. Mash with a fork or potato masher until well combined and nearly smooth. Set aside some of the chopped tomatoes for garnish. Add the remaining tomatoes to the yolk mixture and stir gently to combine. Spoon the yolk mixture into the egg whites. Top with the reserved pepper slices and tomatoes. Sprinkle with black pepper.

TIP To hard-cook eggs, place eggs and enough water to cover in a small saucepan. Bring to a boil and boil for 1 minute. Cover the saucepan and remove from the heat. Let stand for 12 minutes. Drain the eggs and rinse under cool water.

GUACAMOLE-STUFFED MINI PEPPERS

These crunchy little peppers filled with creamy, spicy guacamole make terrific party food. Not only are they delicious, but an assortment of bright yellow, orange, and red peppers with a swath of creamy green avocado in the centers visually pop on a platter.

SERVES 4

PREP: 20 minutes   **TOTAL:** 20 minutes

1 ripe avocado, halved, pitted, and peeled

2 tablespoons finely chopped tomato

1 tablespoon chopped green onion, plus more for serving

1 tablespoon chopped fresh cilantro, plus more for serving

2 teaspoons finely chopped serrano chile pepper

1 tablespoon fresh lime juice

⅛ teaspoon salt

Dash of cayenne pepper

10 mini sweet peppers, halved lengthwise and seeded

4 slices Whole30-compatible bacon, cooked until crisp, drained, and crumbled

Mash the avocado with a fork in a medium bowl. Stir in the tomato, green onion, cilantro, serrano, lime juice, salt, and cayenne.

Spoon the guacamole filling into the mini pepper halves. Top with the crumbled bacon. If desired, sprinkle with additional sliced green onion or chopped cilantro.

TIP To perfectly crisp-cook bacon, preheat the oven to 375°F. Line a baking sheet with aluminum foil. Place a wire rack on top of the foil. Arrange bacon slices in a single layer on the rack. Be careful not to overlap—use two baking sheets if necessary. Bake for 15 to 20 minutes, depending on the thickness of the bacon. Transfer to a paper towel–lined platter to drain. Cool completely before crumbling.

SMOKY BARBECUE-SPICED KALE CHIPS

A blend of chili powder, garlic powder, onion powder, smoked paprika, and black pepper gives these crispy chips real BBQ flavor. The recipe makes more than you need for one batch of chips. Store seasoning leftovers in a tightly sealed container in a cool, dry place for the next time you need to whip up some spicy kale chips, fast.

SERVES 6

PREP: 15 minutes   **COOK:** 25 minutes   **TOTAL:** 40 minutes

1 bunch kale (about 1 pound)

2 tablespoons extra-virgin olive oil

¼ teaspoon salt

¾ teaspoon chili powder

½ teaspoon garlic powder

¼ teaspoon onion powder

¼ teaspoon smoked paprika

¼ teaspoon black pepper

Preheat the oven to 300°F. Line two large baking sheets with parchment paper.

Wash the kale leaves to remove any dirt or sand. Thoroughly dry both sides of each leaf using paper towels. Remove and discard the thick stems from the kale leaves and tear the leaves into bite-size pieces. In a large bowl, combine the kale, oil, and salt. Use your hands to massage the oil and salt into the kale until it's thoroughly coated. Arrange the kale leaves in a single layer on the large baking sheets. Bake for 20 minutes. Stir gently and bake for 5 to 10 minutes more, or until the chips are dry and crisp.

Meanwhile, in a small bowl, combine the chili powder, garlic powder, onion powder, paprika, and pepper.

When the kale chips are finished baking, immediately sprinkle them with the desired amount of the seasoning mixture and toss gently to coat. Let cool completely before serving.

SPICY CACAO-ORANGE ALMONDS

Cacao is native to the Amazon Basin, and has been domesticated in the southern hemisphere for centuries. The combination of cacao with the vitalizing properties of almonds and warming spice make it the perfect portable snack. These almonds are best the day after they're made, and crunchiest after they've cooled completely.

SERVES 2 TO 4

PREP: 5 minutes   **COOK:** 10 minutes   **TOTAL:** 15 minutes

¼ cup fresh orange juice

1 tablespoon ghee, Clarified Butter (page 289), or coconut oil

2 teaspoons unsweetened cocoa powder (100% cacao)

½ teaspoon coarse salt

¼ teaspoon ground cinnamon

⅛ teaspoon cayenne pepper

½ teaspoon orange zest

1 cup raw almonds or macadamia nuts

Preheat the oven to 350°F.

In a small saucepan, bring the orange juice to a boil. Reduce the heat and simmer, uncovered, until the juice has reduced to 2 tablespoons, 3 to 5 minutes. Add the ghee and whisk until melted. Remove the saucepan from the heat. Add the cocoa powder, ¼ teaspoon of the salt, the cinnamon, cayenne, and orange zest. Whisk until well combined. Add the nuts and stir well to coat. Spread the nut mixture in a shallow baking pan.

Bake for 10 to 12 minutes, stirring twice, until the nuts are toasted and nearly dry. Transfer the nuts to a sheet of parchment paper. Sprinkle with the remaining ¼ teaspoon salt. Let cool completely before eating. Store leftover nuts in an airtight container in the refrigerator for up to 3 weeks.

SPINACH-STUFFED MUSHROOMS

What's a party without stuffed mushrooms? These savory caps are filled with a yummy combo of fresh spinach, shallot, garlic, almond meal, mayo, and hot sauce—and crowned with crisp crumbled bacon.

SERVES 6

PREP: 20 minutes   **COOK:** 15 minutes   **TOTAL:** 35 minutes

18 medium white or cremini mushrooms (about 1½ inches in diameter)

2 slices Whole30-compatible bacon

1 medium shallot, finely chopped

3 cloves garlic, minced

1 bag (5 ounces) fresh baby spinach, roughly chopped

2 tablespoons almond meal

2 tablespoons Basic Mayonnaise (page 287)

2 teaspoons Whole30-compatible hot sauce

½ teaspoon salt

Preheat the oven to 375°F. Line a large rimmed baking sheet with foil.

Clean the mushrooms; remove and discard the stems. Place the mushroom caps, stem side down, on the prepared baking sheet. Bake, uncovered, for 8 to 10 minutes. Turn the mushroom caps stem side up.

Meanwhile, in a large skillet, cook the bacon until crisp. Drain the bacon on paper towels, reserving the drippings in the skillet. Crumble the bacon and set aside. Cook the shallot and garlic in the bacon drippings over medium heat, stirring frequently, until tender, about 3 minutes. Add the spinach and cook, stirring, until wilted, about 1 minute. Drain if needed.

Combine the spinach mixture, almond meal, mayonnaise, hot sauce, and salt in a medium bowl. Spoon the spinach mixture into the partially baked mushroom caps. Bake for 8 to 10 minutes, until the mushrooms are tender and the filling is hot. Top with the crumbled bacon.

CUCUMBER-PINEAPPLE SPARKLERS

Cucumber—composed of upward of 96 percent water—is naturally thirst quenching. Served with a splash of pineapple and lime and sparkling water, it refreshes and revives on a hot summer day. If you don't have a muddler, use the handle of a wooden spoon.

SERVES 2

PREP: 5 minutes **TOTAL:** 5 minutes

8 slices English cucumber

½ cup unsweetened pineapple juice, chilled

2 tablespoons fresh lime juice

1 cup sparkling water, chilled

Cucumber slices and lime wedges (optional)

In a large heavy-bottomed glass or cocktail shaker, muddle the cucumber slices. Add the pineapple juice and lime juice and stir or shake to mix well. Strain the mixture into two glasses. Top with ½ cup of the sparkling water. Garnish with the cucumber slices and lime wedges, if desired.

PEACH-ORANGE-BASIL AGUA FRESCA

Agua fresca means "fresh water" in Spanish. These blends of fruit with water and fresh lime juice are popular throughout Mexico, Central America, and the United States and are usually made with cane sugar. This light, no-sugar version is especially quenching.

SERVES 4

PREP: 10 minutes **CHILLING:** 2 hours **TOTAL:** 10 minutes plus chilling

4 cups ripe cubed, peeled peaches (about 4 peaches)

2 cups fresh orange juice

2 tablespoons fresh lemon juice

1¼ cups water

8 large fresh basil leaves, torn, plus whole leaves for serving

Orange slices

Whole fresh basil leaves

Combine the peaches, orange juice, and lemon juice in a blender. Cover and blend until smooth. Pour the peach mixture into a pitcher. Stir in the water. Add the torn basil leaves. Cover and steep in the refrigerator for at least 2 hours.

To serve, remove and discard the torn basil leaves. Serve in ice-filled glasses with orange slices and whole basil leaves.

MANGO-MINT TEA SPRITZER

The refreshing flavors of mint, mango, and ginger infuse a blend of chilled green tea and coconut water. It's topped off with fizzy water for a festive touch.

SERVES 2

PREP: 10 minutes   **CHILLING:** 30 minutes   **TOTAL:** 40 minutes

¼ cup fresh mint leaves

¾ cup simmering water

1 green tea bag (see Tip)

2 thin slices fresh ginger

¾ cup chopped fresh mango

¾ cup unsweetened coconut water

Ice

¾ cup sparkling water

Fresh mint sprigs

Place the mint leaves in a mug and use a wooden spoon to gently bruise them. Add the simmering water, tea bag, and ginger. Cover and steep for 5 minutes. Remove the tea bag, squeezing gently. Chill the tea for 30 minutes. Strain the tea and discard the mint and ginger.

Meanwhile, in a blender, combine the mango and coconut water. Cover and blend until smooth. Pour the mixture through a fine-mesh sieve or through a nut milk bag into a 1-quart glass measuring cup, pressing with the back of a large spoon or squeezing the bag to remove all the liquid. Discard the pulp.

Stir the chilled tea into the mango liquid. Fill two tall glasses halfway with ice. Pour the tea mixture over the ice. Add sparkling water and stir gently. Garnish with fresh mint sprigs. Serve immediately.

TIP If desired, use herbal tea for a caffeine-free drink.

To prepare fresh mango, stand the mango upright on a cutting board and cut down along each side of the large pit in the center. Place each mango half skin side down on the cutting board and cut a crosshatch pattern in the flesh down to the skin. Run the knife closely between the flesh and skin to create cubes of fruit.

SPARKLING BLACKBERRY LIME TEA

Try this with raspberries in place of the blackberries—or make a mixed-berry tea with both kinds of berries.

SERVES 2

PREP: 10 minutes   **CHILLING:** 30 minutes   **TOTAL:** 10 minutes plus 30 minutes chilling

2 green or white tea bags

1 cup boiling water

1 cup fresh blackberries

2 tablespoons fresh lime juice

4 fresh mint leaves

Ice

1 cup chilled sparkling water

Lime twists and fresh mint leaves (optional)

Place the tea bags in the boiling water and steep for 2 to 3 minutes. Remove and discard the tea bags. Cover and chill the brewed tea.

Puree the blackberries and lime juice in a blender until smooth. Pour the blackberry mixture through a fine-mesh strainer set over a bowl. Press the berries to extract as much puree as possible (you should have about ½ cup). Discard the solids left in the strainer.

Muddle the mint leaves in the bottoms of two glasses. Fill the glasses with ice. Pour the blackberry-lime juice, chilled tea, and sparkling water over the ice in the glasses and stir gently to mix.

Garnish with lime twists and additional fresh mint, if desired.

BASICS

CHICKEN BONE BROTH

MAKES 1 GALLON

PREP: 15 minutes   **COOK:** 12 to 24 hours   **TOTAL:** 12 to 24 hours

Carcass from a roasted 3- to 4-pound chicken

2 carrots, roughly chopped

3 stalks celery, roughly chopped

2 onions, roughly chopped

5 or 6 sprigs fresh parsley

1 sprig fresh thyme

2 tablespoons apple cider vinegar

10 whole black peppercorns

1 teaspoon salt

Put all the ingredients in a large stockpot, add water to cover, and bring to a boil over high heat. Cover and reduce the heat to low. Simmer for 12 to 24 hours without stirring. (You can also do this in a slow cooker. Set the cooker to high until the water comes to a boil, then turn the temperature down to low and simmer for 12 to 24 hours.)

Strain the broth through a fine-mesh strainer set over a large bowl or clean pot. Discard the solids. Transfer the broth to multiple containers to speed up cooling—don't freeze or refrigerate it while it's hot! Allow the broth to sit in the fridge, uncovered, for several hours, until the fat rises to the top and hardens. Scrape off the fat with a spoon and discard it.

Refrigerate the broth in airtight containers for 3 to 4 days or freeze for up to 6 months.

A properly prepared chicken broth might look a little jiggly when cold. That's just the gelatin from the collagen in the bones. When ready to use the broth, gently heat it and it will return to a liquid state.

BEEF BONE BROTH

MAKES 1 GALLON

PREP: 15 minutes   **COOK:** 12 to 24 hours   **TOTAL:** 12 to 24 hours

3 to 4 pounds beef bones

2 carrots, roughly chopped

3 stalks celery, roughly chopped

2 onions, roughly chopped

5 or 6 fresh sprigs parsley

1 sprig fresh thyme

2 tablespoons apple cider vinegar

10 whole black peppercorns

1 teaspoon salt

Put all the ingredients in a large stockpot, add water to cover, and bring to a boil over high heat. Cover and reduce the heat to low. Simmer for 12 to 24 hours without stirring. (You can also do this in a slow cooker. Set the cooker to high until the water comes to a boil, then turn the temperature down to low and simmer for 12 to 24 hours.)

Strain the broth through a fine-mesh strainer set over a large bowl or clean pot. Discard the solids. Transfer the broth to multiple containers to speed up cooling—don't freeze or refrigerate it while it's hot! Allow the broth to sit in the fridge, uncovered, for several hours, until the fat rises to the top and hardens. Scrape off the fat with a spoon and discard it.

Refrigerate the broth in airtight containers for 3 to 4 days or freeze for up to 6 months.

A properly prepared beef broth will look solid but jiggly when cold—think "meat Jell-O." That's just the gelatin from the collagen in the bones. When ready to use the broth, gently heat it and it will return to a liquid state.

COCONUT CREAM

This is the easiest thing you will do in this entire book, but it's a game-changer for so many recipes. Adding coconut milk to soups or sauces is a great way to add thickness and texture, but sometimes coconut milk can water down a dish. That's where coconut cream comes in.

Take a can of full-fat coconut milk and put it in the refrigerator for an hour or two—although we recommend leaving at least one can in the fridge at all times for emergency coconut cream situations (something that can actually happen on the Whole30).

When you open the can, the cream will have risen to the top and become solid, while the coconut water remains at the bottom of the can. Just scoop out the thick stuff at the top and use it in recipes that call for coconut cream.

You can also find prepared coconut cream or "culinary coconut milk" at some health food stores, but why would you pay extra when the only thing required to make your own is opening your refrigerator?

BASIC MAYONNAISE

MAKES 1½ CUPS

PREP: 10 minutes   TOTAL: 10 minutes

1¼ cups light olive oil

1 large egg

½ teaspoon dry mustard

½ teaspoon salt

Juice of ½ lemon

Place ¼ cup of the olive oil, the egg, mustard, and salt in a blender, food processor, or mixing bowl. Mix thoroughly. While the food processor or blender is running (or while mixing in a bowl with an immersion blender), slowly drizzle in the remaining 1 cup olive oil. After you've added all the oil and the mixture has emulsified, add the lemon juice and blend on low or stir to incorporate.

TIP The key to this emulsion is making sure all the ingredients are at room temperature. Leave your egg out on the counter for an hour, or let it sit in a bowl of hot water for 5 minutes before mixing. Keep one lemon on the counter at all times for the express purpose of making mayo—trust us, you'll be making a lot of this. The slower you add the oil, the thicker and creamer the emulsion will be. You can slowly pour the oil by hand out of a spouted measuring cup, or use a plastic squeeze bottle to slowly drizzle it into the bowl, food processor, or blender. If you're using an immersion blender, pump the stick up and down a few times toward the end to whip some air into the mixture, making it even fluffier.

EGG-FREE MAYONNAISE

MAKES 1¼ CUPS

PREP: 10 minutes   TOTAL: 10 minutes

½ cup coconut butter, slightly warmed

½ cup warm water

¼ cup light olive oil

2 cloves garlic

1 tablespoon fresh lemon juice

¼ teaspoon salt

If you plan on using this egg-free mayo as a base for dressings and sauces, skip the lemon juice. You then have a neutral-flavored base to which you can add any kind of acid (like a citrus juice or vinegar) based on the dressing or sauce you select.

Place all the ingredients in a food processor or blender and blend on high until the mixture thickens, 1 to 2 minutes.

WHOLE30 KETCHUP

Don't expect the familiar "Heinz 57" from this recipe. Grocery store ketchup is thick and sweet thanks to sugar—nearly 4 grams per tablespoon. In fact, Heinz 57 uses both high-fructose corn syrup and corn syrup to sweeten their paste. We could use date paste to make our ketchup sugary, but that's not really in line with the spirit of the Whole30. This ketchup will have a lighter vinegar flavor, different but still delicious on eggs, burgers, and baked potato "fries."

MAKES 1 CUP

PREP: 5 minutes   **COOK:** 10 minutes   **TOTAL:** 15 minutes

1 cup Whole30-compatible tomato paste

½ cup apple cider

½ cup apple cider vinegar

1 teaspoon garlic powder

½ teaspoon salt

⅛ teaspoon ground cloves (optional)

Heat a medium saucepan over medium heat. Add the tomato paste, apple cider, and vinegar. Stir to combine and let the mixture come to a simmer, but do not allow it to boil. Add the garlic powder, salt, and cloves (if using) and cook, stirring frequently to prevent scorching—you may need to turn the heat down to low or simmer here—until the ketchup has thickened enough to evenly coat the back of a spoon, 5 to 8 minutes. Remove from the heat and allow to cool. Serve when cool, or store in an airtight container in the refrigerator for up to 2 weeks.

CLARIFIED BUTTER

Plain old butter isn't allowed on the Whole30 because it contains traces of milk proteins, which may be problematic for dairy-sensitive individuals. Clarifying butter is the technique of simmering butter slowly at a low temperature to separate the milk solids from the pure butterfat. The end result is a delicious, pure, dairy-free fat, perfect for flavoring dishes or cooking (even on high heat).

You'll also see ghee in the recipes—ghee is just a different form of clarified butter, simmered longer until the milk proteins begin to brown, clump, and drift to the bottom of the pan. Ghee has been an Indian staple for millenia, and means "clarified butter" in Sanskrit. It originated in the ancient states of what is now called India and is a common ingredient in the contemporary cuisines of Middle Eastern and Southeast Asian cuisine. The heat of subcontinental India was not conducive to storing fresh butter for long periods of time. Heating the butter until the water evaporated and the milk solids separated away lent the product a longer shelf life. Incidentally, the removal of these milk solids is what makes it an indispensable fat source on the Whole30.

You can purchase pastured, organic ghee at most grocery stores and online, but making it yourself is much cheaper, and quite easy.

MAKES 1½ CUPS

PREP: 5 minutes   **COOK:** 20 minutes   **TOTAL:** 25 minutes

1 pound (4 sticks) unsalted butter

Cut the butter into 1-inch cubes. In a small pot or saucepan, melt the butter over medium-low heat and let it come to a simmer without stirring. As the butter simmers, foamy white dairy solids will rise to the surface. With a spoon or ladle, gently skim the dairy solids off the top and discard, leaving just the pure clarified butter in the pan.

Once you've removed the majority of the milk solids, strain the butter through cheesecloth into a glass storage jar, discarding the milk solids and cheesecloth when you are done. Allow the butter to cool before storing.

Clarified butter can be stored in the refrigerator for up to 6 months or at room temperature for up to 3 months. (With the milk solids removed, clarified butter is shelf-stable for a longer period of time than regular butter.)

COMPOUND BUTTER

Compound butter is a mixture of butter and herbs, spices, toasted nuts, or other flavorful ingredients. These tasty butters can be melted on top of meats or vegetables, adding a totally new dimension to your meal. This is also one way to fancy up a simple dinner for company—a slice of compound butter on your Grilled Halibut (page 191) is sure to impress.

SERVES 4 TO 8

PREP: 10 minutes   **COOL:** 2 hours   **TOTAL:** 2 hours 10 minutes

½ cup (1 stick) Clarified Butter (page 289) or ghee

¼ cup hazelnuts

1 clove garlic, minced

2 teaspoons fresh thyme leaves

½ teaspoon salt

¼ teaspoon black pepper

Place the butter in a small bowl and leave it on the counter until it reaches room temperature.

Heat a dry pan over medium heat. When the pan is hot, add the hazelnuts and toast, shaking the pan often to prevent burning, until lightly browned, about 5 minutes. Transfer the hazelnuts to a cutting board, allow to cool, then chop.

Gently fold the chopped hazelnuts, garlic, thyme, salt, and pepper into the softened butter. Place a large piece of plastic wrap on a flat surface and place the butter mixture in the center. Form the butter into a rough log about 1½ inches in diameter. Wrap the plastic wrap tightly around the butter and refrigerate until firm, about 2 hours. You can do this ahead of time if prepping for an event or dinner party—wrapped in plastic, compound butter made with fresh ingredients will keep in the fridge for 2 to 3 days.

Compound Butter Combinations

Here are some of our favorite compound butter combinations. Make sure all the ingredients are finely minced.

- ¼ cup sun-dried tomatoes, ¼ cup black olives, pitted, and 2 teaspoons minced fresh rosemary leaves

- ¼ cup minced fresh parsley, ¼ cup toasted pine nuts, and 1 tablespoon fresh lemon juice

- 1 minced garlic clove, 2 teaspoons chopped fresh rosemary, 2 teaspoons fresh oregano, and 2 teaspoons minced fresh chives

SIMPLE CAULIFLOWER RICE

This rice is very subtly flavored with just a little bit of onion (and a little parsley, if you like) so it is adaptable to many dishes and flavor profiles. You can serve it as is or stir in additional herbs, seasonings, chopped toasted nuts, or dried fruits.

SERVES 2

PREP: 15 minutes   **COOK:** 15 minutes   **TOTAL:** 30 minutes

1 large head cauliflower, cut into florets

3 tablespoons Clarified Butter (page 289) or ghee

½ onion, finely chopped

½ cup Chicken Bone Broth (page 284) or Whole30-compatible chicken broth

1½ teaspoons minced fresh parsley (optional)

½ teaspoon salt

¼ teaspoon black pepper

Place half the cauliflower florets in a food processor and pulse until they have broken down to a rice-like consistency, 15 to 20 pulses. (Don't overcrowd the cauliflower in the food processor, and don't overpulse or the "rice" will get mushy.) Transfer to a bowl and rice the remaining cauliflower.

In a large skillet, melt the butter over medium heat and swirl to coat the bottom of the pan. When the butter is hot, add the onion and cook, stirring, until translucent, 2 to 3 minutes.

Add the riced cauliflower to the skillet and mix thoroughly to combine with the onion. Add the broth, cover the pan, and steam the cauliflower for 10 to 12 minutes, until tender but not mushy or wet.

Remove the pan from the heat and mix in the parsley, if using. Season with the salt and pepper.

BONUS RECIPES

In celebration of the release of this updated paperback edition, we've chosen five talented kitchen creatives to each showcase two of their favorite recipes. From inspired remakes of classic family favorites to the reimagination of culturally significant dishes, these exclusive bonus recipes feature bold, bright flavors and creative ingredient combinations, serving up delicious Whole30 dishes your whole family will love.

MEXICAN PICADILLO

FROM JESSICA MCMULLEN OF *DASH OF COLOR AND SPICE*

Here's a Mexican version of a hearty potato and meat dish that is sure to keep you satisfied! Full of flavor, it's a great dish on its own or perfect as a stuffing for chiles rellenos. Picadillo is a must-try for a quick and delicious meal.

SERVES: 4

PREP: 15 minutes **COOK:** 35 minutes **TOTAL:** 50 minutes

1 large russet potato, peeled and diced (¼ inch)

2 medium carrots, peeled and diced (¼ inch)

1 tablespoon extra-virgin olive oil

1 medium yellow onion, chopped

1 pound ground beef, or ground meat of choice

1 teaspoon kosher salt

½ teaspoon freshly ground black pepper

1 teaspoon ground cumin

3 Roma tomatoes, chopped

1 jalapeño, finely chopped (seeded if desired)

2 garlic cloves, minced

Juice of 1 lime

½ cup chopped cilantro

Place the potatoes and carrots in a pot with enough water to cover. Bring to a boil and cook just until they start to soften, 3 to 4 minutes. Drain and set aside.

Heat a large skillet over medium heat and add oil. Once hot, add the onion and ground beef. Cook, breaking meat apart with a wooden spoon, for about 5 minutes. Add salt, pepper, and cumin and cook for 5 minutes more.

Add the tomatoes, jalapeño, and garlic and cook, stirring frequently, for about 5 minutes. Add the potatoes and carrots and lime juice. Reduce heat and simmer for 10 minutes, stirring occasionally.

Stir in the cilantro.

TIP This can be made in advance and stored in a tightly sealed container in the refrigerator for up to 5 days.

JESSICA MCMULLEN

Jessica McMullen is a nurse and a Whole30 Certified Coach. She is the founder of *Dash of Color and Spice*, a food blog known for recreating traditional Mexican dishes with a healthy twist. Her recipes stem from her grandma's and mom's shared love and passion for cooking, and she encourages her readers to try something new through her delicious, flavorful food.

CHILES RELLENOS

FROM JESSICA MCMULLEN OF *DASH OF COLOR AND SPICE*

Chiles rellenos are a labor of love, but are absolutely delicious and satisfying. Chiles rellenos were a staple in our Mexican household growing up, and the filling possibilities are endless. Stuff them with picadillo, chicken tinga, or any protein or veggie mix your heart desires. This traditional Mexican dish is sure to be a hit with everyone!

SERVES: 6

PREP: 50 minutes   **COOK:** 50 minutes   **TOTAL:** 1 hour 40 minutes

---

FOR THE PEPPERS

6 large poblano peppers

3 cups Mexican Picadillo (page 293) or preferred filling (see Tip)

Olive oil

7 large egg whites

¼ teaspoon kosher salt

5 large egg yolks

2 tablespoons tapioca flour

FOR THE SAUCE

1 (14-ounce) can fire-roasted diced tomatoes

½ cup Whole30-compatible chicken broth

½ yellow onion, coarsely chopped

2 large cloves garlic, crushed

¼ teaspoon kosher salt

¼ teaspoon freshly ground black pepper

½ teaspoon ground cumin

¾ teaspoon ancho chile powder

1 tablespoon olive oil

1 teaspoon white wine vinegar

MAKE THE PEPPERS: Heat the oven to 425°F. Line a large rimmed baking pan with paper towels. Place a wire rack over the paper towels. Line another large rimmed baking pan with foil. Arrange the peppers on the foil-lined pan. Roast about 20 minutes or until peppers are charred.

MEANWHILE, MAKE THE SAUCE: In a blender, combine tomatoes, broth, onion, garlic, salt, pepper, cumin, and chile powder. Blend until smooth. In a small saucepan, heat the oil over medium-high heat. When hot, carefully add the tomato mixture. Bring to a boil. Reduce heat and simmer, stirring frequently, until slightly thickened and reduced, 5 to 7 minutes. Stir in the vinegar. Set aside.

Turn oven down to 300°F. Transfer roasted peppers to a large bowl. Cover with plastic wrap. Let stand about 20 minutes or until cool enough to handle. Use a small knife to scrape away the charred skin. Carefully cut a slit down one side of each pepper, leaving a ½-inch margin at the top and bottom of the pepper. Gently open each pepper and use a teaspoon to scrape out the seeds, leaving the stems intact. Gently fill each pepper with picadillo just until pepper is full but you are still able to close it at the opening.

In a very large skillet, heat ½ inch of the oil over medium-high heat. In a large bowl, beat egg whites and salt until stiff peaks form. In another bowl, beat egg yolks about 1 minute or until light in color and slightly thickened. Gently fold egg yolk mixture into egg whites (the batter will be light and airy). Pour the batter into a large shallow dish.

Place the tapioca flour on a large plate and gently roll stuffed peppers in it to coat, making sure stuffing stays in place. (This will help the batter to adhere better.)

Gently place a filled pepper, seam side up, into the batter. Using a spoon, gently spoon batter over the top of the pepper until coated. Use one hand to hold onto the pepper stem and the other hand to place a large metal spatula under the coated pepper. Carefully transfer the coated pepper to the hot oil, seam side up. Fry, two at a time, about 4 minutes or until golden brown, turning once. Using a slotted spoon, transfer fried peppers to the rack on the prepared baking pan. Keep fried peppers warm in the oven while coating and cooking the remaining peppers.

Serve topped with the sauce (warm the sauce if necessary).

TIP Substitute ground meat of choice seasoned with your favorite seasonings for the picadillo. You can also use your favorite shredded chicken recipe as a substitute.

SPICY SHRIMP TWICE-BAKED POTATOES

FROM ERICA NKANSAH OF *THIS AFRICAN COOKS*

This is a recipe that can be served as a side or a main dish: a twice-baked potato, topped with crispy shrimp and drizzled with a creamy sauce made from mayo, sriracha, and coconut aminos.

SERVES: 6

PREP: 30 minutes   **COOK:** 1 hour 15 minutes   **TOTAL:** 1 hour 45 minutes

FOR THE POTATOES

3 extra-large russet potatoes

Extra-virgin olive oil

¾ cup coconut cream (see page 286)

2 tablespoons nutritional yeast

1 teaspoon garlic powder

1 teaspoon kosher salt

½ teaspoon freshly ground black pepper

½ teaspoon onion powder

FOR THE SAUCE

½ cup plus 2 tablespoons Basic Mayonnaise (page 287) or Whole30-compatible mayo

3 tablespoons Whole30-compatible sriracha (see page 295)

2 tablespoons coconut aminos

1 teaspoon apple cider vinegar

1 large clove garlic, minced

½ teaspoon dried parsley

FOR THE SHRIMP

1 cup tapioca flour

1¼ pounds extra-large shrimp (26/30 count), peeled and deveined, tail removed

1½ teaspoons Old Bay seasoning

1 egg + Whole30-compatible hot sauce + 1 tablespoon water

Coconut oil

Sliced green onion, for garnish

MAKE THE POTATOES: Preheat the oven to 400°F. Pierce the potatoes in a few places with a fork. Rub the skins with a little bit of olive oil. Bake potatoes directly on oven rack until tender, about 45 to 60 minutes. Remove from oven and allow to cool. Turn oven to 350°F.

MAKE THE SAUCE: In a small bowl, combine the mayonnaise, sriracha, coconut aminos, vinegar, garlic, and parsley. Cover and refrigerate until ready to serve.

When the potatoes are cool enough to handle, cut in half lengthwise. Carefully scoop the flesh of the potatoes into a medium bowl, leaving ⅛- to ¼-inch shells. Add the coconut cream, nutritional yeast, garlic powder, salt, pepper, and onion powder. Use a potato masher to blend until smooth. Place shells on a rimmed baking pan. Divide the mashed potato evenly among the potato skins, flattening the tops as much as possible. Bake filled potatoes until heated through and lightly browned, about 15 to 20 minutes.

MAKE THE SHRIMP: Place the tapioca flour in a large plastic bag. Wash the shrimp and pat dry. Cut in half crosswise to create bite-size pieces. Sprinkle with the Old Bay seasoning and gently toss to evenly distribute the seasoning.

In a medium bowl, whisk together the egg, hot sauce to taste, and water. Place half of the shrimp in the egg mixture. Stir to coat. Using a slotted spoon, remove a spoonful of shrimp from egg mixture, tapping the spoon on the edge of the bowl to shake off excess. Transfer to the bag. Close and shake to evenly coat. Remove the shrimp to a plate, shaking off the excess flour. Repeat with remaining shrimp.

In a large deep skillet, heat coconut oil to a depth of about ¼ inch over medium-high heat. When hot, add half of the shrimp to the skillet, being sure not to overcrowd the pan. Cook for about 3 minutes. Using tongs, turn and cook on the other side until shrimp are browned and cooked through. Remove to a large baking sheet lined with two layers of paper towels. Add more oil to the skillet, if necessary. When hot, cook remaining shrimp.

Transfer all of the shrimp to a large bowl. Drizzle with half of the sauce. Stir gently to coat all of the shrimp with the sauce.

To serve, divide shrimp among the potatoes (about ⅔ cup per potato). Drizzle with additional sauce and top with green onions.

AIR FRYER METHOD: To cook potatoes in an air fryer, preheat fryer to 400°F. Cook the potatoes for 30 minutes. After 30 minutes, wrap the potatoes in foil and return to the air fryer for an additional 15 minutes. Remove potatoes from air fryer, remove foil, and place on a cooling rack for 10 to 15 minutes or until cool enough to handle. Proceed with recipe as directed. To finish, bake filled potatoes in air fryer at 370°F until heated through and lightly browned on top, 5 to 7 minutes.

WHOLE30 SRIRACHA: If you can't find compatible sriracha, you can make your own. In a high-powered blender, combine 1 pound stemmed, seeded, and roughly chopped Fresno chile peppers; 5 cloves garlic, smashed and peeled; 2 tablespoons cider vinegar; 2 tablespoons tomato paste; 1 medium dried Medjool date, pitted; 2 tablespoons Red Boat fish sauce; and ½ teaspoon kosher salt. Blend until smooth. (Note: If using a regular blender, chop the peppers into smaller pieces and mince the garlic for a smoother consistency.)

Transfer to a small saucepan and bring to a boil. Reduce heat and simmer, stirring occasionally, for 10 minutes. Taste and adjust for salt. If sauce is too thick, add water, 1 tablespoon at a time, until it reaches desired consistency. Let cool. Use immediately or store in an airtight container in the refrigerator for up to 1 week.

TIP The filled potatoes can be stored in a tightly sealed container in the refrigerator for up to 2 days. Bake at 350°F until heated through and lightly browned on top, 20 to 25 minutes, before topping with the shrimp.

ERICA NKANSAH

Erica Nkansah, a registered nurse based in Michigan, created *This African Cooks* as a way of managing her anxiety. She knows meal prep and cooking can be a great way to relieve stress, and believes everyone has the ability to be a good cook. Erica encourages her readers to involve friends and family in the kitchen, try new recipes, and enjoy flavorful, healthy food together.

TOSTÓN CHICKEN GYROS WITH COCONUT CREAM TZATZIKI SAUCE

FROM ERICA NKANSAH OF *THIS AFRICAN COOKS*

This recipe calls for plantains, which originated in South Asia, and are used in many different ways in dishes throughout Africa and South America. This recipe utilizes both ripe and unripe plantains. Tostones, or fried plantains, is one way they are prepared in South America. In this recipe, they are topped with marinated cooked chicken and creamy Whole30 Tzatziki Sauce. Every bite is a bite of flavor. Depending on the size of your tostones, you may have some leftover chicken and sauce.

SERVES: 4 AS A MAIN DISH; 8 AS AN APPETIZER

PREP: 45 minutes   **COOK:** 30 minutes   **TOTAL:** 1 hour 15 minutes

FOR THE CHICKEN

1½ pounds boneless, skinless chicken thighs, cut into thin strips

1 tablespoon red wine vinegar

2½ teaspoons coconut aminos

1½ teaspoons garlic powder

1½ teaspoons dried parsley

1½ teaspoons dried thyme

1½ teaspoons smoked paprika

1½ teaspoons Old Bay seasoning

4 tablespoons olive oil, divided

FOR THE SAUCE

¼ cup coconut cream (see Tip)

¼ cup Whole30-compatible mayonnaise

½ cup finely chopped English cucumber

1 tablespoon finely chopped dill

1 large clove garlic, minced

1 teaspoon lemon zest

3 tablespoons lemon juice

½ teaspoon extra-virgin olive oil

¼ teaspoon kosher salt

FOR THE TOSTONES

1 teaspoon kosher salt, plus more to taste

2 green (unripe) plantains, peeled (see Tip), ends trimmed on the diagonal, each cut on the diagonal into 4 equal pieces

2 yellow (ripe) plantains, peeled (see Tip), ends trimmed on the diagonal, each cut on the diagonal into 4 equal pieces

Coconut oil or extra-virgin olive oil

Chopped cucumber, chopped tomatoes, finely chopped red onion (all optional), finely chopped fresh dill, for serving.

MAKE THE CHICKEN: Place the chicken in a large resealable plastic bag. In a small bowl, combine the vinegar, coconut aminos, garlic powder, parsley, thyme, smoked paprika, Old Bay seasoning, and 2 tablespoons of the olive oil. Stir until the mixture is the consistency of a paste. Pour evenly over the chicken in the bag. Seal the bag and thoroughly massage the marinade into the chicken until all of the chicken is evenly coated. Marinate in the refrigerator at least 30 minutes while you make the sauce and tostones.

MAKE THE SAUCE: In a small bowl, stir together the coconut cream, mayonnaise, cucumber, dill, garlic, lemon zest, lemon juice, olive oil, and salt. Cover and refrigerate until ready to use.

MAKE THE TOSTONES: Pour 2 cups of water in each of two medium bowls and add ½ teaspoon salt to each bowl. Stir until dissolved. Soak the green plantain pieces in one bowl and the yellow plantain pieces in the other for 10 minutes. Drain and pat the pieces as dry as possible to avoid spattering when they are cooked, keeping the green and yellow plantains separate.

Add coconut oil to create a depth of about ¼ inch to a large skillet over medium heat. When hot, add the green plantains and cook until lightly browned all over, about 3 minutes per side. Remove to a paper towel–lined plate. One at a time, place the plantain pieces between two pieces of parchment paper. Firmly press with the back of a plate until you get a small, flat disk. Return the smashed plantains to the pan, a couple at a time, and cook until deeply browned and crisp, 2 to 3 minutes more per side. (Add more oil as needed to maintain a ¼-inch depth, but be sure it is hot before you add the plantains.) Season to taste with salt.

Repeat the same steps with the raw yellow plantains. Cook them in hot oil until browned and crisp, 3 to 4 minutes per side.

Wipe the skillet out with clean paper towels. Heat the remaining 2 tablespoons olive oil over medium heat. When hot, add the chicken. Cook, stirring occasionally, until chicken is cooked through, 10 to 12 minutes.

To assemble the gyros, place a green tostón on a plate. Top with a yellow tostón, about ½ cup chicken, and any optional vegetables. Drizzle each with about 2 tablespoons sauce and sprinkle with chopped dill. Repeat with remaining ingredients.

TIP Empty the entire can of coconut cream into a bowl and whisk to completely incorporate the solids and liquids before you measure. Store leftovers in a tightly sealed container in the refrigerator for another use.

TIP Make sure the yellow plantain is not over-ripe, but some black spots are OK. To peel the plantains more easily, lightly score them with a sharp paring knife from tip to tip in one or two places. Tostones are best eaten the same day they are made.

CHILI-LIME PORK RIBS

FROM JEAN CHOI OF *WHAT GREAT GRANDMA ATE*

I didn't realize how amazing dry rub ribs could be until I had these chili-lime pork ribs. They are perfectly tender with a crispy outer crust, and you'll love them if you love spicy and tangy flavors. They take a bit of time in the oven, but they are very easy to prepare and totally worth it!

SERVES: 2 TO 3

PREP: 10 minutes   **COOK:** 3 hours   **TOTAL:** 3 hours 10 minutes

2½ to 3 pounds pork spareribs

1 tablespoon avocado oil

1 tablespoon chili powder

1 teaspoon paprika

½ teaspoon garlic powder

¼ to ½ teaspoon kosher salt

¼ teaspoon freshly ground black pepper

¼ teaspoon cayenne

Zest of 2 limes

Preheat the oven to 300°F. Line a large rimmed baking sheet with aluminum foil. Place a roasting rack on the prepared pan. Place the rib rack on the roasting rack.

Pat the ribs dry with a paper towel. Drizzle the oil over the top of the ribs and rub to coat.

In a small bowl, combine the chili powder, paprika, garlic powder, salt, pepper, cayenne, and lime zest. Sprinkle the rub evenly over the ribs and press into the meat.

Roast until ribs are juicy and tender on the interior and browned and crisp on the outside, about 3 hours.

Let ribs cool slightly before cutting between the bones to serve.

JEAN CHOI

Jean Choi is a nutritional therapy practitioner and recipe developer at *What Great Grandma Ate*. She loves to create recipes that are approachable while being flavorful and delicious. She's the author of *Korean Paleo* and her cooking style is influenced by her Korean-American background. Jean lives in Southern California with her husband, daughter, and two dogs.

CLAM CHOWDER

FROM JEAN CHOI OF *WHAT GREAT GRANDMA ATE*

This ultra-creamy clam chowder is made with blended cauliflower to boost nutrients and thicken the soup, but it tastes like the real deal. It's chock-full of clams, potatoes, and veggies, and you'd never know that it's dairy-free and gluten-free.

SERVES: 4

PREP: 20 minutes   **COOK:** 30 minutes   **TOTAL:** 50 minutes

4 cups cauliflower florets

3 cups peeled and diced (½ inch) russet potatoes

3 cups bone broth or chicken broth, plus more to taste

1 teaspoon kosher salt

4 slices Whole30-compatible bacon, chopped

1 medium yellow onion, chopped

2 stalks celery, chopped

3 garlic cloves, minced

1 teaspoon fresh thyme leaves

½ cup full-fat coconut milk

3 (6.5-ounce) cans chopped clams, undrained

Freshly ground black pepper

Chopped parsley and/or chives, for garnish (optional)

In a large saucepan, combine the cauliflower florets, 1 cup of the potatoes, broth, and salt. Bring to a boil over medium-high heat. Reduce the heat to medium, cover, and simmer until cauliflower and potatoes are tender, about 10 minutes. Remove from the heat.

Use an immersion blender to blend cauliflower mixture in pot or transfer to a blender and blend until smooth. Set aside.

Heat a Dutch oven or a large pot over medium heat and fry the bacon until crisp, about 5 minutes. Transfer bacon to a paper towel–lined plate. Remove all but 1 tablespoon of the bacon grease from the pot.

Add the onion, celery, garlic, and thyme to the pot and cook, stirring occasionally, until celery is crisp-tender, 5 to 7 minutes.

Add the remaining 2 cups diced potatoes and the cauliflower mixture. Bring to a boil. Reduce heat to medium-low and simmer, stirring occasionally, until potatoes are tender.

Stir in the coconut milk and clams with juices and cook for 3 to 4 minutes until the soup is heated through.

Season with black pepper to taste.

Serve hot, topped with bacon and parsley and/or chives, if using.

CREAMY GREEN PEA DIP

FROM BRAD VANDYKE OF *A PINCH OF PRIDE*

Introduce peas into your Whole30 with this thick and creamy hummus-style dip. It gets better with time and will keep in your refrigerator for up to a week. Serve with your favorite freshly sliced vegetables.

SERVES: 4 TO 6

PREP: 20 mins   **CHILL:** 1 hour   **TOTAL:** 1 hour 20 minutes

1 (16-ounce) bag frozen peas, thawed and drained

2 garlic cloves, crushed

¼ cup tahini

3 tablespoons lemon juice

½ teaspoon grated lemon zest

½ teaspoon kosher salt

¼ teaspoon freshly ground black pepper

Pinch cayenne pepper

¼ cup parsley leaves

1 tablespoon extra-virgin olive oil, plus more for garnish

Paprika

Flaky sea salt

Cut-up raw vegetables, such as radishes, peppers, carrots, cucumber, cauliflower, and broccoli florets, for serving.

In a large blender or food processor, combine peas, garlic, tahini, lemon juice, lemon zest, salt, black pepper, cayenne, parsley, and the olive oil. Add 2 tablespoons of cold water and blend for 30 to 60 seconds or until smooth, scraping down the sides of the blender occasionally. Add 1 more tablespoon of water if needed and blend until smooth.

Cover and refrigerate for 1 hour to allow the flavors to blend. Right before serving, drizzle with olive oil and sprinkle with paprika and flaky sea salt. Serve with your favorite raw vegetables.

TIP Out of parsley? Substitute ¼ cup fresh basil leaves or cilantro leaves, or 1 to 2 teaspoons fresh dill.

BRAD VANDYKE

Brad VanDyke is a self-taught home cook who finds joy in sharing a meal with others by using thoughtful and intentional ingredients to develop his recipes. He believes food has the power to connect individuals and inspire creativity. His passion for experimenting in the kitchen is rivaled only by fighting for social justice and advocacy for the LGBTQ+ community.

VELVETY FONDANT POTATOES

FROM BRAD VANDYKE OF *A PINCH OF PRIDE*

These decadent potatoes have a crispy crust and creamy inside texture. The flavors of the ghee and chicken broth are absorbed throughout the potatoes with hints of garlic and thyme. This fan favorite is perfect for your dinner parties or for a simple night in.

SERVES: 4 TO 6

PREP: 15 minutes   **COOK:** 40 minutes   **TOTAL:** 55 minutes

6 medium russet potatoes (as uniform in size as possible)

3 tablespoons avocado oil

3 tablespoons ghee

4 garlic cloves, crushed

3 to 4 sprigs fresh thyme

Kosher salt and freshly ground black pepper

½ cup Whole30-compatible chicken broth, plus additional if necessary

Flaky sea salt

Fresh thyme leaves, for garnish

Scrub the potatoes under cold running water, then pat dry using paper towels. Peel potatoes, then cut off the ends to create uniform cylinders. Cut each cylinder in half crosswise to make 12 total potato cylinders, each 1½ to 2 inches tall.

Soak the potatoes in cool water for 5 minutes to remove excess starch. Drain and pat as dry as possible with a paper towel to avoid spattering.

Preheat oven to 425°F.

Add the avocado oil to a 10- to 12-inch cast-iron skillet over medium heat. When oil is hot, stand potatoes upright and cook until bottoms are nicely browned, about 5 to 6 minutes. Use tongs to turn and repeat on the other end.

Remove from heat. Transfer potatoes to a plate. Wipe out the skillet with a paper towel. Add the ghee and garlic cloves to the skillet. Arrange the potatoes in the skillet. Using the thyme sprigs, brush some of the ghee from the skillet over the potatoes. Place the thyme sprigs in the skillet. Season with kosher salt and black pepper to taste. Cook over medium heat for about 2 minutes. Remove from heat and carefully add chicken broth to the skillet.

Transfer the skillet to the oven and roast until the potatoes are tender (use a small sharp knife inserted in the sides of a few of the potatoes to test doneness), 30 to 35 minutes, adding a little more broth the skillet if it gets dry.

Cool slightly, then garnish with flaky salt and thyme leaves before serving.

TIP Russet potatoes work best since they crisp up nicely and have a light, fluffy interior to soak up maximum flavor. There should be hardly any chicken broth left in the skillet after roasting.

JERUSALEM SALAD

FROM ABEER NAJJAR

As the daughter of Palestinian refugees, my connection to my heritage is deeply rooted in food and storytelling. My ancestors in Palestine were farmers and that is reflected in the cuisine that has been passed on through generations; the table reflects the season's bounty and inspires honor for the land that sustains them. Variations of this salad are made across the Middle East and North Africa, though it's popularly referred to as Jerusalem Salad. But in my house, it's just "salata" (salad), because that's how central this dish is to our daily meals and cuisine. Its simplicity and bold flavors will make it a regular on your table as well.

SERVES: 4 TO 6

PREP: 30 minutes

4 Roma or on-vine tomatoes, coarsely chopped

5 small Persian cucumbers, ends trimmed, halved lengthwise, and sliced (see Tip)

½ cup finely chopped red onion

¼ cup finely chopped fresh parsley

2 tablespoons finely chopped fresh mint

1 small serrano chile pepper, seeded (if desired) and finely chopped (optional)

¼ cup fresh lemon juice

1 teaspoon kosher salt

2 tablespoons extra-virgin olive oil

TIP The salad can be prepared ahead by chopping all the vegetables and herbs. Refrain from dressing the salad in advance, as the salt and acid draw liquid out of the tomatoes and make the salad very wet. Dress right before eating so both the flavor and texture of this salad can shine.

In a large bowl, combine the tomatoes, cucumbers, onion, parsley, mint, and chile pepper, if using. Add the lemon juice, salt, and olive oil. Mix the salad thoroughly to ensure everything is evenly distributed and dressed.

TIP Persian cucumbers are often packaged as "mini" cucumbers in the supermarket. They are virtually seedless and have a crisp, firm texture.

ABEER NAJJAR

Abeer Najjar is a chef, food writer, and the founder of Huda Supper Club. A Chicago native and child of Palestinian immigrants, her culinary approach reflects her family's heritage and city upbringing. Abeer works to preserve culture and stimulate conversation about identity by using food as a canvas for storytelling.

SHEET PAN 7-SPICE CHICKEN & POTATOES

FROM ABEER NAJJAR

I came up with this recipe during a visit to see my sisters in California. While their kitchens are becoming the setting for teaching our Palestinian culture to the next generation, some days we just need a quick meal so we can spend time catching up and catching some sun. I threw together this sheet pan of chicken and potatoes with some common ingredients and seasonings we always have on hand. One bowl to prep and one pan to cook, so this recipe is easy and low-maintenance from start to finish.

SERVES: 4 TO 6

PREP: 15 minutes   **COOK:** 45 minutes   **TOTAL:** 1 hour

1½ pounds boneless, skinless chicken thighs

1½ pounds Yukon Gold potatoes, cut into 1½- to 2-inch chunks

1 medium yellow onion, halved and thinly sliced

2 cloves garlic, smashed

¼ cup extra-virgin olive oil

2 teaspoons kosher salt

½ teaspoon freshly ground black pepper

1½ teaspoons 7-spice blend (baharat; see Tip)

1 teaspoon ground sumac (see Tip)

2 teaspoons dried oregano

¼ cup finely chopped fresh parsley

1 lime, halved

Line a large rimmed baking sheet with parchment paper; set aside. Preheat the oven to 400°F. In a large bowl, combine the chicken, potatoes, onion, and garlic. Drizzle with the oil and season with the salt, pepper, 7-spice, sumac, and oregano. Use your hands or tongs to combine until evenly coated. Remove the chicken to a plate.

Spread the potato mixture over the prepared baking pan in a thin layer. Lay the chicken on top. (This way, while the chicken cooks, the juices will baste and flavor the potatoes.)

Bake for 45 to 50 minutes, or until browned and slightly crispy. The potatoes should be tender and the juices of the chicken should run clear.

Remove the pan from the oven. Sprinkle with parsley. Squeeze fresh lime juice over the chicken and potatoes.

Serve with Jerusalem Salad (left) for a complete meal.

TIP Seven spice blend (also called *baharat*, the Arabic word for "spice") is a warm and sweet seasoning used throughout the Arab world. It varies from cook to cook, but is usually some combination of paprika, black pepper, cumin, coriander, cinnamon, cloves, star anise, and nutmeg. Sumac is also widely used in the Arab world. It is made from dried and ground sumac berries and has a tangy, lemony flavor. Look for both in specialty markets or online.

WHOLE30 RESOURCES

This first part of this resources section includes websites, cookbooks, and social media feeds we really like, from people with whom I have developed a close personal and professional relationship. They're smart, talented people who are Whole30 experts in their own right. They've done the program, offer specific resources for your Whole30 success, and really get the spirit and intention of the Whole30.

Not everything in their website, cookbook, or social media feed is Whole30 compatible, so read your website content, recipes, and social media hashtags just as carefully as you have to read your labels.

A good rule of thumb: Unless it's coming from me (the Whole30 website, my books, or our social media feeds), don't take any label of "Whole30 compatible" at face value. Use your critical thinking skills, read your labels/ingredients/recipes carefully, and decide for yourself whether the item in question really is "Whole30."

Websites

Whole30

whole30.com
The official home of the Whole30 program. This is where you'll find our free Whole30 Forum, all our free downloads, Whole30 Approved products and affiliates, and more Whole30-related articles than you could possibly hope to read in thirty days. Spend lots of time exploring here before, during, and after your Whole30—this is the very heart of our community.

> Facebook: whole30
> Instagram: @whole30, @whole30recipes, @whole30approved
> Twitter: @whole30
> YouTube: whole30
> Pinterest: @whole30

Nom Nom Paleo: Michelle Tam

nomnompaleo.com
Nom Nom Paleo is the creation of *New York Times* best-selling author and self-described "culinary nerd" Michelle Tam. Her books feature a large number of Whole30-friendly meals, and her website features a Whole30 recipe filter.

> Facebook: nomnompaleo
> Instagram: @nomnompaleo
> Twitter: @nomnompaleo
> Pinterest: nomnompaleo
> Snapchat: michitam

Against All Grain: Danielle Walker

againstallgrain.com
Danielle Walker is a *New York Times* best-selling author and photographer who shares her grain-free, gluten-free, and Whole30-approved recipes on her blog and in her cookbooks. Her website also includes a Whole30 recipe filter.

> Facebook: AgainstAllGrain
> Instagram: @daniellewalker
> Twitter: @againstallgrain
> Youtube: AgainstAllGrain
> Pinterest: @Againstallgrain

Primal Palate: Hayley & Bill Staley

primalpalate.com

Hayley and Bill are the dynamic cooking duo behind the Primal Palate website, cookbooks, and Whole30 Approved spices. They also offer a Whole30 recipe filter on their website.

> Facebook: thefoodlovers
> Instagram: @primalpalate
> Twitter: @primalpalate
> YouTube: primalpalate
> Pinterest: @thefoodlovers

Well Fed: Melissa Joulwan

meljoulwan.com

Melissa Joulwan is the author of three Whole30-friendly cookbooks and a food, fitness, health, and lifestyle blogger with hundreds of Whole30-compliant recipes, meal plans, and resources.

Whole Sisters: Nan and Nicole

whole-sisters.com

Nan and Nicole are sisters and mothers who love to eat and cook with their families. They know firsthand that the food you eat can and will make a difference in your life, and their recipes prove that eating healthy can still taste amazing.

Pretend It's a Donut: Jenn Bumb

pretenditsadonut.com

Jenn Bumb lives in the San Francisco Bay area with her husband and five kids. Her blog focuses on Paleo and Whole30 family-friendly recipes and sticking to a healthy-eating budget when you have a plethora of mouths to feed.

Rubies & Radishes: Arsy Vartanian

rubiesandradishes.com

Arsy Vartanian's experience healing her own body with a Paleo-style diet led her to pursue her passions and interests: a love of cooking; shopping for fresh, organic, grass-fed ingredients; and creating delicious meals for her family and blog readers.

Paleo Paparazzi: Kendra Cardoza

paleopaparazzi.com

Kendra Cardoza is a self-taught real-food chef who started her journey after her husband had a stroke and she was diagnosed with an autoimmune condition. She lives in Northern California, where she pursues her passion of recipe development, nutrition, cooking, and food photography.

What Great Grandma Ate: Jean Choi

whatgreatgrandmaate.com

Jean Choi is a nutritional therapy practitioner and recipe developer. She is the author of *Korean Paleo* and her cooking style is influenced by her Korean-American background. Jean lives in Southern California with her husband, daughter, and two dogs.

Dash of Color and Spice: Jessica McMullen

dashofcolorandspice.com

Jessica McMullen is a nurse and a Whole30 Certified Coach. She is the founder of Dash of Color and Spice, a food blog known for recreating traditional Mexican dishes with a healthy twist. Her recipes stem from her grandma and mom's shared love and passion for cooking.

A Pinch of Pride: Brad VanDyke

Instagram: @apinchofpride

Brad VanDyke is a self-taught home cook who finds joy in using thoughtful and intentional ingredients to develop his recipes. His passion for experimenting in the kitchen is rivaled only by fighting for social justice and advocacy for the LGBTQ+ community.

Abeer Najjar

abeernajjar.com

Abeer Najjar is a chef, food writer, and the founder of Huda Supper Club. A Chicago native and child of Palestinian immigrants, her culinary approach reflects her family's heritage and city upbringing. Abeer works to preserve culture and stimulate conversation about identity by using food as a canvas for storytelling.

This African Cooks: Erica Nkansah

thisafricancooks.com

Erica Nkansah, a registered nurse based in Michigan, created This African Cooks as a way of managing her anxiety and relieving stress. Erica encourages her readers to involve friends and family in the kitchen, try new recipes, and enjoy flavorful, healthy food together.

Cookbooks

There are only five books where 100% of the recipes featured are guaranteed Whole30 Approved—you're reading one of them right now! Here are the other four:

The Whole30: The 30-Day Guide to Total Health and Food Freedom

Although *The Whole30* features more than 100 delicious and totally compatible recipes, it's more than just a cookbook—it's a complete Whole30 handbook, start to finish. If you're loving the recipes in *The Whole30 Cookbook* but want a full game plan for preparing for and completing the program itself, *The Whole30* is all you'll need.

The Whole30 Slow Cooker

This follow-up to *Cooking Whole30* contains 150 recipes designed to get you out of the kitchen fast, with delicious, no-fuss dinners; roasts that transform into tacos, salads, and soups; and satisfying one-pot meals. As an added bonus, it also features recipes and directions for the Instant Pot!

The Whole30 Fast & Easy

This Whole30 cookbook is packed with 150 delicious Whole30 recipes, perfect for weeknight cooking, lunches in a hurry, and hearty breakfasts that still get you out the door on time, most of which can be made in 30 minutes or less using ingredients found in any supermarket.

The Whole30 Friends & Family

Our newest cookbook is packed with full menus and Whole30 recipes for all of life's special moments, from birthdays to baby showers, barbecues to brunches, designed to mix and match to create the perfect menu whether you're hosting or contributing as a guest. It also provides tips to make every social situation a success.

We also have a line of official Whole30 Endorsed cookbooks from authors who love creating Whole30 fare *and* showcasing their Food Freedom favorites. The Whole30-compatible recipes are clearly marked in each of these books.

The Whole Smiths: Michelle Smith

This cookbook offers 150 recipes to keep Whole30 devotees going strong. Many recipes are fully Whole30 compatible, and all are gluten-free, but you'll also find recipes with a careful reintroduction of grains, legumes, and desserts.

No Crumbs Left: Teri Turner

Teri leads readers through a discovery of new flavors and spice combinations and teaches you to trust your cooking instincts. Most recipes are gluten-free, grain-free, dairy-free, and Whole30 compatible, including Teri's signature Magic Elixirs and Marinated Red Onions.

The Defined Dish: Alex Snodgrass

With gluten-free, dairy-free, and grain-free recipes that sound and look way too delicious to be healthy, this is a cookbook you can turn to after completing a Whole30. Each dish is clearly marked as Whole30 compatible, Paleo, gluten-free, dairy-free, and more.

Buck Naked Kitchen: Kirsten Buck

Kirsten won the first "Next Whole30 Star" competition, and is now a certified holistic nutritionist sharing delicious and beautiful recipes this cookbook. She creates gluten-free, grain-free, and dairy-free recipes that prove that healthy eating doesn't have to break the bank.

The Primal Gourmet: Ronny Joseph Lvovski

Ronny creates gourmet-quality meals following Paleo guidelines. His first cookbook includes more than 120 recipes, with blog fan-favorites plus all-new dishes such as Mojo Loco Chicken Wings, Short Rib Ragu, and Jerk Ribs, proving healthy diets really can be delicious.

Meal Planning

Real Plans

w30.co/w30realplans

Delicious, totally compatible Whole30 meals in a weekly plan to fit your taste and schedule. Fully customizable; choose which days of the week and meals to plan, exclude ingredients to which you are allergic or just don't like, prioritize recipes using specific kitchen gadgets like a slow cooker or Instant Pot, and generate an automated shopping list and meal prep instructions for each week. Features more than 1,000 Whole30-compatible recipes to build into your family's perfect weekly meal plan.

Health Care

SteadyMD

steadymd.com/whole30

No co-pays. No office visits. No waiting. Just 24/7 access to your own personal Whole30 doctor, completely online. Partner with a primary care doctor who will support and encourage you during your Whole30 journey and beyond. Securely text your doctor for a quick answer or have more in-depth conversations over the phone or video chat. With SteadyMD, you'll get dedicated personal attention day or night, and true preventative care tailored to your medical needs and lifestyle.

WHOLE30 APPROVED®

This is a list of our official Whole30 Approved partners, with the addition of some Whole30-friendly products from brands we love. These companies make a variety of products to support your Whole30 journey, but in many cases, not *every* product they make fits our guidelines. Read your labels, or look for the official Whole30 Approved logo on their website or packaging. Visit whole30.com/whole30-approved for the full roster.

Whole30 Curated Kits

Thrive Market Whole30 Curated Kits (l.thrv .me/whole30-25p1): Whole30 Approved curated kits, our Made by Whole30 line of dressings and sauces, and more than 150+ compatible pantry staples delivered to your door, all at up to 50% off retail. New members get a 30-day risk-free trial with our affiliate link.

Barefoot Provisions Whole30 Kits (w30.co/ w30bpkits): Whole30 Approved curated kits for emergency foods and healthy fats, shipped throughout the world, no membership required.

Natura Market Canada Whole30 Kits (w30 .co/naturamarket): Your Canadian source for Whole30 Approved curated kits and over 100 compatible items delivered to your door.

On-the-Go and Travel Food

Ayoba (ayobafoods.com): Premium grass-fed beef snacks, spiced to perfection using an authentic South African recipe.

Brooklyn Biltong (brooklynbiltong.com): Seasoned, all-natural dried beef snacks.

DNX Bar (dnxbar.com/whole30): Great tasting, grass-fed meat bars packed with organic ingredients to fuel your on-the-go lifestyle.

EPIC Provisions (epicprovisions.com): Grass-fed/pastured jerky bars, bits, strips, and bacon bites for salads and soups. Most varieties are Whole30 compatible (read your labels).

Chomps Snack Sticks (chomps.com): Protein-packed grass-fed and free-range beef, venison, and turkey snack sticks.

Nick's Sticks (nicks-sticks.com): 100% grass-fed beef and free-range turkey and chicken meat snack sticks.

RXBAR (rxbar.com): Egg white protein–based bars. Most flavors are Whole30 compatible; read your labels and don't use these as treats, please.

Meat and Produce

ButcherBox (butcherbox.com/whole30): 100% grass-fed and -finished beef, organic chicken, heritage breed pork, and wild Alaskan salmon delivered to your door for under $6 per meal.

Happy Egg Co. (happyeggco.com): Happy Egg free-range eggs are pasture-raised on over eight acres, resulting in remarkable nutrition.

Applegate (applegate.com/whole30): More than twenty Approved natural and organic humanely raised meat products. No antibiotics and no GMO ingredients ever.

Teton Waters Ranch (tetonwatersranch.com): Certified humane, 100% grass-fed and -finished beef hot dogs, dinner sausages, hamburgers, and breakfast sausages in a variety of flavors.

True Story Foods (truestoryfoods.com): Sugar-free, organic, and non-GMO deli meats.

Tribalí Foods (tribalifoods.com): Organic 100% grass-fed beef and chicken patties, plus mini breakfast sliders, made with only real ingredients.

U.S. Wellness Meats (grasslandbeef.com): Grass-fed and free-range meats from family farmers.

Western Grassfed Beef (westerngrassfedbeef .com): Grass-fed beef from certified organic family farmers.

Country Natural Beef (countrynaturalbeef.com): Certified Step 4, pasture raised by Global Animal Partnership's animal welfare program.

Pre Brands (eatpre.com): Always grass-fed, grass-finished, and raised with care.

Nature's Rancher (naturesrancher.com): Certified humane, all natural, nitrate- and nitrite-free pork, beef, poultry, and lamb.

The Honest Bison (honestbison.com): Grass-fed and humanely raised bison offerings, including soup bones.

Northstar Bison (northstarbison.com): Bison raised on native grasslands and field harvested for zero stress.

Pederson's Natural Farms (thesimplegrocer .com): Certified humane and sugar-free bacon, sausages, hot dogs, and ham.

Naked Bacon (nakedbaconco.com): Sugar-free, nitrate- and nitrite-free, all-natural bacon and breakfast sausage.

Hungry Harvest (hungryharvest.net): Recovered farm-fresh produce and organic produce, delivered to your door CSA style in the mid-Atlantic (and rapidly growing).

SeaSnax (seasnax.com): Nutrient-packed roasted seaweed sheets in a variety of flavors.

Cece's Veggie Noodle Co. (cecesveggieco.com): Fresh, riced veggies from cauliflower and broccoli, and raw spiralized veggie noodles made from zucchini, butternut squash, sweet potatoes, and beets.

Tio Gazpacho (tiogazpacho.com): Chef-crafted drinkable soups made with super clean non-GMO ingredients.

Jica Foods (jicafoods.com): Crisp and refreshing jicama wraps and sticks.

Love Beets (lovebeets.com): Premium, all-natural, ready-to-eat delicious beets without the mess and fuss.

Olive My Pickle (olivemypickle.com): Saltwater brine, fermented pickles, kraut, kimchi, veggies, and olives.

Pantry Staples

Safe Catch (safecatch.com): Wild-caught tuna and salmon in cans and pouches, featuring the lowest mercury content of any brand—safe even for pregnant women.

Safe Harvest Soups (safeharvest.com): Tasty, healthy twists on classic soups with clean, wholesome ingredients.

Cucina Antica Pasta Sauces (cucina-antica .com): Cooking sauces made with imported Italian San Marzano tomatoes.

Monte Bene (montebene.com): Pasta sauces made without preservatives, added sugar, gluten, water, or tomato paste.

Organico Bello (organicobello.com): USDA Organic and Non-GMO Verified pasta sauces, salsas, and canned tomatoes made with 100% imported organic Italian tomatoes.

Lucina Italia (lucini.com): The leading producer of premium Italian extra-virgin olive oils, and the creator of organic, Italian-made tomato sauces.

Otamot (otamot.com): Nutritious and delicious, veggie-filled tomato sauces packed with nutrients from ten organic vegetables and healthy oil.

Big Tree Farms Coconut Aminos (bigtreefarms .com): A soy sauce substitute made from brewed and naturally fermented coconut blossom nectar and sea salt.

Red Boat Fish Sauce (redboatfishsauce.com): All-natural, first-press, "extra-virgin" Vietnamese fish sauce made without MSG or preservatives.

Kettle & Fire (kettleandfire.com): Grass-fed, organic beef and chicken bone broth in shelf-stable packaging.

EPIC Broth (epicprovisions.com): The first-ever ready-to-heat pasture-raised and grass-fed beef, chicken, and turkey broth, from their Whole Animal Project.

Bonafide Provisions (bonafideprovisions.com): Organic, grass-fed, pasture-raised chicken and beef bone broth and soups.

Bare Bones Broth (barebonesbroth.com): Nutritious, pasture-raised and grass-fed organic chicken and beef bone broths.

Brodo (brodo.com): High-quality ingredients and century-tested craftsmanship create the finest bone broth available.

Laila Ali Spice Blends (shop.lailaali.com): Flavorful, perfectly balanced spice blends that were created for everyday use.

Primal Palate Organic Spices (primalpalate.com): Organic, gluten-free, non-GMO, non-irradiated high-quality spices and spice blends, including an AIP-friendly spice pack.

Paleo Powder Seasonings (paleopowderseasoning.com): All-purpose Paleo, MSG-free, and gluten-free seasonings.

Natural Fats

Primal Kitchen (primalkitchen.com): Heart-healthy avocado oil and avocado oil–based sugar-free mayonnaise, plus egg-free vegan formulations.

California Olive Ranch (californiaoliveranch.com): Highest quality extra-virgin olive oil rooted in California.

Tin Star Ghee (tinstarfoods.com): Cultured, handmade pastured ghee and brown butter ghee made from the milk of grass-fed cows.

Fourth & Heart (fourthandheart.com): Five grass-fed ghee and cooking oil varieties.

Pure Indian Foods Ghee (pureindianfoods.com): Grass-fed, organic, non-GMO ghee and cooking oils.

Fatworks (fatworksfoods.com): Traditional handcrafted cooking fats, including tallow (beef, buffalo, and lamb), lard, leaf lard, duck fat, goose fat, and chicken schmaltz.

Georgia Grinders (georgiagrinders.com): Handcrafted, premium almond, cashew, pecan, and hazelnut nut butters made out of simple, all-natural ingredients.

Revival Food Co. (revivalfoodco.com): Craft almond butter with incredible flavor and stone-ground texture.

Freezer Meals

Great Value Freezer Meals (walmart.com): Exclusively at Walmart, Whole30 Approved Great Value freezer meals come in eight varieties.

GRANDCESTORS Meals (grandcestors.com): Individual serving sizes of prepared frozen meals with hearty portions.

Primal Kitchen Frozen Bowls & Skillets (primalkitchen.com): Chef-crafted, Whole30 Approved frozen bowls and skillets.

Primitive Feast (primitivefeast.com): Hearty, flavorful frozen entrees, shipped nationwide.

Dressings and Sauces

Made by Whole30 (whole30.com/products): Our NEW line of salad dressings and dipping sauces, with flavors your whole family will love on or off the Whole30.

Noble Made (thenewprimal.com): Marinades, Buffalo and BBQ sauces, and delicious dressings from The New Primal.

Primal Kitchen Dressings (primalkitchen.com): Extensive variety of avocado oil–based, sugar-free dressings and marinades.

Tessemae's All Natural (tessemaes.com): All-natural and certified organic dressings, sauces, and condiments from their family to yours.

Organicville (skyvalleyfoods.com): Organic, all-natural, and fully flavored dressings, condiments, sauces, and marinades.

Yai's Thai Sauces (yaisthai.com): Thai-inspired, hand-crafted salsas, sauces, almond sauce, and curry sauces.

Mesa de Vida Recipe Starters (mesadevida.com): Concentrated shortcut sauces to help transform simple ingredients into amazing meals.

Nummy Nibbles (nummynibbles.com): Delicious Indian cooking sauces in three amazing regional flavors.

Yellowbird Foods (yellowbirdfoods.com): Spicy, organic condiments with spunky character made deep in the heart of Texas.

Saucy Lips (saucylips.com): Handcrafted, gourmet sauces created with fresh, clean ingredients.

Ricante–Pura Costa Vida (ricante.com): Versatile Everything Sauces and hot sauces made with the freshest ingredients and bold flavors.

Good Food for Good (goodfoodforgood.ca): Organic ketchup, BBQ sauces, and cooking sauces. Available in Canada and from Thrive Market in the U.S.

Cedar Valley Selections (cedarvalleyselections.com): Canada's first Whole30 Approved salad dressings. Unique and ethnic varieties inspired by cultures around the world.

Beverages

Lacroix Water (lacroixwater.com): Sugar- and calorie-free naturally flavored sparkling waters.

Waterloo (drinkwaterloo.com): A bold taste on sparkling water, focusing on true-to-fruit flavor & aroma and delivering a rich, authentic taste in 100% BPA-free cans.

Rethink Water (drinkrethinkwater.com): The first ever zero-sugar, zero-sweetener, zero-calorie, certified organic, flavored water for kids.

Sound (drinksound.com): Sparkling water infused with organic tea botanicals and fruit extracts. Completely unsweetened and certified organic.

nutpods (nutpods.com): Unsweetened, carrageenan-free almond and coconut milk coffee creamers in four delicious varieties and seasonal offerings.

MALK Organics (malkorganics.com): Cold-pressed nut milks made with sprouted nuts and no binders, colors, or sweeteners.

New Barn Organics (newbarnorganics.com): Unsweetened almond milk and non-dairy creamer with only simple, organic ingredients.

Four Sigmatic (foursigmatic.com): Functional mushroom powders to help you relax, be well, energize, and support productivity.

MUD\WTR (mudwtr.com): Made with organic, earth-grown ingredients, MUD\WTR is packed with adaptogenic mushroom compounds for optimal health and performance benefits.

Rasa Koffee (wearerasa.com): Three delicious varieties of nourishing, adaptogenic coffee and coffee alternative blends created with great-tasting herbs to provide lasting energy.

Jade Leaf Matcha (jadeleafmatcha.com): Farm-direct, organic Japanese matcha–always at a fair price.

Hoplark Hoptea (hoptea.com): Clean, simple ingredients that deliver brilliant hop flavors and aromas without the additives.

Teecino (teecino.com): Bold-tasting roasted herbal coffees and teas made from intentionally blended botanicals.

Turmeric Teas (turmericteas.com): Tea and latte blends with turmeric that help heal you from within.

Lifestyle

Vital Proteins (vitalproteins.com): Pasture-raised collagen peptides and gelatin for healthier skin, nails, and hair; to promote joint and bone health and aid in athletic performance.

BUBS Naturals Collagen & MCT Oil Powder (bubsnaturals.com): Grass-fed, pasture-raised collagen and non-GMO coconut MCT oil powder.

Mindbodygreen (shop.mindbodygreen.com): Organic sea veggies and antioxidants to balance hormones and blood sugar; organic grass-fed bovine collagen plus essential nutrients to support beauty, gut health, and inflammation.

Doc Parsley's Sleep Remedy (docparsley.com): Developed by sleep expert Dr. Kirk Parsley, Sleep Remedy aims to lay the foundation for the best sleep possible.

Lyteline Electrolytes (lyteline.com): Healthier hydration products, including a sports drink, electrolytes, and trace minerals.

Restaurants and Meal Delivery (National)

Chipotle (chipotle.com): Order the official Whole30 Salad Bowl, exclusively at Chipotle.com or on the Chipotle app.

Zoës Kitchen (zoeskitchen.com): Fresh-made Mediterranean with a robust Whole30 Approved menu in more than 250 locations nationwide.

The Good Kitchen (thegoodkitchen.com): High quality, fully prepared Whole30 Approved meals shipped nationally. Farm to table in three minutes.

Paleo on the Go (paleoonthego.com): Handcrafted, chef-prepared meals with an AIP focus. Shipped frozen and available across the U.S.

Visit **whole30.com/whole30-approved** for dozens of local catering, meal delivery, and restaurant options in every region of the U.S.

Whole30 Support

Resources to give you Whole30 support, motivation, and accountability.

The Whole30 Forum
forum.whole30.com

If you have a question, we can almost guarantee it's been answered. Find those answers, solicit expert advice from our moderators, and get support from fellow Whole30'ers on our free forum.

Wholesome
whole30.com/wholesome

Our free newsletter filled with Whole30-related recipes, events, media, testimonials, discounts, giveaways, and more.

XO, MU
whole30.com/xomu

My personal weekly newsletter on relationships, self-care, boundaries, fitness, and personal growth.

Do the Thing
whole30.com/podcast

My podcast, where we explore what's been missing every time you've tried to make a change and make it stick. Covering Whole30, food freedom, and much more.

Free Whole30 PDF Downloads
whole30.com/pdf-downloads

Our helpful PDF downloads (including our shopping list, meal template, label-reading guide, pantry-stocking guide, and more).

Connect with Melissa

I love hearing your stories, answering your questions, and tough-loving you (heavy on the love) when you need it.

melissau.com
Instagram: @melissau
Facebook: /melissau.author
Twitter: @melissa_urban

ACKNOWLEDGMENTS

To Sarah Pelz and Jacqueline Quirk, thank you for helping me revise this book into a work that truly represents our communities and DEI initiatives. To my original editor, Justin Schwartz, your years of support, editorial expertise, and friendship will never be forgotten.

To the entire Houghton Mifflin Harcourt team, thank you for 6 years of support of the Whole30 program and my community. I love being a part of the HMH family.

To Andrea Magyar and Tonia Addison at Penguin Canada, I'm beyond thrilled to share these recipes with all of Canada. My community and I thank you for your continued support.

To Christy Fletcher, Lisa Grubka, Alyssa Taylor, and the Fletcher & Company team. I love working with you all, thank you for all your hard work.

To C. Redwood Hill, working with you as our cultural editor on this project was a blessing. I have enjoyed the education, energy, and expertise you provided, and know this is the start of an ongoing, beautiful relationship. I am incredibly grateful for you.

To Dr. Carrie Kholi-Murchison, thank you for immediately grasping the vision and potential of this project, and infusing our DEI focus into every page. You led us down this path, and we are so lucky to have you.

To Brent Herrig, you shared my vision and my passion every step of the way, and the end results are more beautiful than I could have imagined. Thank you.

To Suzanne Lenzer, it was a pleasure to work with you again. You and your team made these delicious recipes look as gorgeous as they were tasty, and I thank you all so much for lending your talents to this book.

To Maeve Sheridan, not only are you an incredibly gifted prop stylist, you were an absolute joy to have on set. Thank you for giving these photographs just the right finishing touches.

To my Whole30 team: thank you for giving so much of yourselves to this program and our community. I am lucky to have you, and grateful for your talents.

To Nicole Bangertner, Kirsten Buck, Jenn Bumb, Kendra Cardoza, Jean Choi, Nan Jansen, Melissa Joulwan, Jessica McMullen, Abeer Najjar, Erica Nkansah, Michelle Smith, Michelle Tam, Brad VanDyke, and Arsy Vartanian, thank you for everything you have contributed to the Whole30 community, and sharing your tasty fare with us for this book. I am blessed to call you all friends.

To my family and friends, thank you for your love, support, and encouragement. You've been my biggest cheerleaders, and I am so proud to be able to share this moment with you.

For my son, everything is for you.

Finally, to YOU, my Whole30ers. You inspire me, energize me, and keep me motivated to do even more to help you succeed. Thank *you* for all that you have given to *me*.

COOKING CONVERSIONS

Metric weights listed here have been slightly rounded to make measuring easier.

Weight

U.S.	METRIC
¼ oz	7 grams
½ oz	15 g
¾ oz	20 g
1 oz	30 g
8 oz (½ lb)	225 g
12 oz (¾ lb)	340 g
16 oz (1 lb)	455 g
2 lb	900 g
2¼ lb	1 kg

Oven Conversions

FAHRENHEIT (degrees F)	CELSIUS (degrees C)	GAS NUMBER	OVEN TERMS
225	110	¼	Very Cool
250	130	½	Very Slow
275	140	1	Very Slow
300	150	2	Slow
325	165	3	Slow
350	177	4	Moderate
375	190	5	Moderate
400	200	6	Moderately Hot
425	220	7	Hot
450	230	8	Hot
475	245	9	Hot
500	260	10	Extremely Hot
550	290	10	Broiling

Volume

U.S.	METRIC	IMPERIAL
¼ tsp	1.2 ml	
½ tsp	2.5 ml	
1 tsp	5 ml	
½ Tbsp (1½ tsp)	7.5 ml	
1 Tbsp (3 tsp)	15 ml	
¼ cup (4 Tbsp)	60 ml	2 fl oz
⅓ cup (5 Tbsp)	75 ml	2½ fl oz
½ cup (8 Tbsp)	125 ml	4 fl oz
⅔ cup (10 Tbsp)	150 ml	5 fl oz
¾ cup (12 Tbsp)	175 ml	6 fl oz
1 cup (16 Tbsp)	250 ml	8 fl oz
1¼ cups	300 ml	10 fl oz (½ pint)
1½ cups	350 ml	12 fl oz
2 cups (1 pint)	500 ml	16 fl oz
2½ cups	625 ml	20 fl oz (1 pint)
1 quart	1 liter	32 fl oz

INDEX

Note: Page references in *italics* indicate photographs.

CHANGE YOUR LIFE WITH THE BEST-SELLING BOOKS FROM

THE WHOLE30®

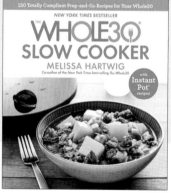

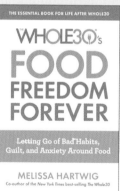

HMH

WHOLE30.COM